ROUTLEDGE LIBRARY EDITIONS: LINGUISTICS

Volume 22

PRODUCTION AND COMPREHENSION OF UTTERANCES

PRODUCTION AND COMPREHENSION OF UTTERANCES

I. M. SCHLESINGER

LONDON AND NEW YORK

First published in 1977

This edition first published in 2014
by Routledge
2 Park Square, Milton Park, Abingdon, Oxfordshire OX14 4RN

Simultaneously published in the USA and Canada
by Routledge
711 Third Avenue, New York, NY 10017

Routledge is an imprint of the Taylor and Francis Group, an informa business

First issued in paperback 2015

©1977 Lawrence Erlbaum Associates, Inc.

British Library Cataloguing in Publication Data
A catalogue record for this book is available from the British Library

ISBN 978-0-415-64438-9 (Set)
eISBN 978-0-203-07902-7 (Set)
ISBN 978-0-415-72376-3 (hbk) (Volume 22)
ISBN 978-1-138-98386-1 (pbk) (Volume 22)
ISBN 978-1-315-85737-4 (ebk) (Volume 22)

Publisher's Note
The publisher has gone to great lengths to ensure the quality of this reprint but points out that some imperfections in the original copies may be apparent.

Disclaimer
The publisher has made every effort to trace copyright holders and would welcome correspondence from those they have been unable to trace.

To the Memory of my Mother and Father

Contents

Preface

It is often hard to say when work on a book has begun. In this case, some of the focal notions had been presented in previous publications but had to be rethought and reformulated. Others are based on some stray ideas, jotted down years ago, shelved, and then taken up again. The studies reported here for the first time were carried out long ago with the partial support of the Human Development Center of the Hebrew University, Jerusalem, whose assistance is gratefully acknowledged. The last three chapters are a revision and extension of an unpublished paper, "Structural and nonstructural processes in decoding: A preliminary model." Then, an earlier version of the book was circulated among colleagues in mimeograph, and the comments they made led to rewriting it in its present form.

There are many people to whom I am deeply indebted for stimulation and advice. Owing to the meandering course of the book's development, described above, it is difficult to tell where the list ends. But I should certainly include Sidney Greenbaum, who read the previous version and made numerous valuable comments, Moshe Anisfeld, Dwight Bolinger, Richard Cromer, Charles Fillmore, Jerry Fodor, Patricia Greenfield, P. N. Johnson-Laird, John MacNamara, David Olson, and an anonymous reviewer. They gave much of their time, and their perceptive comments were extremely helpful. The students in seminars in which I discussed the subject matter of the book helped me to clarify to myself what I thought.

My greatest intellectual debt, however, is to the late Yehoshua Bar-Hillel, who for many years was a stimulating teacher, discerning critic, and true friend. Before his illness and subsequent death he read previous versions of the above paper and of Part One, and as always, I benefited enormously from his detailed comments, often followed by animated discussion leading to new insights. Most of all, I owe to him the formative influence of his uncompromising attitude towards loose and shallow thinking. He was the man with "the lowest threshold of tolerance for nonsense" (someone's characterization of him, which he once quoted to me with visible satisfaction). I do not think I will ever write a paper without asking myself what he would have thought of it.

I also want to express my gratitude to Lawrence Erlbaum for his sustained encouragement, which made the last revision of the manuscript less of a chore and more nearly a pleasure than it would have been without him.

Lila Namir and Etha Frenkel gave very helpful advice in matters of style and presentation and deserve my warmest thanks. So do Haya Gratch, Marcy Sherver, and Sharon Ronis, the typists, who unflinchingly struggled with labyrinthine handwritten drafts.

My concern with psycholinguistics goes back many years and may be traced ultimately to the influence of my parents, who both had a deep, humanistic interest in language. This book is dedicated to their memory.

I. M. SCHLESINGER

Jerusalem

Introduction

A model of language production and comprehension must deal, among other things, with two topics:

1. What is the nature of the rule system which the speaker has internalized:
2. How are these rules applied in production and comprehension?

It might be argued that the first of these problems is within the province of linguistics. The linguist describes deep structures and transformation rules, and what is left for the psycholinguist, therefore, is to deal with the second problem: he must show how the latter are applied by the speaker in uttering sentences. And since there are currently two competing schools of grammar, the psycholinguist may have to lean back and wait for the outcome of the ongoing tournament between generative and interpretive semanticists before setting out to develop his performance model.

Such has indeed long been the predominant approach in psycholinguistics, despite the warning already sounded by Chomsky in 1961 against the "utterly mistaken view that the generative grammar itself provides or is related in some obvious way to a model for the speaker" (Chomsky, 1961, footnote 16). For a long time this warning was conveniently ignored with the hope, perhaps, that if the linguist takes care of content, performance will largely take care of itself. This approach may also have been encouraged by some of Chomsky's casual remarks on the competence–performance distinction which left room for an interpretation which essentially equates a generative grammar with the internalized rule system and the generation of sentences with the way the internalized rules operate (see Derwing, 1973, pp. 259–270; Greene, 1972, pp. 94–100; Schlesinger, 1971a for a discussion of Chomsky's writings on this issue).

In recent years, however, it has become increasingly clear that the equation of grammatical and psycholinguistic processes is untenable. Experimental findings of discrepancy between transformational complexity and difficulty of processing have accumulated. For years now Fodor and his associates have insisted that the relationship between rules of grammar and psycholinguistic processes is more "abstract" than has often been assumed (Fodor, 1971; Fodor & Garrett, 1967). A somewhat more extreme claim has been forwarded by Watt (1970, 1972), who argues persuasively that the grammar internalized by the hearer—speaker cannot be identical with the linguist's grammar. This view is shared by Elisabeth Ingram (1971), who has also shown that the rules of language performance cannot be those of a grammar, and also by McNeill (1975b).

This study endorses that view. To develop a performance model we must let go of the linguist's apron strings and look at linguistic functioning from a new vantage point. Research should no longer be aimed at finding proof for the psychological reality of linguistic constructs, as it has been for over a decade, but at confirming or disconfirming hypotheses arrived at by considerations of what the processes of speaking and understanding might be like. Of course, this does not imply that we can avoid taking into account insights gained through research on transformational grammar, as some psychologists still seem to believe. There can be no turning back of the clock, and the days before the linguistic revolution, when one could rest content with simplistic theories of stimulus—response chains bolstered by stimulus equivalence classes and what not, are no more. For better or for worse, any theory of performance today will have to be more mentalistic than was dreamed of in the fifties.

Any attempt at constructing a model of language production and comprehension will have to be constrained by what linguists tell us, but we cannot stop at that and simply argue that the linguist's grammar is "incorporated" into such a model. There was a time when any discrepancy between what a grammar might predict and empirical findings about the speaker—hearer's behavior was shrugged off as resulting from "performance factors." When this practice continues for too long and in the face of too many discrepancies, the grammar is in danger of becoming enshrined as dogma. Against this approach it should be realized that there is no a priori reason why the grammar that the speaker has in his mind must be isomorphic to the linguist's grammar as currently conceived.[1] In fact, as is shown in this text, there is every reason to suspect that in many respects it is constructed quite differently.

---

[1] The tables have been turned recently by writers who argue that a grammar should be "performance oriented" (Chafe, 1970; Kay, 1970; Schlesinger, 1967). While it seems reasonable to expect that linguistic theorizing will be affected by considerations of performance, it is possible to defend an approach which denies this. For the time being, at least, linguists have their hands full giving a reasonably satisfactory account of language which squares with linguistic intuitions, without burdening themselves (it might be argued) with accounting for facts from other domains. (For a divergent view see Derwing, 1973.) If this approach is followed, psycholinguistic theorizing will diverge increasingly from linguistics. Ultimately, of course, linguistics and psycholinguistics will have to converge on one overall theory.

Recent years have witnessed a breaking away from this undue reliance on linguistic theory. In the development of computer programs for language comprehension taking over the apparatus of any of the current models of generative grammar was not feasible. A somewhat different type of grammar, called augmented finite state transition network grammar, which is suitable for computer parsing of sentences, has been proposed by Woods (1970) and employed in several programs written since.

Computer simulation, however, is susceptible to that error which previous psycholinguistic research has fallen into. As stated above, the fact that grammar can generate the sentences of a language has lured investigators into the unwarranted conclusion that it also describes human language use. Likewise, the fact that a computer program can process sentences does not imply that the human processor is programmed in the same way. Those engaged in computer simulation of natural-language comprehension have typically taken care to indicate from time to time that their program models the way humans presumably function, and they sometimes adduce an argument or two to this effect. Still, one is often left with the impression that their work tends to be dominated to an extent by the exigencies arising from the nature of the computer with usually only more or less perfunctory attention being paid to the human use of language which it intends to simulate. It is, after all, only natural that in working with the computer the thinking of these investigators should gradually accommodate itself to this medium.[2] Traces of this effect on recent programs discussed at various places in this book will be noticed by the reader. It will be argued that current work in programming has failed to take to account several important aspects of human processing. Let us examine here briefly one of these aspects.

One of the main themes of our present proposal is that in production and comprehension of utterances various alternative routes are available to the human processor. The "noisy" conditions in which human communication usually takes place and the nature of the organism, more fallible than the computer, require that the processor be versatile. In comprehension, there is the additional requirement that there be redundant cues in the utterance which the processor can select from. There can be no royal road to understanding an utterance or to producing it – contrary to what is currently assumed in computer programming. Rather, many alternatives are open to the speaker and hearer, the choice between them being determined by such momentary factors as focus of attention and saliency of various aspects of the message. It is little wonder that such capricious conduct is not congenial to computer programming.

However, the difficulties of simulating such versatility are not impossible to overcome. The way will be open to devising more sophisticated computer

---

[2] At least one of these investigators is clearly aware of this himself. He states candidly: "Since I have, in some sense, been 'thinking' in Planner [the computer language] ... The method ... which was in the back of my mind while writing this thesis is the method which is most natural to Planner" (Charniak, 1972, pp. 51, 52).

programs, once one has a clear conception of what a model of the human use of language is like. Theoretical investigations of language behavior, then, must precede computer simulation, not merely be accessory to it.

This summing up of the present state of affairs suggests that we have come to the point at which we need to pause and take stock. If laboratory experimentation is not to become aimless busy work and if computer simulation is to refrain from traipsing around without approaching an understanding of human processing, we must attempt to gain a clear notion of what a sensible model of language production and comprehension must look like. The course of psycholinguistic research in the past 15 years or so should at least have taught us that it is not enough to take care of the facts: their theoretical import will not take care of itself. Since current linguistic models can no longer serve as a paradigm for performance, new theoretical foundations must be developed.

This realization has guided the attempt made here to rethink many of the basic issues. But this book is only a first step in this direction, and the reader should be warned not to expect from it what it does not profess to offer. Presented here is not a theory, in the sense that it directly yields testable predictions, but rather what one might prefer to call a framework for a theory. This framework must be developed further; it must gain substance before one will be justified in talking of it as of a verifiable theory. However, this does not mean that it is immune to debate at its present stage. On the contrary, since the claims made here are based on the evidence of already existing data and on a priori considerations, they can be examined and tentatively accepted, amended, or rejected. Previous versions of the manuscript of this book circulated among colleagues have, in fact, been so discussed, and this has already led to various clarifications and revisions.

But, one may ask, what is the point of publishing a forensic that is only on the way to becoming a testable theory? It seems to me that, as matters now stand in this field, a stronger theory is not necessarily a better one. True, a loose formulation like the one presented here has the obvious methodological disadvantage of not being easily refutable. On the other hand, there is some merit in leaving various options open, since this may provide a kind of master plan for theory construction. It will hopefully engender specific research hypotheses, the testing of which may lead to increasingly tighter formulations. It would be quixotic to attempt such a tighter formulation already at this point: it stands hardly any chance of being true. The book, then, will have achieved its objective if it provides a perspective for future discussion and research.

Theorizing about language processing, like all theorizing, implies concentrating on certain kinds of phenomena and considering them in relative isolation from others. Where the boundaries are drawn between what is being considered and what is not depends on the theorist, his interests and his intuition as to what can safely be disregarded for the time being. His decision may turn out to have been a good one; or it may later be found to have led to an impasse, as when psycholinguists gradually came to realize that early attempts to study linguistic performance without regard to semantic variables were futile. As for a model of speech production, it seems obvious that we can not afford to disregard what happens when speaking goes wrong. In discussing production of utterances I have therefore paid attention to the possible implications of recent work on such malfunctions as hesitation phenomena and speech errors. Aphasic disturbances, on the other hand, have not been dealt with here. The reason is not that they seem to be any less relevant and important, but simply that I have not managed to clarify to myself what the currently available data reveal about normal functioning.

My account is also incomplete in that it merely mentions but does not discuss in depth the final phase of production—conversion of words into speech sounds — nor the first phase of comprehension: perception of speech sounds and their organization into words. These are relatively well-studied areas and I had nothing to contribute to them.

Other areas neglected here are those usually studied by sociolinguists. Ultimately a theory of production and comprehension will have to deal with various aspects of the interaction between speaker and hearer; and, likewise, it will have to encompass motivational factors which interact with linguistic functioning. All these have been left out of account here. At this stage, it seems both possible and necessary to exclude such factors from the deliberations leading to theory construction and to examine only the cognitive processes which lead to the emission of utterances and to understanding them.

There is one area, however, which can not be dismissed in this manner even in a preliminary attempt like the present one. One of the premises of this study is that a model of linguistic performance must take into account the child learning his native language. Conversely, since the child ultimately develops an adult performance mechanism, a theory of language development must cope with the problem of how he acquires the rules according to which this mechanism operates. The genetic viewpoint has, therefore, been attended to throughout this study. In fact, by posing both the above problems jointly some of my ideas first took shape. These were published in a paper entitled accordingly: "Production of utterances and language acquisition" (Schlesinger, 1971b).

In that paper some of the central notions of the following chapters were first proposed. It was claimed, in opposition to the then prevalent view, that the structures underlying speech are semantic. The semantic presentations which were assumed to form the input to the production model were called input-markers. The short term for these, which has since gained some currency, is I-MARKERS.[3] But in introducing this acronym I then intimated that it might also

---

[3] A note on terminology. The term I-marker was intended as a contrast to P-MARKER, or phrase-marker, a term used (previously more than now) for the underlying structure in transformational grammar. In dealing with linguistic performance it seems wise to use a terminology differing from that used in generative grammar, so as to avoid confusion and the illusion that one can borrow uncritically from linguistics. I have therefore introduced quite a few new terms and avoided many of the current ones, including "competence" and

stand for "intention-marker." This double entendre has turned out to be not too felicitous because, as has meanwhile become clear to me, I-markers should be taken to represent only some, but by no means all, of the aspects of the speaker's intentions.

The latter issue is discussed in the first chapter of this book, which deals with I-markers. In Chapters 2 and 3 I then deal with the mechanism that converts the I-marker into an utterance. The form of the so-called realization rules operative here is essentially that proposed in the above-mentioned paper (Schlesinger, 1971b). The remaining two chapters of Part I treat of additional components of the production model, which together with the I-marker component, may be said to embody the speaker's intentions. The first part thus deals with the production process. Comprehension achieves the reverse of production: it leads from the utterance to a reconstitution of the speaker's intentions. That this is not a mere retracing of the steps taken by the speaker becomes clear in Part II. It is better, however, not to burden the reader at this point with an overview of the second part (such an overview is given at its beginning), but leave him free to proceed to the first chapter.[4]

"meaning." The term "competence" has undoubtedly fulfilled an important role in psycholinguistic thought. At the same time it has been beset with misinterpretations engendered by a lack of precise definition (Schlesinger, 1971a). It has been thought best, therefore, to eschew the use of this term, as well as that of the much-abused "meaning," as far as possible. If I have to make mistakes, I prefer them to be my own rather than have them compounded with those of others. The term "utterance" will be used for the linguistic output: following Bar-Hillel (1969), "sentence" should be reserved for the abstract linguistic structure which is realized by an utterance.

[4] Of the studies reported in this volume some were partly supported by the Human Development Center of the Hebrew University, Jerusalem, and by the Social and Rehabilitation Service of the United States Department of Health, Education and Welfare under Project No. VRA-ISR-32-67, carried out at the Psychology Department, Hebrew University of Jerusalem in cooperation with The Association of the Deaf and Mute in Israel and the Helen Keller House.

Part I

From Intention to Utterance

1
I-Markers

1A. I-MARKERS AND RELATIONS

A production model makes explicit the processes by which the speaker expresses his intentions by utterances, and the structures involved in these processes. One of the central components of our model involves semantic representations. These are formalized as INPUT-MARKERS or I-MARKERS, so called because they serve as input to a mechanism which produces utterances. The rules according to which this mechanism operates will be called REALIZATION RULES.

The claim that the structures underlying utterances are semantic rather than syntactic in nature is motivated in part by considerations of language learning. It has been proposed that in learning the native language the child infers such semantic structures by observing how the relations he perceives in the environment correspond with the adult's utterances (Schlesinger, 1971b). In this way he acquires rules, which he then uses in his utterances.

That the structures underlying speech must be conceptual in nature is recognized by several investigators. Schank (1972, 1973) proposes a comprehension model with a conceptual base, Osgood's (unpublished) semantically based performance model starts with intentions; and Carroll (1973) has adopted the term I-marker for his production model. The ongoing debate in linguistics, whether the base is semantic or whether its semantic representation results from an interpretative component operating on a syntactic base, concerns only the competence model. As far as performance is concerned, even the spokesmen for the interpretative semantics theory recognize that the speaker must start with semantic representations (Katz & Postal, 1964, pp. 169 ff.).

The nature of the concepts which figure in I-markers is discussed below. In this section we discuss the relations holding between these concepts. As an example consider the relations expressed in (1.1) and (1.2):

(1.1)   The witch rides.

(1.2)   The witch has been burned.

Example (1.1) states that the action of riding is performed by the witch. We shall say that the agent—action relation holds between "witch" and "ride" (quotes being used here for concepts), or

(1.3)   (AGENT – ACTION witch, ride)[1]

Note that the name of the relation is capitalized. The arguments of the relation are ordered: according to our convention the action concept is the second argument.

In Example (1.2) 'burn' is an action having 'witch' as its goal, or – again with the action concept as second argument –

(1.4)   (GOAL–ACTION witch, burn)

Consider now an I-marker of a somewhat more complex sentence like

(1.5)   Alice kicks poor Bill.

Here we have three dyadic relations[2]: the AGENT–ACTION relation which holds between 'Alice' and 'kick', the GOAL–ACTION relation between 'Bill'

---

[1] The terminology employed in logic might be more consistent and precise, and I have in fact been advised to use it. However, it remains uncertain to what extent a classification based on this terminology comes close to describing underlying psychological processes. The moral to be drawn from the domination of the psycholinguistic scene by terminology of generative grammar seems to be that an established formalism may have a stultifying influence. A new terminology carries no air of finality and may therefore be expected not to obstruct a fresh look at things. Another reason for adopting the present symbolism is that I believe it to be more self-explanatory than logical symbolism, and dealing with it seems to be a less exacting task for psychologists, including myself.

[2] There are of course other possibilities, as for instance a triadic relation with "Alice", "kick", and "Bill" as arguments, and the possibility that "kick" is the relation holding between "Alice" and "Bill." So far, however, I see no good reason to abandon the notion of a hierarchically organized base structure, following in this respect the current practice in linguistics. But in contrast to the usual treatment of attributes, which introduces them by a transformation from an embedded sentence, ATTRIBUTE is regarded here as a dyadic relation on a par with AGENT–ACTION and GOAL–ACTION. In this connection it is of interest to note Bolinger's (1967) linguistic arguments against the derivation of attributives from *be* predications. From the viewpoint of performance, this treatment seems to be intuitively more satisfactory. See also Section 4C, where it is argued that attribution and the corresponding predication have the same underlying I-markers.

Sidney Greenbaum (personal communication) has correctly pointed out that a term like ATTRIBUTE–ATTRIBUANT might be more in keeping with the other names of relations. But this is so awkward that I prefer to abandon consistency in this case.

and 'kick' and the **ATTRIBUTE** relation between 'poor' and 'Bill':

(1.6) (ATTRIBUTE poor, Bill)

That Examples (1.1) and (1.5) are in the present tense must also be represented in the I-marker. Presumably the present tense of Example (1.5) indicates
that the action referred to is habitual. HABITUAL is best viewed as a relation.
Unlike the relations discussed so far, which hold between two independent
concepts, HABITUAL is meaningful in relation to one other concept; i.e., it is a
monadic relation, a relation with one argument ('kick'). The same goes for a
concept like PLURALITY, which in English is also realized by inflection.[3]
Henceforward the term "relation" will be used to refer to monadic relations
(which are often called "properties") as well as to dyadic (two-argument) ones
(or to relations between more than two arguments, if there are such).

It is proposed, then, that I-markers are constituted of relations similar to those
which appear in semantically based grammars (Chafe, 1970; Fillmore, 1968,
1971). But there are a great number of relations which can be perceived in a
situation to which a given utterance pertains. Which of these are to be included
in the I-marker is a question. Linguists are far from agreeing on the 'cases' that
should be included in the grammar and how these should be defined. In addition
to linguistic considerations there may be those relevant to a production model.
What, then, should our criteria be for specifying I-marker relations?

One of the criteria is quite simple, although its application in any specific case
may be anything but that. The function of an I-marker is to serve as input to
realization rules; and hence only those relations which affect the form of the
utterance should be included in the I-marker. I-markers therefore contain only
those relations which are linguistically relevant. In principle, then, I-markers
cannot be investigated independently of realization rules. These two types of
constructs can be meaningfully formulated only within one overall system. In
English the I-marker must contain (where applicable) PLURALITY, which results in a noun being realized in the plural form, whereas certain other languages
which lack a singular—plural distinction ipso facto do not include this informa-

---

[3] However, the way the relation is realized — whether by inflection or as two words — is
not a criterion for classification into monadic and dyadic relations. Monadic relations may
be expressed by the addition of a word, and on the other hand some dyadic relations can be
signalled by affixes (for example, *give it* can be translated by one word in some inflected
languages). The boundary line between monadic and dyadic relations is not quite clear:
should RECURRENCE, for instance, be viewed as a dyadic relation holding between two
concepts which are realized as in the utterance *more cake,* or as a relation with the single
term *cake*? That the distinction between monadic and dyadic relations has psychological
relevance is shown by the finding that small children differ in their strategies of language
acquisition (Bloom, 1973, pp. 111–123). Some children use at first only recurrence and
monadic relations, whereas others start out with dyadic relations like the goal and agent
relations.

tion in the I-marker. On the other hand, the distinction between an action reported by hearsay and one reported as an eye witness, and many other distinctions which may be expressed by some languages, are not expressed in English and not represented in I-markers of English speakers. To an extent, then, I-markers are language specific. This by no means obvious claim is discussed further in Section 5C.

Many more relations can be perceived in the event or object being talked about than are linguistically relevant. A speaker is certain to notice when there is more than one thing spoken about, even if the grammar of his language does not make the singular—plural distinction. Similarly, the speaker of English will be aware that he knows about an action from hearsay, although there is no realization rule in English which expresses this information. It appears, therefore, that when I-markers are viewed as containing only linguistically relevant material they can not be identified with that level at which utterances originate. Rather, prior to I-markers there must be a level representing the way we perceive what we talk about. It is from this level of COGNITIVE STRUCTURES that I-markers are formed.

In Chapter 5 a fuller account will be given of the nature of cognitive structures and of the motivation for distinguishing between them and I-markers. Here it is important to point out that it would be wrong to identify I-markers, tout court, with the intention of the speaker, or as embodying the "meaning" or the "message" of the utterance, or any such pretheoretical notion. The I-marker is a theoretical construct which can be meaningfully conceived of only as a component of the production model, that component which mediates between cognitive structures and the utterance.[4]

This intermediary level is, as stated, semantically based. This means that I-markers, too, are intimately related to the way we organize the world cognitively. The relations in cognitive structures are classified into I-marker relations (Schlesinger, 1974). In addition to perceiving – in our cognitive structures – people moving and pushing things, writing, and talking, these events may be classified – in the I-marker – as involving people doing something, that is, instances of an AGENT—ACTION relationship (as opposed to other events in which, for example, something is happening to them).

Another important requirement for the formulation of I-marker relations is, therefore, that they must be compatible with intuitive notions about the way we perceive the world. The formulation of I-markers must make sense. In principle,

---

[4]One might be tempted to call it *i*ntermediary marker, since it is *i*nput only to realization rules and not to the production mechanism as a whole. Some confusion in this matter may have arisen from a previous treatment of I-markers as representing the *i*ntentions of the speaker (Schlesinger, 1971b). It now seems that this needs to be qualified, since "intention" is a global notion which in a performance model is represented in at least three components: cognitive structures, I-markers and the component of communicative considerations about which more will be said further on.

it is possible that a certain formulation of I-markers and realization rules may account for the production of utterances in a given language but will nevertheless have to be rejected on the grounds that it involves an incongruous picture of the world (it might lump together I-marker relations that are cognitively unrelated).

These two criteria, linguistic relevance and "making sense" cognitively, are still in need of being explored in specifying I-marker relations. For the time being any suggestion as to I-marker relations must be regarded as tentative. One may ask, for instance, whether one and the same GOAL–ACTION relation is employed in talking about moving a picture and painting a picture, or whether 'much sugar' and 'white sugar' exhibit the same or different relations. These and similar questions remain open to investigation. A discussion of a few such problems are found in Sections 2A and 2B.

Let us return now to the structure of the I-marker. For Example (1.5) three relations have been identified. It is now proposed that these are organized hierarchically. Figure 1.1 may give a general idea of this hierarchical arrangement, although it presents only the concepts and not the relations of Example (1.5), and the monadic relation HABITUAL is omitted.

The first argument of the GOAL–ACTION relation is not merely 'Bill', but 'poor Bill'. The first argument of the AGENT–ACTION relation is 'Alice', and the second argument comprises all the remaining concepts. Schematically:

(1.7) AGENT–ACTION Alice, $\overbrace{\hspace{5cm}}$
$\qquad\qquad\qquad$ GOAL–ACTION $\overbrace{\hspace{3.5cm}}$, kick
$\qquad\qquad\qquad\qquad\qquad$ ATTRIBUTE poor, Bill

This can be convently symbolized by parentheses as:

(1.8) (AGENT–ACTION Alice, (GOAL–ACTION
$\qquad\qquad\qquad\qquad\qquad\qquad$ (ATTRIBUTE poor, Bill), kick))

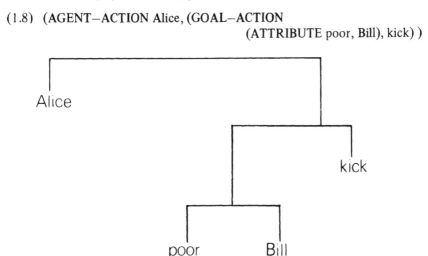

Figure 1.1 Hierarchical structure of *Alice kicks poor Bill*.

In the following, the AGENT–ACTION relation will also be called AGENT RELATION for short, and the GOAL–ACTION relation – GOAL RELATION. (ATTRIBUTE poor, Bill), (GOAL – ACTION (ATTRIBUTE poor, Bill), kick), and in general any section of an I-marker between a pair of parentheses belonging together, will be called I-MARKER CONSTITUENT.

As the following examples show, an argument in a dyadic relation may be a conjunction of two concepts:

(1.9)   John and Paul write articles and film scripts.

(1.10)   John and Paul write and sell film scripts.

(1.11)   John and Paul write articles and film scripts, respectively.

(1.12)   John writes scripts and Paul sells them.

The conjunction of the agent terms in the I-markers underlying Examples (1.9) and (1.10), that of the action terms in Example (1.10), and that of the goal terms in (1.9) must of course be represented in the I-marker. Further, the terms of the I-marker may have to be indexed so as to distinguish, for instance, Example (1.9) from Example (1.11), and to indicate that the goal of 'write' is identical to that of 'sell' in Example (1.12).

Moreover, whole I-markers may be conjoined like the one underlying Example (1.12). The application of certain realization rules will result in this I-marker being realized as Example (1.12); if certain other rules are applied, the result will be an utterance of two independent sentences. While a grammar assigns an underlying structure to each sentence, there is no a priori reason why each I-marker must be expressed by a single sentence.

In addition to conjunctions realized by *and*, there are those realized by *but*, *or*, and other connectives, each of which must be represented in the I-marker. Further, the I-marker must reflect certain forms of subordination. All this presents no special problems and hence will not be explained in further detail here.

The I-markers are mapped into utterances by realization rules. For a given I-marker there will often be more than one mapping. The I-marker underlying Example (1.12) may be alternatively realized by two sentences, or as (one conjoined, or two) passive sentences, or as

(1.13)   It is John who writes scripts and Paul who sells them.

and in several other ways. Various considerations influence the choice between these alternatives. Our model must include a component that determines which of several possible realization rules are to operate on a given I-marker. This component of COMMUNICATIVE CONSIDERATIONS is discussed in Chapter 4. Realization rules and their manner of operation are dealt with in Chapters 2 and 3. But first some further issues pertaining to I-markers must be taken up in this chapter.

1B. THE ELEMENTS OF I-MARKERS

So far we have called the elements between which I-marker relations hold "concepts." It would seem desirable to replace, if we could, this fuzzy notion with a better defined one. "Word" would suggest itself here but there are good reasons against settling for this.

As is shown in Section 3B, certain hesitation phenomena cannot be explained as due to an indecision concerning the way I-marker relations are expressed, but are caused by a search for an appropriate word. This is borne out by introspection: we often find ourselves at a loss for a word appropriate for the concept we have in mind. Karl Bühler (1934, p. 253) reports an experiment in which subjects were asked to introspect on their experiences in producing a sentence and reported on an awareness of a "leeres syntakisches Schema" (empty syntactic scheme) which had later to be filled out by words. These subjects must have had a general idea of what they were going to write about. Their "Schema" therefore must have included those concepts which they later replaced by words.

It is proposed therefore that the elements in I-markers are not words but the stuff words are made of. "Concept" is not quite an appropriate term here, because it is not restricted to the use of language. Those concepts which figure in I-markers and are converted into words will be referred to as PROTOVERBAL ELEMENTS . Let us now see what can be said about the nature of these elements, besides that they are the predecessors of words.

Protoverbal elements are neutral as to grammatical category (form class). When the speaker intends to say something involving the concept 'good', the rules of grammar will prescribe whether this concept will be expressed by the word 'good' or 'well' or 'goodness'. Grammatical category (form class) is introduced by realization rules; it does not reside in the I-marker.[5]

This is a negative characterization of protoverbal elements. What can be positively said about their nature? Here we find ourselves in the midst of an ongoing controversy. Some recent work on the componential analysis of words may be relevant here. According to some investigators (Bierwisch, 1967; Katz, 1972), words may be analyzed as bundles of features or components. Thus, *man* may have the components: male, adult, human. When they involve opposites, components may be marked '+' and '−'. This permits analyzing *woman* as −male, +adult, +human, and *boy* as +male, −adult, +human. Conceivably, protoverbal

---

[5] This is also the reason why the notation of Fillmore (1968) and Chafe (1970) which introduce grammatical categories into the base are inappropriate for our purpose here. Schank (1972) classifies the concepts in his conceptual network into nominals (picture producers), actions and two kind of modifiers: 'picture aids' and 'action aids.' Schank intends his conceptual representations to be 'interlingual,' but it seems doubtful whether his classification may be consistently applied, unless the linguistic realization in a given language is considered a criterion. For instance, 'wind,' 'snow' and 'rain' can be nouns in English, but there is no other reason why these should be nominals rather than actions; 'green' could be a nominal (referring to 'green thing') or a modifier.

elements are not unanalyzed wholes but may be regarded (like words) as bundles or hierarchies of components that have been claimed by Bierwisch (1967) to "represent . . . deepseated innate dispositions of the human organism and the perceptual apparatus (p. 3)." Doubts as to the 'cognitive reality' of the components proposed in recent analyses have been voiced, however, by Lyons (1968, pp. 477–480).

The feasibility of this program of word analysis has also been questioned. The criticisms of Bar-Hillel (1969; see also Bar-Hillel, 1967) and Bolinger (1965) of Katz' semantic theory have not been fully and successfully answered, as far as I see, in the latest revision of the theory (Katz, 1972). It appears that this type of analysis is appropriate mainly for 'institutional facts', such as Katz's standard example of *bachelor* and kinship terms (Bierwisch, 1970a), and for verbs of motion (see Ikegami, 1969, whose analysis is within the framework of stratificational grammar, however). Imagine, on the other hand, what a semantic analysis would be like of words designating items of furniture (*table, chair, cupboard,* etc.) or breeds of dogs, and in fact, any number of objects encountered in everyday life. Here the main burden of analysis will have to be borne by so-called distinguishers, which, according to Katz (1972), "mark purely perceptual distinctions (p. 84)."[6] An extreme case is that of the distinction between color terms which seems to rest entirely on such distinguishers. This reliance of much of componential analysis on perceptual aspects seems to suggest that protoverbal elements are perhaps constituted, in varying degrees, of imagery. Introspection seems to bear this out. We often have an image of an object we want to talk about and only subsequently do we find a word for it – perhaps only after we are halfway through uttering the sentence.[7]

Images may contain more information than is accommodated by semantic markers. In most cases they contain at least some of the factual, contingent information that Katz insists must be ruled out of dictionary entries, as, for instance, the information that a bachelor is over one inch tall (Katz, 1972, pp. 73–77; see also Section 9C of this volume). And why shouldn't they? Katz's arguments in this respect are irrelevant as far as the production process is concerned. He proposes that only that information should be included which predicts semantic properties and relations between sentences, such as ambiguity, synonymy, and redundancy. This criterion is relevant for semantic theory, which intends to predict these properties and relations, but there is no reason why a performance model should summarily exclude such information from protoverbal elements. However, the suggestion that protoverbal elements consist of

---

[6] This is not to say that Katz's distinction between conceptual and perceptual can be upheld; see Bierwisch (1969) for arguments against the distinction between distinguishers and semantic markers, which are not invalidated by anything Katz (1972) says.

[7] Note, however, that this fact can be interpreted in two ways: the images may be either in the I-marker or in the cognitive structure out of which the I-marker is formed (see Section 1A).

images, at best, points at a solution of the problem; it does not solve it. Are these images unanalyzable wholes or are they complex entities subject to analysis? That images are the precursors of words was suggested by introspection, and introspection also tells us that these images change from time to time, gaining detail or losing vividness. This makes it rather unlikely that they should be treated as primitives; but if they are complex, the question is how they are to be analyzed. So we are back where we came from.

Another proposal concerning the analysis of words – and one which also suggests a parallel treatment of protoverbal elements – is based on the observation that a word often means the same as a whole phrase. A well-known example is *kill*, which is claimed to be synonymous with *cause to die*. This has led to the suggestion that words may be derived from transformations of underlying phrases. There are important counterarguments to this 'transformationalist' approach, however, which we cannot go into here. (See Fodor, Bever & Garrett, 1974, pp. 197–212, for a discussion of the relative merits of this approach and that of componential analysis, the 'lexicalist' approach.)

Among psychologists word meaning is usually viewed as a mediational process. Osgood (1953, pp. 695–699) has stressed the connotational aspects of the mediational process engendered by a word, but his account leaves room also for perceptual aspects (imagery). Mediational processes can be linked not only to overt stimuli and responses but also to each other. This approach is therefore compatible with the notion of protoverbal elements which are linked by relations in the I-marker.

This brief review of current positions shows how far we are from anything like a definite answer to the problem of word meaning. The question as to the nature of protoverbal elements must therefore be left open. This problem's solution is fortunately not an indispensible prerequisite for theorizing about a performance model: we can regard protoverbal elements as given, and proceed to examine the way they function in the model. Those definite statements which can be made about protoverbal elements concern therefore their role in the production process. One of these is the claim made above that protoverbal elements are neutral as to grammatical category, and the other is considered below.

Protoverbal elements are constructs which figure in I-markers. Just as only those relations are included in I-markers which are relevant to the way the latter are expressed in utterances (see Section 1A), the system of protoverbal elements contains only those distinctions which result in different lexicalizations. Cognitively we often make far finer distinctions, but any distinction that cannot be expressed by choosing a different lexicalization is not represented by different protoverbal elements. Protoverbal elements are therefore language dependent: languages differ in the way their vocabularies classify experience. Examples of this are legion. An extreme case is the Israeli Sign Language, which often has an indefinite number of signs for what in some languages may be expressed by only one word (hence, it has only one protoverbal element). Thus, there are different ways of signing what the speaker of English calls *to carry*, depending on whether the thing carried is an umbrella, a heavy box, a cigarette holder, a baby, etc. (Cohen, Namir & Schlesinger, in press). In this language, then, there are correspondingly many protoverbal elements for the action of carrying. Of course these distinctions are perceptually conspicuous enough for the speaker of English to be aware of, but since they are linguistically irrelevant for him, they do not function in his system of protoverbal elements. Finally, it should be evident that since speakers of any one language differ in the vocabulary at their disposal, they likewise differ in their system of protoverbal elements.

1C. ORDER AND SALIENCY IN THE I-MARKER

The notation for I-markers introduced in Section 1A imposes a certain kind of order: if the sequence of elements and relations in the I-marker in Example (1.8) is changed, a different I-marker results, the realization of which will be a different sentence. However, this sequence does not imply any temporal order of processing or any other kind of behavioral primacy of one relation over another. Evidently, adoption of a different notational convention – for example, in AGENT–ACTION *a, b* the action term is symbolized by *b* instead of *a* – would result in a different left-to-right sequence in the I-marker, but this has nothing to do with the way I-markers are ultimately expressed by utterances.

This may seem to be an obvious point to make, but as far as the order of base structures postulated by transformational grammar is concerned, there has been some confusion on this issue in the literature. Base structures do not contain words but abstract elements (including PAST and PASSIVE) and there can therefore be no sense in which base structures themselves are uttered, as has been suggested (McNeill, 1970, p. 32). The order of morphemes in the base structure does not imply anything about the actual uttering of the corresponding sentence (the point of Chomsky's, 1965, pp. 123–127, claim that base structures are ordered being that this permits a more parsimonious description of transformations). It is therefore incorrect to speak of "serial and left-to-right" processing of base structures (Trabasso, 1972). The same applies also to I-markers. Ordering in the I-marker is not dependent on the choice of notation. Parts of the I-marker indeed differ in saliency, and hence in availability for processing. The studies cited below are of sentence comprehension rather than production, but since I-markers must also be retrieved by the listener, these studies are pertinent here.

In a series of concept learning experiments, Trabasso and Gough (Trabasso, 1972) showed that it is easier to classify sentences according to the agent (deep structure subject) than according to the patient (deep structure object). This effect could not be accounted for by the sequence of words in the surface, because it held up to some extent also in passive sentences where the deep structure object precedes the deep structure subject. Blumenthal (1967) found that in the recall of passive sentences the agent appearing in a *by*-phrase (as *by tailors*) is a better prompt than the instrument appearing in a *by*-phrase (as *by machine*), which suggests that the former relation is more salient (see also Blumenthal & Boakes, 1967). In a replication it was found that this factor interacts with degree of imagery (Danks & Sorce, 1973). Further, learning studies have found differential recall for various sentence parts. While a number of studies have come up with conflicting results (see Wearing, 1970, for a summary of these), and confounding factors such as imagery may have been at work, it seems likely that these effects are due, in part at least, to differential saliency in the I-marker which has been constructed during learning and is processed at the time of recall.

These effects might be laid down to our experience with language. A large proportion of sentences uttered have an agent, fewer express the goal (the deep structure object) or the instrument. This use of language phenomenon is likely itself to be an outcome of our cognitive organization.

In his early one-word utterances, the small child signals relations, and the word he utters is the one expressing the argument which is most informative at the time (Greenfield & Smith, 1976). There also seems to be a tendency in the early multiword utterances of small children to place first the word standing for the most salient element in the situation (Schlesinger, in press). Perhaps this is what also accounts for the preferred word order in most languages, in which the subject precedes the object (Greenberg, 1963). In the sign language of the Israeli deaf, which has no fixed order for subject and object, there is nevertheless a tendency for the agent to be mentioned first in the sentence (Schlesinger, 1971a; Namir & Schlesinger, in press).

The above experimental results and observations converge on the conclusion that there is a difference in saliency between various parts of the I-markers (see also Section 6E and Appendix A). Saliency, however, may vary with situational and linguistic context, and there are various ways in which this may be reflected in the utterance so that the information as to what is salient for the speaker is communicated to the hearer (see Section 4A).

SUMMARY

I-markers are semantic representations constituted of protoverbal elements and relations holding between them. These are hierarchically organized. Relations may have one argument (like PLURALITY) or two or more arguments. We are in no position to make definite statements as to which relations are to be included in the I-marker, but there are at least two criteria for such inclusion: (1) Since it is the function of the I-marker to serve as input to realization rules, all relations must be linguistically relevant; and (2) since the I-marker is a way of categorizing experience for the purpose of utterance production, the relations must 'make sense' semantically.

Protoverbal elements are the concepts figuring in I-markers. In the course of the realization process these are converted into words, but they themselves are neutral as to grammatical category. I-marker relations and protoverbal elements have this in common, that they may vary from language to language. This is so, because only those distinctions are represented in the I-marker of a given language which are expressed in it.

There is no spatial or temporal left-to-right order in the I-marker (or any other order for that matter); such an order is a property only of utterances. However, various experimental findings suggest that I-marker elements and relations may differ among themselves in degree of saliency.

2
Realization Rules

2A. THE RULE SYSTEM IN A PRODUCTION MODEL

The term REALIZATION RULES has been proposed for the rules mapping I-markers into utterances (Schlesinger, 1971b). Among realization rules we distinguish the following: (1) RELATION RULES which determine how the relations of the I-marker are expressed by means of word order, affixes, function words and grammatical category; (2) the LEXICON which "translates" protoverbal elements of the I-marker into words and phrases; (3) CONCORD RULES which assign inflections to words according to the requirements of inflectional linkage of the language (Hockett, 1958, pp. 214–218); (4) INTONATION RULES which impose intonation contour; and (5) PHONOLOGICAL RULES which determine the phonological shape of the utterance. The last three are not discussed here at length; most of our discussion is devoted to relation rules and the lexicon. But first some general questions concerning the nature of the rules in the production model have to be clarified.

It is becoming increasingly recognized that the rules by which linguistic performance proceeds cannot be identical with the transformational rules of generative grammar. More and more evidence has accumulated that difficulty in comprehension often fails to be predicted by the derivational history of the sentences in question (Fodor, 1971; Fodor & Garrett, 1967; Watt, 1970, pp. 169–171). Dingwall (unpublished manuscript) also found no support for predictions derived from transformational rules in four experiments employing four different tasks.

According to Fodor (1971), the grammar internalized by the hearer–speaker does not permit prediction of behavior, because its effects are overlaid by perceptual strategies. However, he sees no reason to discard the assumption that what is internalized must be the grammar arrived at by linguistic research. This assumption is rejected by Watt (1970, pp. 179–189; 1972) who argues persuasively that it is implausible on a priori grounds that what he calls the "mental grammar" should be identical with the linguist's grammar. This is because the two must employ quite different criteria of economy. Economy for the linguist is economy of the overall system, in terms of rules and other constructs, whereas in the mental grammar quite a different principle of economy must be operative, according to which the number of rules employed in the production of any single utterance ought to be kept at a minimum. Watt shows that these two principles of economy necessarily conflict and that the mental grammar must be constituted by some compromise between them.

What the compromise might be in each individual case is, of course, far from clear, but in some cases relevant data are available. Watt discusses the example of the truncated passive, which runs roughly as follows. There are good reasons for the linguist to assign to the truncated passive a more complex derivation than to the full passive, with the former requiring a deletion transformation in addition to the transformations required for the latter. Now, this apparently does not hold for the child learning to speak who masters the truncated passive before the full passive and therefore cannot have derived it from the latter. The child presumably derives a truncated passive like *the chair is pushed* in the same way as an adjectival predicate, such as, *the chair is green*. Later he acquires the full passive.[1] But, argues Watt, it is unreasonable to suppose that the child then discards the above simple derivation of the truncated passive for a more complex one which relates it to the full passive, only in order to achieve more economy in his overall system of rules (see also Schlesinger, 1967, p. 401). Instead, he presumably remains with two derivations: the simple one for the truncated passive (which is the same as for sentences with adjectival predicate) and a somewhat more complex one for full passives. The fact that for adults, too, the truncated passive is easier to process than the full passive corroborates this hypothesis. In this case, then, economy in the performance of a single construction overrides the linguist's economy.

Watt's argument has been gone into in such detail here because of its importance in theorizing about linguistic performance. In the past psycholinguistic theorizing has been too much constrained by the rule system of generative grammar. If progress toward a viable performance model is to be made, we must learn to look at performance with fresh eyes, drawing on all the psychological knowledge we can muster, without, of course, disregarding linguistic findings which describe the product a performance model must produce.

It must be concluded that the performance model follows a principle of economy which is not based exclusively on the number of constructs in the

---

[1] Bolinger (1967) has pointed out that the passive participle may designate characteristics rather than the passive of actions. Thus, *the stolen jewels* refers to a characteristic of the jewels, unlike *the jewels stolen*, which is the passive of the action; and the truncated passive *the jewels were stolen* is ambiguous between the latter two.

grammar as a whole. This conclusion is relevant to the question of the place of syntactic constructs in a performance model. The problem has been raised by some writers (e.g., Brown, 1973) how a semantically based deep structure, like that proposed by Schlesinger (1971b) for child language, can eventually develop into an adult grammar. More specifically, it has been argued by Bowerman (1974) that it is doubtful whether one can do away with syntactic constructs altogether, since the latter achieve greater simplicity of the rule system. For instance, there are a number of semantic relations which are expressed by the grammatical category "subject of," as the agent, the instrument, and the person affected, as in

(2.1) John cut the meat.

(2.2) The knife cut the meat.

(2.3) The boy wants (sees, likes . . .) the knife.

There are various transformation rules, such as passivization, which are statable in terms of the "subject of" category (or the equivalent formulation in terms of syntactic categories; see Chomsky, 1965, pp. 68–74). If this category were to be discarded, the respective rule would have to be stated redundantly several times, once for each of the corresponding semantic concepts. Bowerman therefore suggests that while the child starts out with semantic categories, he soon learns to subsume these under more abstract syntactic categories.

Now, if it is correct that for the adult as well as for the child the input to utterance production involves semantic relations representing the speaker's intentions, then Bowerman's suggestion implies the following. In addition to semantic concepts like agent, instrument, and person affected, the adult production model includes also syntactic concepts, like subject. Realization rules operate on semantic concepts in the I-marker (like the former) and convert them into utterances via syntactic constructs, like subject.

For a child learning his native language, two-stage rules like these would be presumably more difficult to master than one-stage rules, in particular since syntactic concepts are involved. The grammar of the native language is learned essentially by observing coocurrences of linguistic structures with certain relations perceivable in the environment (Schlesinger, 1971b). Purely syntactic constructs devoid of any referent in the world around him would be inaccessible to this learning strategy, and it is not clear how he could acquire them. Note that the motivation for Bowerman's suggestion is the overall simplicity of the rule system achieved by the introduction of syntactic categories. This is based on the linguist's economy criterion. But this economy is achieved at the expense of complicating the task of the child learning language. One may therefore wonder, with Watt, whether this is the economy criterion according to which the performance model is constructed. It does not seem at all implausible that the performance model duplicates its rules – for the agent, for the instrument, and for the person affected – in order to make it easier for the child to acquire his grammar. "Missing a generalization," which is regarded as a cardinal sin by some linguists, may at times be a virtue in a performance model.

Apart from these considerations, it can be shown that the specific examples given above—the agent, instrument, and person affected—admit of another interpretation. There are various ways in which the relations we perceive to hold in the world around us can be categorized. As already has been pointed out in Section 1A, the relations suggested there should be considered only as tentative (and so should their names). It may be the case, therefore, that the agent relation in the I-marker should be conceived of as a wider and more inclusive relation than that which we commonly call by this name. The instrument in Example (2.2) above may perhaps be conceived of, somewhat metaphorically, as a kind of agent, and a similar process may perhaps occur for other relations. Let this be called the SEMANTIC ASSIMILATION HYPOTHESIS. Some of its empirical consequences are explored below, where it is shown by some linguistic observations that the instrument, when it is realized as subject as in Example (2.2), has some of the connotations of the agent. This permits us to subsume the instrument (in some cases) and the agent under one semantic relation. To the extent that this solution is applicable to other semantic relations commonly expressed as subjects, there no longer is a reason for hypothesizing a routine of realization rules through the syntactic construct "subject of." How much further simplicity in the overall system can be achieved by formulating the semantic relations in the I-marker in a maximally "efficient" manner remains to be seen.

2B. SEMANTIC ASSIMILATION

The agent is defined by Fillmore (1971) as "the instigator of the action" and the instrument as "the stimulus or physical cause of an event." Hence, the subject of Example (2.4) expresses the agent case, whereas the subjects of Examples (2.5) and (2.6) express the instrumental case:

(2.4) John smashed the shop window.

(2.5) The car smashed the shop window.

(2.6) The storm smashed the shop window.

The rationale for this distinction is that cars and storms do not "instigate" events. Now, while this is true for the educated adult, the young child probably treats cars and other vehicles as animate (Bowerman, 1973a, pp. 87–88) and the wind as instigator of action. Primitive thought is similarly animistic. Constructions like Examples (2.5) and (2.6) came into being at a period where the relations involved were presumably viewed as not very different from those in Example (2.4). In Greenlandic one does not say *I shot the arrow* but *the arrow is flying away from me* (Waisman, 1962), apparently crediting the arrow with "instigating the action" rather than being the goal of the action. And it is most likely that for all our twentieth-century mentality we may still think of cars and storms and other instruments, like knives and brooms, as sorcerers' apprentices doing the job by themselves. In Fillmore (1968) the agent was still defined as "typically animate," but in Fillmore (1971) this characteristic no longer appears in the definition of the agent. I assume that this is because Fillmore realized that there are too many personifications like *the nation* and *the robot* which may serve as agents (see Fillmore, 1968, p. 31, fn. 24). Now, just as the animate—inanimate distinction becomes obliterated by personification, the instigator—instrument distinction may be disregarded in a quasimetaphorical manner of speaking (see Lyons, 1968, p. 298).

It is suggested, then, that for the purpose of formulating our intentions, the storm is regarded as agent — where this concept is now more broadly conceived than Fillmore's instigator of action — just as John is in Example (2.4). The situation described in Example (2.5) may also be regarded differently so that the car is the instrument by means of which the agent performs the action; but then the intention will be formulated so as to result, for instance, in Example (2.7):

(2.7)   John smashed the shop window with the car.

By contrast, in Example (2.5) *the car* is regarded as agent, like *the storm* in Example (2.6). Unlike Example (2.5) which has its parallel in Example (2.7), Example (2.6) has, of course, no similar alternative.

The proposal that the instrument be treated as a kind of agent receives some empirical support from the observation of some constraints upon what Fillmore views as the subjectivization of the instrument. In certain cases the instrument can be expressed either by an adverbial phrase, or by the subject, as in Examples (2.8) and (2.9); but in other cases it can be expressed only by an adverbial phrase (Example 2.10) and subjectivization as in Example (2.11) would be unacceptable.

(2.8)   The conductor made a few jerky movements with his bow.

(2.9)   The bow made a few jerky movements.

(2.10)   The conductor conducted the symphony orchestra with his bow.

(2.11)   *The bow conducted the symphony orchestra.

A similar example is the following:

(2.12)   John struck the table with the old cards.

(2.13)   The old cards struck the table.

(2.14)   John played poker with the old cards.

(2.15)   *The old cards played poker.

In Example (2.9) *the bow* is viewed as a sort of agent, and therefore it is subjectivized. We can even ask: *What did the bow do?*, and Example (2.9) would be an appropriate answer; which suggests that this is what it does by itself. Conducting a symphony, however, is much too serious an affair to entrust to a bow, even metaphorically; a conductor is needed to do that. It is also too much to demand of cards that they should play a game of poker on their own, as in Example (2.15). Further examples have been given in Schlesinger (1974), showing that when an action requires deliberation, the instrument cannot be subjectivized. The most plausible explanation for this is that the instrument is subjectivized only when it is treated as an agent, and there are limits beyond which one does not go in treating inanimate objects as agents.

Finally, some support for the hypothesis comes from the possibility of conjoining noun phrases. "Only noun phrases representing the same case may be conjoined" (Fillmore, 1968, p. 22), and accordingly Example (2.16) would be unacceptable.

(2.16)   *John and the car smashed the shop window.

This principle of conjunction is the fulcrum of Dougherty's (1970) criticism of Fillmore's case grammar. In addition to what he has to say there is a counterexample (pointed out to me by Sidney Greenbaum) of what case grammar would regard as an instrument being conjoined with what is clearly an agent:

(2.17)   The area was ravaged by floods and by guerilla forces.

According to Fillmore's own criterion, then, *floods* would be an agent (unless *guerilla forces* is analyzed as instrument — but these are animate). Quirk, Greenbaum, Leech, and Svartvik (1972, p. 325), from whom this example is taken, suggest that when different processes are involved, as in Example (2.17), conjoining is possible, but not where the actions carried out by what are expressed by the two noun phrases are one and the same process, as in Example (2.16). This has to be refined, however, as shown by:

(2.18)   *John and the knife cut the bread and the salami, respectively.

Here different processes are referred to and still conjoining is unacceptable. The reason seems to be that while John and the knife could have cut the same object by the same process (John as agent, knife as instrument), guerillas and floods ravage in different ways and guerillas do not ravage areas with floods, as John cuts with a knife. In other words, the conjunction principle shows that the instrument can be viewed as agent, as in Example (2.17). Such a view is naturally ruled out in cases where mention is made of an agent who either actually uses the instrument in performing the action, Example (2.16), or could have used it, Example (2.18), because here we are "reminded" of the fact that these are really instruments and not agents.

The argument for syntactic categories in the performance model in Section 2A was based on the claim that syntactic categories like "subject of," in terms of which transformations are most parsimoniously formulated, may express different semantic categories. The above discussion shows that, as far as the agent and instrument are concerned, this claim is unfounded. Instruments are expressed as subjects when they are viewed as a sort of agent.[2] Matters are less clear for other semantic categories, but I think there is some merit in regarding them, too, as agent whenever they are subjectivized. Thus, a distinction is usually made between the agent who performs actions and the "experiencer" or "person affected" who is in some state, usually expressed by so-called stative verbs like *see, want,* and *know.* But the boundary line here seems hard to draw. In which of the following sentences, for instance, should one regard *John* as agent, and in which as experiencer?:

(2.19)   John knows the answer.

(2.20)   John recalls the answer.

(2.21)   John guesses the answer.

(2.22)   John computes the answer.

Computing seems quite definitely to be an action, but guessing appears to me only slightly less so, and under certain circumstances I would consider recalling to be quite an active process. When something is viewed one way under certain circumstances and another way under others, a fixed boundary must be lacking. The two relations begin to merge and perhaps there is no clear distinction to be made. As Sidney Greenbaum pointed out to me, students need some convincing that verbs like *see* do not designate an action. Perhaps the students are right as far as performance is concerned, and stative verbs like *see* and *know* as well as action verbs like *smash* and *compute* belong with their subjects under one broad agent—action relation (which perhaps deserves a name more neutral between active and stative). Of course their difficulty may also be due to the mutual influence between cognition and language: when different situations are described by the same linguistic construction, they are conceived of as instances of the same relation.

Other cases of Fillmore's grammar can also appear as subject. Some of these, such as the location in Example (2.23), cannot be passivized, and so some of the motivation for introducing the subject category in addition to semantic categories — the parsimonious description of transformations — does not apply here with the same force as in the case of the instrumental.

(2.23)   The hall seats 400 people.

Passivization is possible (though awkward) for:

(2.24)   The road made a right turn.

---

[2] It is in line with this analysis that the *by*-phrase in passive sentences may be used to express either the instrument (*by machine*) or the agent (*by the worker*). The instrument and the agent are expressed identically because they are conceived of in the same way.

What semantic relation is involved here? Fillmore (1971) would, presumably, regard *the road* as "object," a case he defines as "the entity that moves or changes or whose position or existence is in consideration [p. 376]." Now, in Example (2.25) *the car* is also an "entity that moves," and might therefore with similar justification be regarded as "object."

(2.25)   The car made a right turn.

On the other hand, since we have Example (2.26) which is related to Example (2.25) like Examples (2.7) to (2.5), Fillmore could regard *the car* in Example (2.25) with as much reason as instrument:

(2.26)   John made a right turn with the car.

The car would thus be ambiguously object and instrument. Whether this can be made palatable for those interested in linguistic description, I do not know.[3] As far as a performance model is concerned, it appears that since a rigid distinction between object, instrument and agent is difficult to be upheld, these should be subsumed under one comprehensive semantic relation, which can be realized in a single manner: agent + main verb. This, of course, makes it unnecessary to postulate that in the course of production a "subject of" category is made use of.

Fillmore's "location" can be expressed as subject, as in Example (2.23), or as object (the syntactic category "object," not Fillmore's semantic category of the same name):

(2.27)   John climbed the Everest.

(2.28)   John scaled the mountain.

(2.29)   John crossed the ocean.

(2.30)   Strangers filled the room.

Since Examples (2.27)–(2.30) may be passivized, they might serve as an argument for the introduction of a syntactic category "object of," by means of which the two semantic relations, goal and location, are realized. But here, too, there is an alternative similar to that suggested above for the instrument: the "location" in Examples (2.27)–(2.30) is actually conceived of as the goal. The same situation may be viewed, metaphorically, in different ways. This is also shown by the following pairs of sentences, where different ways of choosing an I-marker relation result in realizations with different verbs: *the tree* is location in

---

[3] Additional examples have been given by Haas (1973b), who, however, arrived at quite a different conclusion: that there are semantic tendencies the formulation of which is not the task of syntax. His far-reaching suggestions concern the theory of grammar and leave out of account considerations about linguistic performance.

Example (2.31) and goal in Example (2.32):

(2.31)   The forester wrapped sack cloth around the tree.

(2.32)   The forester enwrapped the tree with sack cloth.

So far we have therefore no evidence for a syntactic category "object of" in the performance model. More investigation will of course be needed to determine whether arguments similar to the above are possible for all instances where a single syntactic category apparently expresses various semantic categories.

To summarize, the semantic assimilation hypothesis claims that various semantic relations have been conceived sufficiently similar to the agent relation to be assimilated by it and to be treated like it by the production mechanism. Other relations may have been viewed as similar to the goal relation and been assimilated by it, and presumably there will be additional I-marker relations which are assimilated by others.

Support for the semantic assimilation hypothesis comes also from developmental studies. Several writers have independently reported that the semantic relations in early child language are at first very narrowly conceived and expand only gradually (Bloom, Miller, & Hood, 1975; Braine, 1976; Brown, 1973; Edwards, unpublished manuscript). McNeill (1975a) has referred to this phenomenon as "semiotic extension." Bowerman (1973b) quotes a report on a Russian child for whom the patient category (the goal relation) at first applied only for objects which moved in space. Later, of course, the child must have expanded this category to include all that is subsumed by the adult category; otherwise he would be unable to apply realization rules in the way the adult does. It seems, then, that a certain type of assimilation process starts to appear already in early childhood as a mechanism of developing adult I-marker relations. The semantic assimilation hypothesis goes further, and claims that, in addition, what seem cognitively to be quite distinct relations may be categorized as one I-marker relation on the basis of some perceived similarity. The hypothesis does not imply, however, that the similarity is noticed by each speaker, who then decides to assimilate one relation into another one. Instead, the similarity may have been felt at some point of time by a large enough number of speakers and this gave rise to constructions such as the one expressed in Example (2.25). Thereafter speakers may have learned, as one of the rules of language, that, for example, turns can be made by cars.

In Section 1A the criteria were discussed for specifying which relations figure in I-markers. Two considerations were claimed to be relevant:

1. The I-marker serves as input to realization rules, and therefore only those relations should be included in it which affect the operation of these rules.

2. The I-marker represents the way we structure what we talk about, and therefore I-marker relations must make sense; they must mesh with our intuitions about how the world may be viewed.

The arguments which converge on the semantic assimilation hypothesis illustrate how these two considerations are applied. Two distinguishable relations (agent and instrument) were found to have similar surface realizations, thus suggesting that the distinction between these relations is not linguistically relevant (see Requirement 1 above). The second requirement was also satisfied, since certain sentences in which one of the two relations was expressed could be viewed as metaphorical extensions. It was concluded therefore that the instrument is assimilated to the agent (but only in certain kinds of sentences; complete collapsing of relations may also occur, as shown by the above treatment of the object relation).

An important consequence of this approach should be pointed out. If the system of I-marker relations is determined in part by considerations of similarities in surface realizations, then the I-marker level differs from the deep structure level of current generative models in being much closer to the surface. Or, in other words, the system of realization rules is simplified thereby. It is no longer necessary, for instance, to have a relation rule assigning to the instrument the position of surface subject, if by semantic assimilation it is treated as an agent; the one rule that accords the position of surface subject to the agent is sufficient. This simplification is achieved at the price of introducing an additional level, the level of cognitive structures, as is seen in Chapter 5. But, as is shown there, such a level is required also for other, independent reasons.

The semantic assimilation hypothesis, of course, does not rule out the possibility of semantic notions besides the agent being realized as sentence subjects. Conceivably, instances can be found of a single syntactic category expressing semantic categories so dissimilar to each other that the hypothesis does not seem applicable in that particular case. From this it would follow that the same realization rules must be stated separately for different semantic relations. The assimilation hypothesis would still retain its advantage, discussed above, of making possible greater economy of the rule system. For instance, the examples discussed in this section require that the rules resulting in passivization of the subject need to be stated only once for the agent relation instead of for several semantic relations separately.

Let us examine some possible objections to the assimilation hypothesis. In commenting on the hypothesis, Bowerman (1974) observes that ". . . the subjects of many sentences resist interpretation as agents or even as extended agents . . . (p. 206)" Among the examples she gives are the following:

(2.33) Health legislation continues to be a problem.

(2.34) John benefited from the assignment.

(2.35) The boat trip resulted in several deaths.

It is indeed difficult to see what the subjects of these sentences have in common with the agent, and perhaps these are examples of other semantic relations which may be realized as subjects. Note, however, that since Examples (2.33)–(2.35) cannot be passivized, a major motivation for introducing a "subject" relation – greater economy in the rule system – does not apply here.

A more serious challenge to the assimilation hypothesis seems to be presented by two other examples given by Bowerman:

(2.36) The situation justifies taking drastic measures.

(2.37) Caution outweighed the need for action.

Here passivization can apply. If it is true that the subjects here indeed "resist interpretation as agent," then one might conclude that the subject category cannot be dispensed with if the rule system is to be kept maximally economical (see, however, Section 2A for a discussion of the economy criterion). Note, however, that the subjects of these sentences express abstract concepts. In talking about abstract relationships, language usually provides us with no other means than that of metaphor. Thus, "the situation" is treated as if it were a person who justifies something, as if it were an agent.

Now, even if the abstract concepts in Example (2.37) are replaced by more concrete ones, as in Example (2.38), we do not seem to have a very active agent, but it is not hard to imagine the scene as it might be described in an animated cartoon. It seems therefore not too farfetched to conceive of Example (2.38) – and by metaphorical extension, of Example (2.37) – as realizations of the agent relation:

(2.38) The mouse outweighed the elephant.

But, it might be objected, this kind of argumentation must ultimately lead to despoiling the notion of agent of any semantic content whatsoever. Not so, because what is really proposed here is that the agent relation (and presumably other I-marker relations as well) has a semantic core which attracts other relations more or less similar to it. Consequently, it will of course be "difficult to pinpoint specific cognitive concepts," as Bowerman (1974) remarks, associated with the agent: only what is in the semantic core can be pinpointed, and not what lies in the conceptual shadows.

Consider what could be a possible alternative to the assimilation hypothesis. Suppose, for the sake of the argument, that we accept Bowerman's suggestion that syntactic relations (like the subject relation) are realized in speech, while admitting that what we talk about is cognized in semantic terms. It is possible to claim that this semantic cognization is subsequently crystallized into syntactic terms. This would account for the facts such as that several semantic notions are realizable as subject. But note that this would only push the problem one step back. Why is it that the agent relation as well as that exhibited in Examples (2.36), (2.37), (2.5), (2.19), and (2.24) etc. are all funneled into utterances through the subject construct? The individual speaker may simply have learned (in accordance with the two-stage hypothesis) that this is so, in the course of acquiring the language. But there remains the question of origins: why should language have decided on just this route? The answer must be that at some point a given semantic relation was perceived as sufficiently similar to the agent relation to treat both as subjects. Now, once similarity is conceded to have such an effect, Bowerman's hypothesis has no longer an edge over the semantic assimilation hypothesis. One may just as well assume that a number of relations were at some point in time considered sufficiently similar to the agent relation to be assimilated by it.

Now remains consideration of Patricia Greenfield's suggestion (personal communication, 1974) concerning syntactic relations. She proposes that relations like "subject of" should be retained, not in the deep structure, but in the surface structure produced by realization rules. People are usually quite good at identifying the surface subject of any sentence, and this linguistic intuition should be accounted for by a model of production and comprehension. Greenfield proposes that in learning the native language the child perceives what is common to those I-marker relations which are realized as surface subjects. As a result of the abstraction process the concept of surface subject is formed. This leads to an alternative explanation of the phenomena discussed above: if the surface subject has psychological reality, the speaker may have learned in each case what term in the I-marker can serve as surface subject (see especially Examples (2.23)–(2.24), (2.33)–(2.37)).

The merit of this solution seems to depend on the possibility of assigning some sort of semantic definition to the surface subject. But it is difficult to see what all surface subjects might have in common. The notion of "topic" is the only one which comes to mind; but the topic is not always the same as the surface subject, since it depends also on intonation. The fact remains that the surface subject seems well established in our intuition, as pointed out by Greenfield, but this may be due to nothing more than an awareness of the formal structure of the sentence: the surface subject is a noun or pronoun which agrees in number with the main verb and either stands first in the sentence, or . . . , and so on.

The implication of Greenfield's suggestion is that there may be more than one semantic level underlying speech, and further investigation may show that this is so. As pointed out in Section 1A, there must be a level of cognitive structure beyond the I-marker level, and it is possible also that one I-marker level will not be enough to account for the mechanism of realization. An additional level closer to the surface may be needed into which relations from the deeper level are categorized. As yet, however, there is no evidence for this.

2C. THE FORM OF RELATION RULES

Those realization rules which operate on I-marker relations are relation rules. Before discussing the form of these rules some general remarks are in order.

In the Chomskyan model, transformations are conceived of as mappings of deep structures as a whole into surface structures. Analogously one might propose that realization rules convert I-markers as a whole into strings which underlie utterances. Such a view seems implausible, however, in the light of the observation that speakers very frequently seem to be making up an utterance as they utter it, which often results in hesitations and false starts. This suggests that the relations in the I-marker are realized not all at once, but sequentially. This is the approach adopted in the following: to each I-marker several relation rules are applied. Since these rules may operate sequentially, hesitations and false starts may occur in the course of speaking.

In addition to observations of how people talk, an argument for such a piecemeal realization can be made on the basis of a consideration of the comprehension process. Comprehension should be assumed, for reasons of parsimony, to involve rules which are the inverse of those operating in production; otherwise the speaker—hearer would have to learn two different sets of rules instead of one set of sound—meaning correspondences (relation rules and their inverses). Now, as shown in Section 6A, the listener, too, usually does not process an utterance as a whole. Each of the rules by which he processes an utterance thus can apply only to a section of the utterance, and has as its output a part of the I-marker, and not the I-marker as a whole. If these rules are inverses of those operating in production, then the latter can not apply to the I-marker as a whole.

It is proposed, therefore, that for each relation in the I-marker there is a separate relation rule which specifies how it is realized in the utterance. Before discussing the form of these relation rules, the following problem must briefly be dealt with. There are several alternative ways of realizing a given relation in the I-marker, and the realization of one relation is dependent on the way other relations are realized. For instance, the action—goal relation is realized in one way in the active form and in a different way in the passive (*has locked the gate* versus *the gate has been locked*). The choice between these alternatives is contingent on the choice between the two alternative ways of realizing the agent—action relation (agent preceding action versus *by*-phrase). The mutual dependency between realizations of the goal relation and the agent relation is taken care of in the current Chomskyan model by transformations applying to the deep structure as a whole: one transformation for the active determines the surface string in its entirety and another transformation for the passive results in a different surface string. But within the present framework, if each relation is realized by a separate rule, the mutual dependency between alternatives requires that realization rules must be context sensitive.

There are various ways in which context sensitivity could be introduced into the production model. For instance, it is possible to specify that before each choice between alternative relation rules a search is to be carried out for certain cues in the I-marker, for example, the cue that the utterance is to be in the form of a passive sentence, and that any such cue acts as an order as to which alternative is to be chosen. Another possibility is that orders are issued by some trace left from the previous application of a realization rule. For instance, if a rule has been applied turning the agent into a *by*-phrase, the order is to choose the rule resulting in *the gate has been locked,* rather than in those resulting in *has locked the gate.* Context sensitivity might also occur post hoc, readjusting the outcome of relation rules (for instance, by permuting order) if it clashes somehow with the outcome of previously applied relation rules. These possibilities are not pursued in greater detail here, because two somewhat different partial solutions are presented in the following chapters.

Constraints on grammatical category by which arguments of relations are realized are built into the system of relation rules, and these obviate certain faulty constructions (see Section 3A). Further, the component of communicative considerations, discussed in Section 4A, selects from the set of possible relation rules a subset of rules which is internally consistent, in the sense that they do not result in faulty constructions. Possibly, however, these two devices do not suffice and additional ways, like those mentioned above, will be necessary to ensure the context sensitivity needed to avoid unacceptable outputs of relation rules.

In addition to the principle that relation rules do not apply to the I-marker as a whole, there is another principle which in the preceding section was shown to follow from considerations pertaining to language acquisition. It would be difficult to account for the acquisition of purely syntactic concepts that do not refer to anything in reality. Relation rules should accordingly operate without recourse to intervening syntactic concepts. There is one apparent exception to this principle, however: relation rules must assign a grammatical category to each protoverbal element (I-marker elements are neutral as to semantic category; see Section 1B). Grammatical categories are syntactic concepts; they can not be identified with any semantically defined class. For instance, there is no referential notion common to all nouns. Evidently, not all nouns refer to "objects" or "things". Compare *courtship, action, obedience* with the verbs *court, act, obey* and *height* with *high.* But while they do not correspond to semantic classes, most grammatical categories do have a semantic core (see Lyons, 1968, p. 317 ff.). Therefore other items may become attached to this core by a process similar to semantic assimilation. Thus nouns like the above may have come to be viewed for the purpose of talking as if they were some sort of "thing" just as the instrument may be viewed, for the purpose of talking, as if it was a sort of agent.

Be that as it may, the introduction of grammatical category by relation rules can not be objected to on the grounds that these categories are difficult for the child to acquire. As shown elsewhere (Schlesinger, 1975a), the child may learn the classification into word classes as part of his earliest rules for expressing relations. The class of nouns, for instance, may be for him that class of words which can express the agent term in agent relations as well as the goal terms in goal relations. Learning this categorization may be facilitated at a later stage by morphological cues: for example, verbs are characterized by certain inflections which they can take, and words ending in *ship, tion* and *ence* are usually nouns.

But apart from grammatical categories, relation rules should not introduce grammatical concepts. This principle and the principle discussed above, that to each I-marker relation a separate relation rule applies, now suggest the following general form for relation rules. The input to a relation rule is one of the relations in the I-marker and the protoverbal elements between which it holds. To these elements the relation rule assigns grammatical categories and relative positions in the utterance; and further the relation rule introduces the inflectional affixes and function words required by the language in which the utterance is made.

Let us illustrate the above by a kind of relation rule which is common for dyadic relations in English. The general form of this rule may be symbolized as Rule (2.39) or Rule (2.40):

$$(2.39) \quad (R \, a, \, b) \rightarrow (R \, a^X + b^Y)^Z$$

$$(2.40) \quad (R \, a, \, b) \rightarrow (R \, b^X + a^Y)^Z$$

Here R stands for any dyadic relation, a and b for the arguments of this relation (protoverbal elements). The arrow indicates that the expression to its left is realized as the expression to its right. Let us call the latter expression a REALIZATE. In the realizate the two arguments appear with a plus sign between them, and the sequence of these arguments corresponds to the sequence in which their lexical realization will appear in the utterance. The superscripts X, Y, Z are CATEGORY MARKERS, X and Y specifying the grammatical categories of the two terms, and Z that of the realizate as a whole. The realizate also preserves the information as to the relation which has been realized (R); as becomes clear in Chapter 3, this is necessary for the operation of concord rules and intonation rules.

Let us illustrate how this works by considering a simplified I-marker:

$$(2.41) \quad \text{(AGENT--ACTION Alice, (GOAL--ACTION (ATTRIBUTE poor,}$$
$$\text{lizards), kick)}$$

The monadic relations PLURALITY and HABITUAL have been omitted here for convenience of exposition, and the form of relation rules applying to such relations are discussed in the following. Among the relation rules applied to Example (2.41) are

$$(2.42) \quad (\text{ATTRIBUTE } a, \, b) \rightarrow (\text{ATTR } a^A + b^N)^N$$

$$(2.43) \quad (\text{GOAL--ACTION } a, \, b) \rightarrow (\text{GOAL } b^V + a^N)^V$$

$$(2.44) \quad (\text{AGENT--ACTION } a, \, b) \rightarrow (\text{AGENT } a^N + b^V)^S$$

(The names of relations are given in abbreviated form in the realizate — right of the arrow — so as to distinguish the latter maximally from the I-marker constituents left of the arrow.)

Relation Rule (2.42) states that if a is an attribute of b, this relation may be realized by an adjective (A) which is listed in the lexicon under a, and a noun (N) which is listed in the lexicon under b, and that the adjective must precede the noun. The category marker N after the parentheses indicates that this realizate is to be treated as a noun in further processing. This parallels the noun phrase of transformational grammar; for our purposes the present notation is more convenient, as will become apparent in a moment. Rule (2.42) realizes the constituent (ATTRIBUTE poor, lizards) of (2.41) as ATTR (poor^A + lizards^N)^N.

For most I-marker relations there will be alternative relation rules. Thus Rules (2.43) and (2.44) result in active sentences; for passives there are different rules. Likewise, in English the adjectival attribute may in some cases follow the noun it modifies, as in *the river navigable*[4]; Rule (2.42) is only one of the relation rules which can be applied to (ATTRIBUTE a, b). The decision between these rules is made by the component of communicative considerations (see Section 4A).

Relation Rule (2.43) states that if a is the goal of b, b may be realized as a verb and precede a, and then the latter is realized as a noun; and further, that this realizate functions as a verb in subsequent processing.

Any expression, a or b in the realizate may be either (1) a single protoverbal element, or (2) a realizate resulting from another relation rule whose category marker is identical to that of a (or b).[5] To illustrate, the realizate of Rule (2.42), (ATTR a^A + b^N)^N may function as a in the realizate of Rule (2.43), because both have the same category marker, N. Applying Rule (2.43), after Rule (2.42) has applied to I-marker (2.41), we therefore obtain

(2.45)   (GOAL–ACTION (ATTRIBUTE poor, lizards), kick →
(GOAL kick^V + (ATTR poor^A + lizards^N)^N)^V

Similarly, the realizate of Rule (2.43), having a category marker V, can function as the b term of Relation Rule (2.44), which has the same category marker. Thus the application of Rule (2.44) to I-marker (2.41) results in Example (2.46), which has the realizate of Example (2.45) as its b term

(2.46)   (AGENT Alice^N + (GOAL kick^V + (ATTR poor^A + lizards ^{N})^N)^V)^S

The category marker for this final realizate is S; realizates with this category marker may be embedded (as "sentences") in more complex constructions.

This is not the only sequence in which Rules (2.42)–(2.44) can be applied; but the above will serve to illustrate their manner of operation, which is to be discussed more fully in Section 3A.

Consider now the monadic relations omitted from I-marker (2.41). For PLURALITY, English has the following relation rule:

(2.47)   (PLURALITY a) → (PLUR a^N + s)^N

This converts the element "lizards" of Example (2.41) — or, more precisely,

---

[4] See Bolinger (1967), whose treatment, however, seems to suggest that there are two different relations instead of the one called here ATTRIBUTE.

[5] There are obvious similarities between this approach and categorial grammars (Bar-Hillel, 1964b).

(PLURALITY lizard) – into *lizards*. Note the s in Example (2.47) is sans serif to indicate that it serves directly as input to phonological rules, in contrast to other arguments in the realizates of Rules (2.42)–(2.44) and in Example (2.47), which are protoverbal elements and have to be converted into words before being uttered.

Another monadic relation omitted from Example (2.41) is HABITUAL. This leads to "kick" being realized in the present tense. Unlike Example (2.47), the relation rule for HABITUAL does not introduce any affix. The realizate is (HABIT a^V)^V and the concord rules operating on the final output of all relation rules supplies the affix of *kicks* (since *Alice* is third person singular).

Other English relation rules introduce function words into the realizate; for example *with* for the instrumental relation, *on, in, under,* and so on for certain locatives.

Relation rules for other languages may of course differ considerably from those for English, described above. To the extent that word order is free in a given language, no relative position will be assigned to arguments of dyadic relations (and of relations with more than two terms, if any).

Concord rules and intonation rules operate on the output of relation rules. This subject and further details about the operation of relation rules is discussed in the next chapter.

Now remains the consideration of an alternative to the relations rules described above. Carroll (1973) has proposed a "performance grammar" in which rules of a different type operate. Before describing these, a word must be said about the semantic representations which are the input to the production rules. These are also called I-markers by Carroll, but their structure differs from that of our I-markers in that they are constituted of unordered sets of elements (such as deep subject, deep object, declarative mode, emphasis on deep subject). The elements are not hierarchically arranged, but Carroll remarks that extension of his performance grammar may necessitate introducing more structure into his I-markers.

A computer program has been developed capable of generating sentences containing a deep subject, a deep object (each of which comprises a single noun or pronoun) and a transitive verb. Sentences can be produced in a variety of interrogative forms, as well as in the declarative form, with different types of emphasis and both in the active and in the passive voice. The central part of the program involves a series of decisions as to which word (or constituent) is to be the output. The process starts with the first word of the sentence and moves from left to right, each decision being determined by the presence of certain elements in the I-marker. For instance, to decide which word comes first in the sentence, rules are applied which can be paraphrased loosely as follows:

1. If the mode element in the I-marker is "declarative," the first word is the theme (either the deep subject or the deep object, whichever is marked as theme in the I-marker).

2. If the mode element is "interrogative" and no particular element is questioned, the first word is the first element of the auxiliary.

3. If the mode element is "interrogative" and a particular element is questioned (for example, *Who chose her?*, questions the deep subject), the first word is the *wh-* word for the questioned element.

From the decision taken as to the first word, the program moves to a decision as to the second word, and so on until all I-marker elements have been considered in determining the output.

While the relation rules presented in this section start from I-marker relations and develop from them the linguistic expression, Carroll's program starts from positions in the output and consults the I-marker as to the words which are to appear at each position. His program proceeds strictly from left to right, whereas our relation rules let the linguistic expression unfold from top to bottom. In Example (2.45) above, for instance, the attribute and goal relations were realized first, and the first word in the utterance, *Alice,* could be uttered only after application of an additional rule in Example (2.46).

Evaluation of these alternative proposals will depend on how they account not only for regular, smooth production of utterances but also for the way things may go wrong. Hesitations and various types of speech errors are viewed in Sections 3B and 3C from the vantage point of the realization rules discussed in this chapter, and it remains to be seen how well these phenomena can be accommodated by Carroll's model. Further, as Carroll himself points out, if production rules have psychological reality, it must be possible to show how they are acquired by the child learning his native language. A theory of the acquisition of relation rules has already been proposed (Schlesinger, 1971b).

Carroll's present program is evidently only a first step. It needs to be developed further so that it can deal with more complex utterance types. Such a development seems possible by adopting some ideas from the augmented transition network grammar (Woods, 1970). One of the basic ideas in Woods' program is that at each step of processing a lower-level program can be transferred to, and after it has been pursued, the main program is reentered at the point it was left. This principle can be made use of in developing Carroll's approach. For instance, according to his rules, when there is a declarative element in the I-marker and the theme is the deep subject, the latter begins the utterance (see Rule 1 above). To take care of deep subjects which are not constituted of just one word, a lower-level program would instead have to be resorted to which specializes in deep subjects (or perhaps in themes, whether these are deep subjects or deep objects). On the basis of the information contained in the I-marker this program decides whether the first word is an article — and if so, which kind of article — or an adjective or a noun. After completing the deep subject, the main program is reentered. Such lower-level programs can be called at each step of the main program.

The relation rules proposed in this section seem to have two advantages over Carroll's production rules, which compute the output from left to right. First, our relation rules allow for greater flexibility. That words of a sentence must be uttered from left to right does not imply that the processes which lead up to articulation must follow any left-to-right order. Since each of our relation rules applies to a single I-marker relation these rules can be applied in various sequences or simultaneously (see Section 3A). One may assume that speakers have at their disposal a variety of production strategies which can be resorted to as required by such factors as saliency, fluctuations of attention, etc.

A second advantage of relation rules is that they are formulated in such a way that they can be employed also in comprehension (applied inversely), thus making for economy in the system of rules that has to be learned and stored in memory. By contrast, rules processing the utterance from left to right are not likely to be employed in comprehension, because, as shown in Section 6A, in comprehending an utterance a left-to-right order need not invariably be followed.

Relation rules have these two advantages not only over rules of the form proposed by Carroll, but also over any program based on an augmented transition network, because such networks require a rigid, unidirectional operation of rules.

2D. THE LEXICON

Realization of an I-marker requires that the protoverbal elements figuring in the I-marker be converted into words, or as we shall say, LEXICALIZED. This is done by referring to the lexicon. Each entry in the lexicon pairs a protoverbal element with one or more words. Often these will include words belonging to different word classes. The grammatical category for each word is indicated by a category marker as in Example (2.48) or (2.49):

(2.48) $good;^A$ $well;^{ADV}$ $goodness^N$

(2.49) $theft;^N$ $steal^V$

In the process of production protoverbal elements are lexicalized by choosing the word whose category marker is the same as that of the realizate of the relation rule. For instance, if the goal relation is realized by Relation Rule (2.43), as $(GOAL\ b^V + a^N)^V$, the action term b can be realized only by $steal^V$, and not by $theft^N$.

As Examples (2.48) and (2.49) show, the words of an entry need not have the same root. Conversely, when two words are derived from each other, they do not necessarily belong in the same entry of the same protoverbal element. Thus, *thief* does not belong together with Example (2.49), because it differs from "theft" and "steal" conceptually. Whether *theft* or *steal* is uttered depends on the relation rules, but whether we say *theft* or *thief* depends on what we intend to say.

The lexicon must contain information about certain constraints on the syntactic constructions a word may enter into. Thus, for every verb its entry must specify the types of complements it may receive; as indicated by experimental results of Fodor, Garrett and Bever (1968), this is a factor influencing processing. (Cromer, 1972, has advanced an interesting explanation of how this information may have been acquired by the child learning language.)

Certain other selection restrictions must also be represented in the entry. Consider, for instance, an I-marker

(2.50) (AGENT–ACTION John, repair)

One might intend to say such a thing without specifying what is repaired, particularly in the context of a conversation. *Repair* requires a direct object in English (its translation equivalent in some languages need not always require one). This is a grammatical constraint on the usage of *repair* which must be registered in the lexicon. By contrast, the selection restriction requiring that *repair* requires an animate subject need not be represented in the lexicon, because normally a speaker will not have an intention formulated as an I-marker whose agent term is inanimate like 'sincerity', and whose action term is 'repair', 'admire', etc. If he does have such an intention he will speak accordingly, and if his utterance sounds odd it is because one does not normally intend to say such things.

If there are several words appropriate for realizing a given protoverbal element, all of them will appear in its entry. Synonyms may be differentiated by certain "stage directions" indicating differences in usage (see also Section 4A). In a given case it may not always be clear whether we have synonyms with "stage directions" or two different protoverbal elements. Are *starry*[A] and *stellar*[A] entries belonging to one protoverbal element with a "stage direction" to the effect that the first, but not the second, word be used as an attribute of *night, banner,* etc. and the second, but not the first, of *influence, astronomy,* and the like? (That these "stage directions" would have to be fairly complicated becomes clear from the discussion of these words in Webster's *New Dictionary of Synonyms,* 1968.) Or do these words refer to different, though related, "concepts" and hence appear in the entries of different protoverbal elements?

In addition to words and their synonyms, the lexicon contains entries of a special form. (These are discussed in the following section. The reader who wishes to get an overall picture of the production process may skip this section, as well as Chapter 3, which deals with details of realization, without detriment to an understanding of Chapters 4 and 5.)

2E. SPECIAL KINDS OF LEXICAL ENTRIES

Looking for a way to express a "concept" or an image we have in mind, a concatenation of words rather than a single word frequently occurs to us. In asking for a certain kind of drink we may utter the phrase *Bloody Mary,* or we may speak of someone as of a *young man.* These are previously learned phrases, and whether they have a synonym (like *youngster* for *young man*) or not (as in the case of *Bloody Mary*) they should be represented as lexical entries. In this connection Bolinger (1965) considers the possibility that some concatenations (as *a spell of warm weather*) are learned as such, and Bierwisch (1970b) concludes on the basis of an analysis of selection errors "that the internal structure of a lexical unit is in principle the same as that of a synonymous syntactic construction [translated from German, pp. 403–404]." Whenever the lexicon specifies that a single protoverbal element is to be lexicalized by a string of more than one word, we shall speak of a STRING LEXICALIZATION.

It is important to point out what string lexicalizations are not. The child seeing a zebra for the first time and calling it *striped horse* or *horse in pajamas* is not using a string lexicalization. This is because these expressions, presumably, have not been learned before, but have been made up for the occasion; and by definition, string lexicalizations, like other entries in the lexicon, are formed beforehand and are available for lexicalization on different speech occasions. This excludes all new coinages, like the one above, made at the zoo. What happened there is that the child saw the zebra, intended to talk about it and formed the I-marker constituent (ATTRIBUTE striped, horse), which was accordingly realized.

The converse of a string lexicalization occurs when a constituent of an I-marker is expressed as a single word. When one looks at a man doing something and then notices that the man is young, an I-marker may be formed with the constituent (ATTRIBUTE young, man), which is then lexicalized as *youngster.* In addition to string lexicalizations, then, the lexicon includes COMPACT LEXICALIZATIONS. The form of these entries presents some problems. One possibility would be to enter compact lexicalizations under I-marker constituents, unlike other entries which appear under protoverbal elements. When the lexicon contains such paraphrases as *youngster* and the string lexicalization *young man,* the latter would be entered under a protoverbal element, and the former under an I-marker constituent (and probably, in addition, under a protoverbal element).

Another possibility would be to enter words and string lexicalizations as translation equivalents: *young man* = *youngster. Youngster* would then be derived not directly from (ATTRIBUTE young, man) but via the concatenation *young man.* Moreover, the string lexicalization *young man* would no longer have to be derived from a protoverbal element, but via the word *youngster* which lexicalizes the protoverbal element. However, by considering how string lexicalizations are used we can arrive at a third, probably better, solution.

String lexicalizations must have category markers, because relation rules must operate on them as they do on words. But it is not enough to assign a category marker to the string lexicalization as a whole: each of the words it comprises must have such a category marker. The reason for this is that only thus is it possible to account for certain grammatical rules of inflection. Take, for instance, a protoverbal element with the following string lexicalization:

$$(2.51) \quad (hold^V + up^{ADV})^V ; (hold^V + up^{ADV})^N.$$

When the past tense is intended, the former expression is lexicalized as *held up* and not as **hold upped*. The relation rule for PAST operates on an element with a category marker V,[6] and in the present case there is both a bracketed expression and its constituent element "hold" which have this category marker. The relation rule for PAST must apply to the constituent element, according to a principle followed by many — or perhaps all — monadic relation rules in English: when a monadic relation rule which requires for its application an element with Category Marker X is to be applied to a string lexicalization $(a^X + b^Y)^X$, it operates on a rather than on the string lexicalization as a whole; and similarly, it operates on b in $(a^X + b^Y)^Y$, when Category Marker Y is required.

The relation rules pluralizing $(hold^V + up^{ADV})^N$, on the other hand, must operate on an element with the category marker N. Since there is no such element inside the bracket, we have *hold ups* and not **holds up* as plural of the expression marked N.

But the form suggested in Example (2.51) is still inadequate to account for the way certain string lexicalizations may be transformed. Sentences with string lexicalizations can often undergo transformations. Suppose that there is a string lexicalization *take legal action* (that is, this phrase has been learned as a whole as referring to a certain activity). If the string lexicalization has the form of Example (2.51), it will not be possible to account for its passive, *legal action is taken,* because this form does not preserve the GOAL—ACTION relation on which the appropriate relation rule must operate. On the other hand, the passive form cannot always be assumed to appear as such in the lexicon, because having once learned *take legal action,* the speaker presumably can produce the passive spontaneously. It appears, therefore, that the entry for a string lexicalization must include both the string of words with their category marker, as in Example (2.51), and the I-marker relations holding between words:[7]

$$(2.52) \begin{cases} (take^V + legal^A + action^N)^V \\ \text{GOAL—ACTION (ATTRIBUTE legal, action), take} \end{cases}$$

To return to the problem of compact lexicalizations, suppose a certain proto-

---

[6] It is assumed that relation rules can apply also after lexicalization has taken place. That this is so is argued on independent grounds in Section 3B.

[7] The second line of the entry would not be sufficient, because any expression synonymous with the string lexicalization (or any string lexicalization with one of its constituent words replaced by its synonym) will not necessarily be a string lexicalization (it may be that it is not stored in the lexicon). Complex words like *attendant* (= one who attends) or *accuse* (= say that ... is guilty) might be viewed as compact lexicalizations. However, Kintsch (1974) has examined the behavioral evidence for this and his results were negative.

verbal element has as its entry both a single word and a synonymous string lexicalization for it, as in:

$$(2.53) \begin{cases} (young^A + man^N)^N \\ \text{ATTRIBUTE young, man} \end{cases} ; youngster^N$$

Then there would be no need for a separate entry for a compact lexicalization under an I-marker constituent, because Example (2.53) already includes the I-marker constituent (ATTRIBUTE young, man), and the latter can be lexicalized as *youngster,* also included in Example (2.53). The lexicon would thus have only entries under protoverbal elements, and there would be a general rule that the I-marker constituent of a string lexicalization can be lexicalized by a single word appearing under the same protoverbal elements. This would be similar to a response equivalence class which learning theorists are familiar with: two responses (in this case, the I-marker constituent and the single word) evoked by a single stimulus come to evoke each other.

We now come to a special kind of string lexicalization which can be described within the above framework, namely, the IDIOM. One of the characteristics of idioms is that certain transformations do not apply to them. Thus, Example (2.54) in its idiomatic sense lends itself neither to passivization, Example (2.55), nor to nominalization, Example (2.56). That is, Examples (2.55) and (2.56) have only a literal meaning. In contrast, Example (2.57) can have an idiomatic meaning (Chafe, 1968):

(2.54)   Geoffrey kicked the bucket.

(2.55)   The bucket was kicked by Geoffrey.

(2.56)   Geoffrey's kicking of the bucket caused some concern.

(2.57)   Geoffrey's kicking the bucket caused some concern.

Presumably *kicked the bucket* is a string lexicalization only in its idiomatic sense. The literal sense is unlikely to have been learned to the extent of forming an entry in the lexicon. Be that as it may, what distinguishes this expression from nonidiomatic ones is that it is stored as a phrase without relations between words; it has a form like Example (2.51) rather than like Example (2.52). In the present case the idiom is entered as

$$(2.58) \quad (kick^V + the^D + bucket^N)^V.$$

For an entry like Example (2.58) there are consequently no relation rules which can operate on I-marker relations within the entry such as are required for the production of Examples (2.55) and (2.56). If the latter utterances occur, they are not a result of idiomatic string lexicalizations; instead they are meant to be literal. However, the relation rule which renders Example (2.57) in its idiomatic sense merely adds *ing* to the action term of (AGENT—ACTION Geoffrey, kick-the-bucket); and since it applies to Example (2.58) as a whole, the principle discussed above for string lexicalizations like Example (2.51) prescribes that this affix must be added to that element within the parentheses which has the category marker V, namely to *kick*. This explains why Example (2.57) can be idiomatic.

Many idioms do not permit even this restricted kind of transformation. Thus, we can refer to *Bloody Mary* but only jocularly to **Bloodier Mary*, we have the idiom *kingdom come* but not **kingdom came*, and *much of a muchness* — meaning, as Gardner (1965, p. 103) glosses Alice in Wonderland, "very much alike" — but not **most of a muchness*. Unlike Example (2.58), these string lexicalizations do not even have category markers within parentheses. In this respect idioms like these and entries of single words are very much alike, or

(2.59)   (*much of a muchness*)^A.

A special effect is achieved by a speaker's resuscitating, as it were, the dead category markers and protoverbal elements of the single words in the idiom, as for instance,

(2.60)   I was served the bloodiest Mary you can imagine.

(2.61)   Geoffrey finally kicked the bucket, but it was not much
         of a bucket to speak of.

This requires a focusing of the speaker's attention to the possibilities inherent in words, and it is just because not everybody thinks of these that the effect is attained.

The final word goes, therefore, to the mad Hatter:

". . . You know, you say things are 'much of a muchness' – did you ever see such a thing as a drawing of a muchness?"

"Really, now you ask me," said Alice, very much confused, "I don't think" –

"Then you shouldn't talk," said the Hatter.

2F.   ARE THERE UNIVERSAL CONSTRAINTS ON REALIZATION RULES?

Realization rules differ from language to language. It has been suggested, by Chomsky (1965, p. 65) that there are universal constraints on the transformations possible in any human language. Such innate constraints on transformations – or, within the framework of this work, on realization rules – might be expected to make the task of the child learning grammar very much easier.

But in specifying which transformations are ruled out by universal constraints, Chomsky's examples include only the absence in any language of a transformation mapping a string into its mirror image, and of mapping *a b c d* into *a b c d c b a*. It seems hardly surprising that a complex operation like this appears in no known language, and for the child learning language such a constraint offers little help. Constraints like these are to be expected from what we know about cognitive abilities in general, and there is no need to postulate a specifically linguistic innate constraint in order to account for the nonoccurrence of something like a string followed by its mirror image. Doubtlessly, some cognitive abilities and constraints are innate, but no linguist is needed to tell us this. The interest of Chomsky's claim lies in that it assumes, in addition, linguistic constraints which are unexplained by known cognitive principles or learning principles.

In a small scale experiment we tried to test this stronger claim by means of two artificial languages, in one of which the agent relation was marked by duplication, and in the other by a suffix.[8] There seems to be no reason why either of these grammatical devices should be easier to learn than the other; both seem about equally complex (or simple) from a cognitive standpoint. However, while suffixes are frequently used in inflectional languages to mark a variety of relations, the reduplication of morphemes is found only for far more restricted purposes, mainly for emphasis or to indicate repetition, the plural and modality (see Sapir, 1921, pp. 60, 76–78, for a treatment of this device). As far as we could ascertain, reduplications do not express relations like "subject of" and "object of" in any known language. Therefore, we have a case of a universal constraint on transformations which cannot be explained on cognitive grounds. It should be pointed out, however, that ideally an experiment testing this hypothesis should compare a nonexistent transformation with an existing one. But I could not find any nonexistent transformation which was not also more complex on purely cognitive grounds.

The question asked in these experiments was whether the languagette using the suffix to indicate the agent relation would be more easily learned than that using reduplication. A positive answer would be a clear confirmation of Chomsky's hypothesis (though some might prefer to formulate the results not in terms of innate constraints but of differences in "preparedness"; Seligman, 1970). It might be argued that if, with linguistic material, an operation A cannot be learned or is much more difficult to learn than another operation B, and if, furthermore, this difference is left unexplained by known learning principles, then this would be proof of a specifically linguistic constraint in the language acquisition device.

Our contrived language consisted of "words" represented in the form of schematic line drawings describing situations each of which involved an agent, an action and a goal. Both the agent and the goal were animate, and hence the "sentences" were reversible. A typical "sentence" translated into English would be *The girl pushes the woman.* The "word" referring to the agent was marked by a suffix (again a line drawing) in one of the languages and by reduplication of the "word" in the other. A free and variable "word" order was used for both

---

[8] This experiment was designed in collaboration with Shulamit Stern and Bina Presser, and I am indebted to them also for carrying out the pretest. M. Rimor ran the experiment.

languages. Subjects were 2 groups of 12 third graders, each group being assigned to the learning of one language by a standardized learning procedure.

Space does not permit to describe the procedure in greater detail, but the results are easily summarized; there was hardly ever an experiment on which the null hypothesis received stronger "support"! By every criterion of learning applied, the performance of the two groups was almost identical. The result of no difference in a single experiment does not suffice for rejecting the hypothesis of innate constraints. With a different experimental procedure, confirmation of this hypothesis might conceivably be obtained. It may also be argued that our subjects were old enough to master any reasonably simple transformation and that differences might be found with children at the age of first language acquisition. This is possible, but it should be noted that our subjects had not yet passed what is usually regarded as the critical age for language acquisition. Another reservation concerns the transformations chosen: inflection and reduplication may not be the appropriate operations with which to test Chomsky's claim of innate constraints, particularly since, as pointed out above, reduplication does occur in some languages (though, to my knowledge, it is used nowhere to express relations like those employed in this experiment). But then the onus seems to be on the proponents of innate constraints to suggest a nonexistent transformation that is not at the same time more complex by known principles having nothing to do with linguistic capabilities. Still another possible objection (suggested to me by Moshe Anisfeld and by Dan Slobin in personal communications) would be that subjects approached the experimental task as if it were one of solving a puzzle. Such puzzle solving should be distinguished from what goes on in language learning. This may be the case, but note that such a move makes the innate constraints hypothesis virtually untestable. In summary, while the hypothesis of innate constraints cannot be regarded as refuted by the present experiment, it has at least been given a fair try and failed.

It should also be pointed out that the hypothesis of specifically linguistic innate constraints has very little a priori plausibility. In the course of their development humans acquire complex reasoning abilities which enable them to play chess and solve arithmetic problems. Why should they require specific constraints on transformations (or realization rules) to enable them to learn them? But the nativist approach seems to be so deeply entrenched that such an "implausibility argument" will have little impact, as long as it is not backed by empirical investigation.

SUMMARY

It is proposed that the rules that map I-markers into utterances involve only semantic notions. The advantage offered by syntactic concepts, like "subject," which permit some simplification of these rules, is offset by the difficulty the child learning language would have acquiring these concepts. The semantic assimilation hypothesis was invoked to account for certain regularities which are usually explained by resorting to syntactic categories. The hypothesis claims situations where a certain semantic relation apparently applies may be treated, metaphorically, as if another semantic relation were involved. Adopting the semantic hypothesis simplifies realization rules and brings the I-marker closer to the surface. Support for this hypothesis comes from observations showing that the metaphor is only dormant and not dead: in certain instances it jars our sensibilities and the metaphorical utterance would be unacceptable. Thus, the instrument can be viewed as if it were the agent only as long as the action does not presuppose creativeness or a considerable degree of deliberation; and there is apparently no simple linguistic explanation for this constraint.

There are several kinds of realization rules. The rules determining how I-marker relations are expressed by word order, function words and affixes are called relation rules. Since we seem to construct our utterances while speaking, these rules do not apply to the I-marker as a whole. Instead, to each I-marker relation and its arguments a relation rule is applied. This conclusion is supported by considerations pertaining to the rules employed in comprehension. Relation rules are conceived of as one-stage rules, which in line with the argument given above, do not involve syntactic concepts. There is one exception, however: category markers, which specify the grammatical category (form class) of the word, are introduced by relation rules. It is shown how these categories can be acquired in native language learning.

Two other types of realization rules operate on the output of relation rules: concord rules, responsible for grammatical agreement; and intonation rules. Finally, phonological rules prepare the output for articulation.

Realization rules comprise also the lexicon, which determines how each protoverbal element is lexicalized (converted into words). Lexicalization takes place relatively independently of the operation of the other kinds of realization rules. A lexical entry for a protoverbal element lists the word or words by which it may be expressed and their grammatical categories. Special kinds of lexical entries are those showing how a protoverbal element may be lexicalized by a string of words (string lexicalizations), or alternatively by a single word (compact lexicalizations). Idioms are treated as a special kind of string lexicalization which constrain the types of transformations applicable to them.

3

The Application
of Realization Rules

3A. THE SEQUENCE OF RULE APPLICATION

In the preceeding chapter realization rules were discussed in general terms. Here it will be shown how these rules can be applied in various different sequences. A plausible assumption about the production process is that there are alternative routes from a given I-marker to one and the same utterance. The human organism is fallible, distractions and other kinds of "noise" are ubiquitous, and hence such alternatives must be available to ensure more or less regular functioning. In this respect the objective in constructing a production model should differ from what is usually considered the immediate objective when performance is simulated. In simulation one more often than not rests content with finding a single way in which a task can be carried out. Subsequently refinements may be made and alternatives may be developed, but actually such alternatives are often not envisaged. In theorizing about linguistic performance it seems to be more strategic to start by postulating as many ways as possible for carrying out the same task, some of which may later turn out to be impracticable. Without detracting from the heuristic value of simulation, one may suggest that a spate of theorizing should precede simulation, so that one can see clearly what it is that should be simulated.

In this chapter I attempt, accordingly, to spell out the various possibilities of realizing an I-marker in the manner described in a general fashion in Section 2C. These are possibilities IN PRINCIPLE; very little knowledge is available bearing on the question which of these possibilities actually occur in the production process. Experimental work bearing on this question is sparse and largely inconclusive (see Lindsley, 1975, for a report of some experiments and a summary of previous research).

In order not to encumber the exposition, let us begin with an I-marker, which has been simplified in that no account has been taken of what is ultimately to be expressed as tense. Further, let us shelve the problem how communicative considerations select the appropriate realizations, which is taken up again in Section 4A. Here it will be assumed that I-marker (3.1) will be realized as a simple active declarative sentence:

(3.1) (AGENT–ACTION(ATTRIBUTE big, Alice),
        (GOAL–ACTION(ATTRIBUTE poor, Bill),kick))

Relation rules (2.42)–(2.44) apply to this I-marker and are presented here again for convenience:

(3.2) (ATTRIBUTE a, b) → (ATTR $a^A + b^N$)^N

(3.3) (GOAL–ACTION) a, b → (GOAL $b^V + a^N$)^V

(3.4) (AGENT–ACTION) a, b → (AGENT $a^N + b^V$)^S

The result of applying these rules to I-marker (3.1) is shown in detail in Table 3.1. Note that the plus sign indicates relative position ('$a + b$' means that a precedes b), whereas the comma implies no such ordering. The former appears in the realizate (right of the arrow in realization rules), and the latter in I-marker constituents (left of the arrow).

Table 3.1 does not describe the operation of concord rules, intonation rules and phonological rules (see Section 2A). These have to be applied before the utterance can be articulated, but they will not be dealt with here.

The rightmost column of Table 3.1 shows which consecutive words may be actually uttered at each step, after lexicalization, concord rules and so forth have been applied. After Step 1 there is already a realizate: (ATTR big^A + Alice ^{N})^N, which will ultimately be lexicalized as *big Alice*. Nevertheless, *big Alice* should not be uttered until the relative position of these two words is determined. Unless this principle is followed, false starts may result. Thus, if *poor Bill* is uttered after Step 2, the speaker will either have to correct himself or he will have to resort to different realization rules which permit uttering a passive sentence beginning with *poor Bill* (see Section 4A, but note that here we consider only actives).

Lexicalization should be distinguished from the actual uttering of words. A speaker may lexicalize a protoverbal element without speaking it out loud. A word should not be uttered before the relevant concord, intonation and phonological rules have been applied. For instance, *kick* must receive the suffix *s* (given that I-marker (3.1) is to be realized in the present tense, a fact not represented in Table 3.1). Moreover, the speaker may store the word for a while till further processing has been done.

It is important for the functioning of the realization process that relation rules assign category markers not only to individual elements but also to the realizate as a whole. For instance, in Table 3.1 the entire expression (ATTR poor^A + Bill^N)^N is marked as N, in accordance with Rule (3.2). Since the first (goal) term of the goal relation must be marked N (see Rule 3.3), the above expression is

TABLE 3.1
How To Produce *Big Alice kicks poor Bill*

Step	Relation realized	Resulting realizate	Words that can be uttered
		(AGENT–ACTION(ATTRIBUTE big, Alice (GOAL–ACTION(ATTRIBUTE poor, Bill), kick))	
1	ATTRIBUTE	(AGENT–ACTION(ATTR big^A + Alice^N)^N, (GOAL–ACTION(ATTR poor, Bill)kick))	—
2	ATTRIBUTE	(AGENT–ACTION(ATTR big^A + Alice^N)^N, (GOAL–ACTION(ATTR poor^A + Bill^N)^N, kick))	—
3	GOAL–ACTION	(AGENT–ACTION(ATTR big^A + Alice^N)^N, (GOAL kick^V + (ATTR poor^N)^N)^V)	—
4	AGENT–ACTION	(AGENT(ATTR big^A + Alice^N)^N + (GOAL kick^V + (ATTR poor^A + Bill^N)^N)^V)^S	*big Alice kicks poor Bill*

eligible to be inserted for the goal term in Step 3. Likewise, realization of the goal relation in Step 3 results in an expression marked $V - (GOAL\ kick^V + (ATTR\ poor^A + Bill^N)^N)^V$ – which can therefore figure as the second term in the agent relation in Step 4.

In this manner constraints are imposed on the process which obviate the production of certain faulty constructions. For example, by applying Rules (3.3) and (3.4) we can obtain Sentence (3.5) (in which x serves as a variable for which appropriate expressions can be substituted):

(3.5) $(AGENT\ x^N + (GOAL\ hurt^V + Bill^N)^V)^S$.

Only expressions marked N can be substituted for x. The following sentences are realizations of I-markers in which this constraint is satisfied:

(3.6)   Alice hurt Bill.

(3.7)   Alice's kick hurt Bill.

(3.8)   The fact that Alice kicked hurt Bill.

By contrast, *Alice kicked* does not result from an expression marked N; conceivably, it is a realization of:

(3.9) $(AGENT\ Alice^N + kick^V)^S$.

The category marker N in Example (3.5) prevents the placement of x by Example (3.9) or by any expression which would result in Example (3.5) being realized as the unacceptable:

(3.10)   *Alice kicked hurt Bill.

This is a partial solution for the problem of context sensitivity of relation rules raised in Section 2C.

There is much room for variations in the process described in Table 3.1. Steps 1–4 may be carried out either sequentially, or alternatively, one or more steps may be performed simultaneously, or partially overlapping in time with another step.

Further, lexicalization of protoverbal elements can take place at any stage, and lexicalization of one element may proceed independently of that of another one. In Table 3.1 (and in the following tables) the third column presents protoverbal elements, but it should be remembered that actually any such element already may have been lexicalized (replaced by a word).[1]

---

[1] This applies at least to those elements which appear in realizates, since these have a category marker and this ensures that a word appropriate in form class is chosen. But perhaps it applies also to elements in I-marker constituents to which relation rules have not yet applied (for example, poor in Step 2). (This would entail the form of relation rules given in Example 3.13.) If the choice then falls on a word belonging to an inappropriate form class, a revision will subsequently have to be made when the category marker is introduced (see also Section 3B).

Finally, Table 3.1 presents only one possible sequence of steps. Note that when this particular sequence of rules is resorted to, words can be uttered only after all the rules have applied. Can relation rules operate in any order which ensures that words may be uttered immediately after their position in the utterance has been determined, without waiting for application of other rules? Table 3.2 shows that this is possible — almost. Here the utterance is processed from left to right, each word being uttered as soon as the corresponding protoverbal element has been dealt with by relation rules. But there are other possibilities as well (see Table 3.3). Equally possible are, in principle, all permutations of the relation rules involved here, at least as far as the present example is concerned, as the reader may easily convince himself. This is because lexicalization may be deferred for any number of steps. In Table 3.1, Steps 1 and 2 can be interchanged; in Table 3.2 the goal relation may be realized before any one of the attribute relations is; and so on. There is thus no need for the child to learn any ordering of relation rules. All that is required is that a record be kept which I-marker relation has been operated on, so as to avoid applying the same rule twice to the same relation.

If there are various ways of ordering relation rules, what determines which order is chosen in any particular case? The answer presumably depends in part on the relative saliency of parts of the I-marker (see Section 1C). If the agent relation is more salient than the goal relation, an ordering like that in Table 3.2 may occur.[2] But saliency may differ from case to case. For instance, where the goal relation is more salient than the agent relation, the process may be ordered as in Table 3.3. Actually, when the goal relation is more salient, the passive form of the sentence will usually be preferred (see Section 4A).

A different view is held by Fodor, Bever, and Garrett (1974, pp. 409–418), who conclude from a few experiments relevant to this problem that production appears to be left to right (not only at the level of uttering words). They point out, however, that the evidence available so far is only indirect. Carroll's (1973) production model is also based on a left-to-right process. Should this be borne out by further research, constraints would have to be imposed on the sequencing of relation rules. First, in any realizate that term which has been accorded first position should be realized first. For instance, in Table 3.2 (ATTRIBUTE big, Alice)^N is accorded first position in Step 1 and dealt with in the next step. This is necessary but not sufficient to ensure left-to-right processing, as an examination of Tables 3.1 and 3.3 should make clear. An additional instruction is needed to the effect that relation rules be applied to higher-order constituents first, or in other words, that a bracketed constituent should not be processed before the constituent which brackets it has been processed. The AGENT–ACTION relation, for instance, should be processed before the GOAL–ACTION relation

---

[2] Note, incidentially, Table 3.2 proceeds from top to bottom of the I-marker (see Figure 1.1), whereas Table 3.1 proceeds from bottom to top.

TABLE 3.2
Another Way of Producing *Big Alice kicks poor Bill.*

Step	Relation realized	Resulting realizate	Words that can be uttered
1	AGENT–ACTION	(AGENT–ACTION(ATTRIBUTE big, Alice), (GOAL–ACTION(ATTRIBUTE poor, Bill), kick)) (AGENT(ATTRIBUTE big, Alice)^N + (GOAL–ACTION(ATTR poor, Bill), kick)^V)^S	
2	ATTRIBUTE	(AGENT(ATTR big^A + Alice^N)^N + (GOAL–ACTION(ATTR poor, Bill), kick)^V)^S	*big Alice*
3	GOAL–ACTION	(AGENT(ATTR big^A + Alice^N)^N + (GOAL kick^V + (ATTR poor, Bill)^N)^V)^S	*big Alice kicks*
4	ATTRIBUTE	(AGENT(ATTR big^A + Alice^N)^N + (GOAL kick^V + (ATTR poor^A + Bill^N)^N)^V)^S	*big Alice kicks poor Bill*

TABLE 3.3

A Third Way of Producing *Big Alice kicks poor Bill*

Step	Relation realized	Resulting realizate	Words that can be uttered
1	GOAL–ACTION	(AGENT–ACTION(ATTRIBUTE big, Alice), (GOAL–ACTION(ATTRIBUTE poor, Bill), kick)) (AGENT–ACTION(ATTR big, Alice), (GOAL, kick^V + (ATTR poor, Bill)^N) V)	—
2	AGENT–ACTION	(AGENT(ATTR big, Alice)^N + (GOAL kick^V + (ATTR poor, Bill)^N) V)S	—
3	ATTRIBUTE	(AGENT(ATTR big^A + Alice^N)^N + (GOAL kick^V + (ATTR poor, Bill)^N)V)S big, Alice	*big Alice kicks*
4	ATTRIBUTE	(AGENT(ATTR big^A + Alice^N)^N + (GOAL kick^V + (ATTR poor^A + Bill^N)^N)V)S poor, Bill	*big Alice kicks poor Bill*

bracketed in it, and the latter before the **ATTRIBUTE** relation bracketed in it. This instruction may perhaps be motivated by differential saliency of the relations in question (see above). Both these priorities are violated in Table 3.3. Only in Table 3.2 are these constraints obeyed and processing is from left to right. However, the left-to-right directionality seems unlikely as an inviolable constraint on processing.

No confirmatory evidence is available so far for the model sketched in this section, but there are some data that are relevant to it: hesitations and errors of speech. These will be discussed in the following sections. While they do not constitute a corroboration of the model, they can be accomodated within the theoretical framework presented here. The very least one should expect from a theory of utterance production is that it should be capable of being extended to account for cases where the smooth flow of speech is disturbed.

3B. LEXICALIZATION, HESITATIONS, AND ERRORS

The protoverbal elements appearing in the I-marker must be converted into words. This involves looking up the lexicon (see Section 2D), which, as argued above, can occur at any place in the process of production.

Hesitation often occurs at phrase structure boundaries. These cases may be the result of uncertainty on the part of the speaker as to which relation rule to apply or how to apply it. Suppose, for instance, that after Step 2 of Table 3.2, the first words of the sentence are uttered, and that difficulty then arises with the application of the relation rule for the goal relation, or that the speaker vacillates between applying this rule or the one applicable to the agent relation. As a result, he will stop after *big Alice* and before continuing *kicks poor Bill.*

But hesitations occur also in the middle of a phrase (Goldman-Eisler, 1968, pp. 12–14, 32–34), and these cannot be due to any uncertainty as to relation rules. Supppose, for instance, that in uttering the above sentence the speaker hesitates before *Alice.* Whether the relation rules are applied as in Tables 3.1, 3.2, or 3.3, the relation rule assigns the relative positions of big^A and of Alice^N simultaneously. If the speaker hesitates before saying *Alice* and after saying *big* there can be only one explanation, namely, that it is the word *Alice* which causes trouble (for instance, he has forgotten the name or is not sure which name to choose; see, however, Section 3C for a different possibility). The same explanation applies in some cases where the speaker hesitates before a frequently occurring noun, as in Goldman-Eisler's (1968, p. 13) example, in which / / indicates a hesitation pause:

(3.11) In each of / / the cells of the body . . .

Hesitations like these are triggered off by lexicalization: something in the process of converting the protoverbal element into a word or a string lexicalization does not go quite as smoothly and fast as usual. ("Usual" is not quite exact:

in many situations our speech is full of hesitations, some of which normally go unnoticed). This may be because there is a choice to be made between two words listed in the lexicon under the protoverbal element in question, or simply because the word is hard to recall. Difficulties of recall may give rise to the "tip-of-the-tongue" phenomenon: the word is, for a moment at least, not available but the speaker has partial knowledge of it; for example, he "recognizes" it as the word he intended as soon as someone else supplies it. As Brown and McNeill (1966) have shown, he may also know some of its properties, as some of its letters, the number of its syllables, and the locations of primary stress. (On the basis of these findings these authors also speculate on the nature of entries in the lexicon.)

It is important to point out that hesitations in these cases occur after relation rules have applied and before the protoverbal element is converted into words, which shows that in some cases at least lexicalization is applied after the relation rule. Conceivably, there will be other instances where lexicalization is applied before relation rules. That is, a relation may apply not only to an I-marker constituent with protoverbal elements as in Example (3.12) but also to the I-marker constituent after all protoverbal elements have been lexicalized, as in Example (3.13), or after some of them have been lexicalized:

(3.12) (ATTRIBUTE poor, Bill) → (ATTR $poor^A$ + $Bill^N$)^N

(3.13) (ATTRIBUTE *poor, Bill*) → (ATTR *poor*^{A} + *Bill*^{N})^N .

One may even speculate that there may be cases where words instead of (all or some) protoverbal elements appear in the I-marker at the outset, lexicalization taking place before the I-marker is formed. Suppose one looks at a scene involving, say, a policeman and a demonstrator, thinks the words *policeman* and *demonstrator,* and only subsequently becomes aware of what is happening between the two. One therefore forms an I-marker involving these two words.

Obviously, to proceed in this way means to gamble. In Example (3.13) the choice of *poor* and *Bill* for the protoverbal elements left of the arrow turns out to be appropriate, because these words belong to the grammatical categories which are specified subsequently by the relation rule. When there are several words belonging to different grammatical categories listed under the same protoverbal element, it may happen that lexicalization which is performed before application of relation rules chooses a word of an incorrect grammatical category. This may lead to a revision in the course of the production process before the word is uttered. Only rarely do speakers utter a word violating grammatical category (Garrett, 1975).

Recently several writers have studied errors of speech and explored their implications for a theory of linguistic performance (e.g., Bierwisch, 1970b; Fodor, Bever, & Garrett, 1974; Fromkin, 1971; Garrett, 1975).

Let us consider first the exchange of words in sentences, which is a common type of speech error. An example given by Garrett (1975) is Example (3.15), which was uttered where Example (3.14) was obviously intended:

(3.14) Make it so the tree has less apples.

(3.15) Make it so the apple has less trees.

In such exchanges the inflectional endings are left behind. In the above examples the plural ending of *apples* in Example (3.14) is left "stranded" (as Garrett calls it), and becomes attached to *tree* in Example (3.15).

The "stranding" phenomon can best be explained by assuming that the exchange occurs in the realizate. For the purpose of explanation, let us introduce the relations POSSESSOR–POSSESSED and QUANTITY (whether this is the best way of viewing the relations in question need not concern us here). Part of the realizate of the I-marker underlying Example (3.14) may be (with some simplifications):

(3.16) (POSS tree^N + (QUAN less^A + PLUR apple^N)^N).

The exchange of 'tree' and 'apple' results in:

(3.17) (POSS apple^N + (QUAN less^A + PLUR tree^N)^N).

Now, PLUR in Example (3.17) ensures that 'tree' will finally be uttered as *trees.*

An essentially similar explanation can be given for the finding that not only affixes but also stress tends to be left behind, as in the following example of word exchange (Boomer & Laver, 1968, quoted in Fodor, Bever, & Garrett, 1974):

(3.18) how *things* bad were

Intonation contour is partly determined by the relational structure of the realizate; protoverbal elements themselves are neither stressed nor unstressed and hence cannot carry stress with them when they are exchanged.

The above explanation has been formulated in terms of protoverbal elements. It is obvious, however, that it can be phrased just as well, mutatis mutandis, in terms of words appearing in realizates. Lexicalization of protoverbal elements does not introduce affixes or stress; rather, the latter result from the operation of relation rules, like PLUR in Example (3.17), and of intonation rules.

A different treatment of the "stranding" phenomenon has been suggested by Garrett (1975). He postulates a "functional level of representation" which is constituted of lexical formatives and the relations holding between them. This level corresponds roughly to the I-marker level, except that it includes lexical formatives rather than protoverbal elements. In addition, Garrett proposed a "positional level of representation" which provides a positional frame with grammatical formatives (function words, affixes) into which the lexical formatives of the previous level are inserted. Exchange errors are due to faulty insertion of lexical formatives, and this accounts for inflectional endings (and, incidentally, also function words), which are part of the positional frame, not being involved in the exchange. Fromkin (1971) postulates an essentially similar process.

It seems to me that when the production process envisaged by Garrett will be spelled out in greater detail, it will turn out to be more complicated than the process described in the previous section. Consider that on the one hand the construction of the positional frame must be guided by the "functional level of presentation" (since there are indefinitely many positional frames for the utterances of the language), and on the other, the material contained in the latter is inserted into the positional frame only after it is completed. Hence, during the construction of the positional frame a place holder apparently must be introduced into it for each element in the "functional level," so that these elements can be correctly inserted. In contrast, no place holder is required for the realizates of Section 3A, since these already include the I-marker elements.

Garrett's proposal has the merit, however, of providing an explanation for the fact that exchange errors occur: something may go awry in the process of inserting lexical formatives. What could cause an exchange error in the realization process described in Section 3A, which involved no such insertion? One possibility is that these errors happen in some instances where two or more protoverbal elements in the realizate are lexicalized simultaneously (tree and apple in the above example). (Note that here lexicalization is assumed to have the effect accorded by Garrett to insertion of lexical formatives, but there are other reasons why protoverbal elements have to be postulated which are subsequently lexicalized; see Section 1B).

In some cases the "stranding" of elements may be due also to the operation of concord rules which apply after the protoverbal elements have been exchanged. (Remember that concord rules apply after relation rules.) Take the speaker of German who uttered Example (3.20) instead of Example (3.19):

(3.19)   Erstens dauert nicht jede Probe vier Stunden.

(3.20)   Erstens dauert nicht jede Stunde vier Proben.

The plural *Stunden* 'hours' in Example (3.19) may have become the singular *Stunde* in Example (3.20) as a result of the operation of a concord rule: *jede* 'each' requires that the noun it modifies be singular.

Bierwisch (1970b), to whom this example is due, reports that words which are erroneously exchanged always belong to the same grammatical category (see also Fromkin, 1971). Thus, *Probe* 'rehearsal' and *Stunde* are both nouns. Garrett (1975) has shown, however, that when the exchanged words are close together or belong to the same surface clause – and these are the great majority of exchange errors – many exceptions occur. One of his examples is:

(3.21)   I'm not in the read for mooding.

(Note again the "stranded" element *ing*.) Only between-clause exchanges are constrained by grammatical category.

To explain this, Garrett suggests that exchanges can occur at either one of two levels in the production process. The errors discussed before were due, according to him, to faulty insertion of lexical formatives in the positional frame. In addition to these, there may be errors occurring already at the "functional level of representation." Such errors may occur only between words that are similar in terms of this level, that is, they must be of the same grammatical category (because for Garrett the relations holding between lexical formatives are represented, inter alia, by grammatical category of the formatives). Between-clause exchange errors belong to this functional level, and hence obey the grammatical category constraint. On the other hand, errors due to faulty insertion of formatives into the positional frame obey a positional constraint: the exchanged words are close together or belong to the same clause (see Example 3.21).

These two types of errors thus differ in the level they occur, according to Garrett. In the terminology of this chapter his explanation says that while within-clause errors occur in the realizate, between-clause errors occur in the I-marker (the closest parallel to Garrett's "functional level"). Now, as has been stated above, the latter type of exchange error is limited to words of the same grammatical category, it follows therefore that the error can occur only after the introduction of category markers, since only these can obviate exchanges of elements belonging to different classes. At first sight this seems to contradict the claim that these errors occur in the I-marker, because in Tables 3.1–3.3 category markers make their appearance only in the realizates. There is no reason, however, why category markers should not be introduced, in some instances, before the operation of position rules; that is, the relation rule may operate in two stages, introducing category markers first. When this happens, the result is an I-marker with the addition of category markers.

It appears, however, that there is no need to postulate different loci for between-clause and within-clause exchange errors, as Garrett does. One can account for both kinds of error, more parsimoniously, as taking place in the realizates, after the operation of relation rules. The latter introduce the category markers, which impose the grammatical category constraint on between-clause errors. The reason why this constraint does not operate on within-clause errors may be simpler than that given by Garrett. Proximity of elements and their similarity are the two factors which contribute to exchange errors. The elements belonging to different clauses are relatively far from each other, and hence, for a between-clause exchange to occur, the elements involved must be similar: they must have the same category marker. Within-clause errors, by contrast, may be occasioned merely by proximity of elements.[3]

---

[3] Since we are not dealing here with surface strings, "proximity" in this context does not refer to spatial or temporal distance, but rather to the place of the exchanged elements in the bracketing of the realizates. That most exchange errors are within-clause errors can also be explained by the tendency of these errors to occur early in the process. There are fewer realizates in the earlier steps, and hence there is a greater chance of two words within the same clause being affected.

Not only words may be exchanged but also, more rarely, whole phrases, as in the following example (Fromkin, 1971):

(3.21)   An end of the sentence occurs at the fall of pitch.

The exchanged sections are both noun phrases, which is in line with the above explanation. Remember that the realizate contains category markers not only for single elements but for whole "phrases" as well.

So far exchange errors have been discussed. A different type of error described by Bierwisch (1970b), Fromkin (1971), and Garrett (1975) involves substitution of words. These are either semantically related, as in *like* instead of *hate, oral* instead of *written, bottom* instead of *top*, and *contemporary* instead of *adjacent* (Fromkin, 1971) or in Bierwisch's German examples: *geheiratet* instead of *geerbt* 'married', 'inherited'; *andere* instead of *verschiedene* 'other', 'various'; or phonetically related like *products* for *projects, chambermaid* for *chamber music* (Fromkin, 1971), and *tabu* for *partout* (both loan words in German; Bierwisch, 1970b). This shows that the lexicon is not a mere list of words but that entries are interconnected in various ways (Bierwisch, 1970b; see also Fromkin, 1971, pp. 46–48; Garrett, 1975).

Above we have seen that inflectional endings are kept intact in exchange errors. These examples show that the same is true of inflectional endings of substitution errors, including endings which result from concord rules (such as the plural ending of the adjectives *andere* and *verschiedene*). The above explanation seems to apply here too: the substituting protoverbal element is introduced into the realizate. An alternative explanation would be that concord rules apply after lexicalization. Still another possibility is that protoverbal elements are first tagged by concord rules in a manner which permits applying the appropriate inflections after the protoverbal elements have been converted into words.

That phonological rules apply after relation rules is shown by the observations of Fromkin (1971) and Garrett (1975) that the phonology "adjusts" itself to the outcome of the error. For instance, in the error *add ups to* the *s* is an unvoiced /s/, unlike the voiced /z/ in the correct *adds up to* (Garrett's example). In Example (3.21) *end* replaced *fall* and the article consequently changed to *an*.

When two words are listed under a protoverbal element (see Section 2E) it may happen that the speaker performs first one lexicalization and then changes his mind and substitutes another one for it. This may or may not result in hesitation phenomena (or self-corrections), depending on the point at which the change of mind occurs. The speaker may also substitute a string lexicalization for a word, and vice versa (or one string lexicalization for another) where both appear under the same protoverbal element (see Section 2E). This is possible, because lexicalization does not imply that henceforward only the word (or string lexicalization) exists, and its meaning is lost sight of; rather, the connection between the word and the protoverbal element carrying the meaning is maintained and the latter can always be reverted to. The situation is similar in regard to compact lexicalizations (see Section 2E). Once a compact lexicalization is decided on, the speaker can still go back to the I-marker constituent which gave rise to it and substitute a different lexicalization (*young man* for *youngster*). The reverse may also occur: protoverbal elements in an I-marker constituent are lexicalized and subsequently a compact lexicalization for the whole constituent is substituted for these. (The communicative considerations which may give rise to such changes are discussed in Section 4A.)

An entirely different process takes place when the speaker changes his mind and substitutes a nonsynonymous expression for the original lexicalization. As a result, hesitations and certain kinds of errors may occur. Since only synonymous expressions are listed under a given protoverbal element, such changes of mind must be due to a change in the protoverbal element itself.

3C. CHANGES IN I-MARKERS

The discussion so far has been based on the assumption that once an I-marker has been formed it remains stable throughout the production process, and that any changes of mind concern only alternative lexicalizations of protoverbal elements given in the I-marker. Introspectively it is quite clear that this is very often not the case. We may change our minds in midspeech not only as to how we want to say something but also as to what we want to say. I-markers are not static structures but must be assumed to be subject to change in the course of production. This erratic behavior of I-markers does not upset the apparatus developed so far. Suppose for instance that in the course of the process described in Table 3.3 the speaker decides he should say that *Bill* is not only *poor,* but also that he is *unlucky.* At any point before Step 4 the I-marker can be changed so that the protoverbal element 'unlucky' is added as an attribute in addition to the protoverbal element 'poor', with the result that Step 4 will render a realizate with 'unlucky^A'. (After Step 4 such a change of I-marker would require a revision of the realizate.) Such a change of I-marker, if it occurs at too late a stage, may result in hesitation or may necessitate self-correction. But if it takes place early enough, it may go unnoticed by the hearer.

Change in the I-marker may permit "tacking on" of words at the end of an utterance, as in the form of a conjoined phrase or a subordinate clause, again often without noticeable speech disturbance. However, the I-marker when thus enlarged may also be realized as two separate sentences. As pointed out in Section 1A, there is no reason for assuming that every I-marker must result in a single sentence.

Instead of adding a protoverbal element, the speaker may delete one. In Table 3.3 'poor' might be deleted from the I-marker before Step 4, which results in a shorter utterance. Of course, if the deletion is made after *poor* has been uttered, he will have to "take back" what he just said (or rest content with an unsatisfactory realization).

Further, the speaker may substitute one protoverbal element for another. For some reason he may decide that 'courageous' is a more apt attribute of Bill than 'poor'. The change may be less extreme, and a protoverbal element may be substituted for a very similar one, perhaps 'helpless' for 'poor' (this is the case alluded to at the close of the previous section: *helpless* and *poor* will not be listed in the lexicon under the same protoverbal element). Such substitution will occur whenever the speaker has difficulty in retrieving the appropriate word for the protoverbal element in question. He will then have to change the protoverbal element and settle for the second best expression. This presupposes that proto-verbal elements are interrelated so that additional ones are readily available. The same assumption must be made to account for substitution errors (see Section 3B). The nature of this interrelation remains to be investigated (see Brown & McNeill, 1966).

The speaker may fail to find a protoverbal element which fits the message he tries to convey, and as a consequence has to choose a somewhat less satisfactory protoverbal element. Note that this assumes a stage in the production process which precedes the formation of I-markers and at which there are "concepts" or notions which have yet to be converted into protoverbal elements (see Chapter 5).

When a change of protoverbal element occurs too late, blends of two words may occur: *swip* (= *swinging* + *hip*), *spirative* (= *spirant* + *fricative*) (Fromkin, 1971); and by a speaker of German: *verweitern* (= *vergrössern* + *erweitern*) (Bierwisch, 1970b). The two expressions from which such a blend presumably originated are either very close in meaning, or else, as pointed out by Garrett (1975), interchangeable in a particular context. Thus *intervene* and *interfere* do not mean the same — they are not listed under the same protoverbal element — but both would have fitted in the same context when the blending error cited by Garrett (1975) occurred:

(3.22) I don't want to intervere.

A blend may occur when a change of the protoverbal element is undertaken so late that the process of uttering a word was already on its way when instructions to utter a different one arrived. Alternatively, the speaker may have vacillated between two protoverbal elements (between two competing I-markers).

The bottleneck leading to such blends must be assumed to occur after category markers have been introduced by relation rules. This is shown by the strong tendency, reported by Garrett (1975), for the two blended words to belong to the same grammatical category. Matters are further complicated by the finding that not only words but whole phrases can be contaminated: *es stellt sich fest* (Bierwisch, 1970b) is apparently a blend of *es stellt sich heraus* and *ich stelle fest.* Here the change seems to have involved a larger portion of the I-marker.

Another kind of error, which also indicates competition between protoverbal elements, is one where the speaker utters an inappropriate word and then, usually, corrects himself:

(3.24) I'm chronically on the fringe . . . on the verge of making a break.

Unlike blends, such substitution errors do not always involve words of similar meaning: substitution of antonyms is common, as in:

(3.25)   I have to leave in at least . . . at most an hour.

But then, of course, antonyms are in a sense semantically similar (which is why young children often confuse them). Garrett (1975), from whom the last two examples are taken, reports that these errors involve words of the same grammatical category, which again, suggests that the locus of the disturbance is after introduction of category markers.

The phenomena discussed in this section strongly suggest a level of processing which precedes the I-marker level, and embodies the general intention to convey a particular message. At this level of cognitive structures (see Section 1A) a change of I-marker is decided on and the competing protoverbal elements arise that result in blends and in substitution errors (whether these are Freudian slips or not). (Additional motivations for this level are discussed in Chapter 5.)

The treatment of errors in the above two sections obviously does not amount to a full explanation of these phenomena. I have merely tried to show how they can be made to fit into the framework outlined in Section 3A. Also, only those findings of error studies have been reported which seemed pertinent to this objective. So far I have not come across any finding that presents a serious challenge to the account of the production process presented in this chapter, but one must agree with Fodor, Bever, and Garrett (1974), who conclude their discussion on speech errors admitting that "theorizing at this stage of investigation is extremely hazardous because it is largely unconstrained [p. 432]."

SUMMARY

In the preceding chapter the general principles of the operation of realization rules and the form of relation rules were discussed. The production process is described in further detail in this chapter. The principle observed here is that there are various alternative routes to emitting an utterance. Relation rules are so constructed that they can be applied to I-markers in any sequence and lexicalizations can be carried out at any point in the process. Speakers may have preferences for some sequences (and it has been claimed that there is a left-to-right preference), but they are not limited to these. The flexibility of the process made possible by the many alternatives is necessary to enable production to proceed in the fact of distractions and other noise factors.

Even so, these factors frequently make themselves felt in the form of hesitations and speech errors. A theory of production must show how such phenomena can occur, and so an account of them has been presented here. A distinction is made between hesitations due to the operation of relation rules and those due to problems in lexicalizing a protoverbal element. Various regularities in exchange errors can be explained by assuming that these arise when two lexicalizations are carried out simultaneously in the course of the production process.

It has been noted in Chapter 1 that the speech act originates on a level beyond I-markers. Some evidence is presented in that chapter that this deeper level does not always lead to the formation of a single I-marker. More than one I-marker may be active and compete for the "attention" of realization rules. Further, changes may be introduced into the I-marker by this "deeper" level in the course of realization. As a result, the speaker may hesitate and substitution errors and blends may occur.

4

The Choice
between Alternative
Realization Rules

4A. COMMUNICATIVE CONSIDERATIONS AND SHUNTING

'For the Duchess. An invitation from the Queen to play croquet.'
'From the Queen, an invitation for the Duchess to play croquet.'
Then they both bowed low, and their curls got entangled together.

(Carroll, *Alice in Wonderland*)

To give an account of linguistic performance one must disentangle the factors determining the choice between different ways of expressing the same idea. Linguists have typically regarded purely stylistic variations as belonging to performance and hence as outside their province. (Chomsky, 1965, p. 147). But where the linguist rests content with stating that there are optional transformations, a theory of performance must explain how an option is taken (Osgood, 1971, p. 521).

There are usually a number of alternative sets of realization rules which can be applied to a given I-marker. The realization may be by one or more sentences (see Section 1A); conjoined words, or phrases may be applied in different sequences; there is often a choice between the active and the passive voice, etc. As for lexicalization, a speaker frequently has his choice between synonymous words, string lexicalizations, or compact lexicalizations (see Sections 2D and 2E). The decision to use one relation rule or intonation rule rather than another, or one lexicalization rather than another, is made on the basis of various COMMUNICATIVE CONSIDERATIONS (of which the speaker may or may not be aware). We propose therefore an additional component for the production model, which together with the I-marker component determines the form of the utterance.

Both the I-marker and communicative considerations represent the message conveyed by the speaker. In fact, in Carroll's (1973) production model communicative considerations like "emphasis" and "theme" are included in the I-marker (see Section 2C). The distinction between two components which is proposed here is motivated by a difference in function between I-marker elements and relations on the one hand and communicative considerations on the other: the I-marker marshals sets of alternative realization rules and communicative considerations determine the choice between the alternatives. These two aspects of the message thus play different roles in the production process and consequently they are assigned to different components in the model.

The effects of communicative considerations have been only very insufficiently investigated. (Since the main intention is merely to illustrate the notion of communicative considerations, a number of relevant experiments are described only summarily.)

A factor influencing the choice between the active and the passive, which has been studied experimentally, is the focus of the utterance: the speaker tends to produce a sentence in which the noun focused upon is the surface subject. When he focuses on the agent he is likely to produce active sentences, whereas he tends to choose the passive when the goal is focused on.[1] This has been found in experiments where focus was manipulated by extralinguistic cues (Carroll, 1958; Turner & Rommetveit, 1968) and by linguistic context (Tannenbaum & Williams, 1968). It is also corroborated by experiments on judgments of the appropriateness of alternative sentences (Johnson-Laird, 1968a), and ratings of the importance of nouns in the sentence (Segal & Martin, 1966). These findings seem to link in with the claim made in Section 1C that aspects of the I-marker may differ in saliency. The choice of active and passive sentences seems to be one consequence of such a difference.

Focus and saliency seem also to be determinants in the finding of Clark (1965) that animate nouns tend to be expressed as surface subject (see also Johnson, 1967). Similarly, James, Thompson, and Baldwin (1973) report that the agent will be chosen as surface subject if it has a higher imagery value than the goal — and consequently the sentence will be active — and conversely, when the goal has higher imagery value it will tend to be expressed as surface subject and the sentence will be passive. Clark (1965) also found that the noun with little uncertainty, in the information theory sense, tends to appear as surface subject and concludes that "people put what they want to talk about [the topic or the theme] in the beginning of the sentence. [p. 369]."

Parallel to the above is Johnson-Laird's (1968b) finding, concerning sentence comprehension, that the formulation of a sentence affects the way the hearer

---

[1] A further difference between active and passive sentences is that they imply different presuppositions (Anisfeld & Klenbort, 1973).

represents it by schematic drawings, the surface subject tending to be drawn larger. Huttenlocher, Eisenberg and Strauss (1968) have shown that children can be better instructed to manipulate objects if the object to be moved, rather than the one which remains fixed, is expressed as surface subject. However, James (1972) has argued that for the listener there are a number of factors, such as imagery and idiosyncratic interest, which determine what he considers the theme.

Considerations of focus or theme affect not only the choice between active and passive, but also that between other constructions. An example given by Kay (1970) is the cleft sentence; compare Example (4.1) with Example (4.2):

(4.1)   It was the lion that was afraid of the unicorn.

(4.2)   It was the unicorn that the lion was afraid of.

Another subset of communicative considerations includes such "stylistic" considerations as simplicity, "avoidance of monotony," "level" of style (colloquial or formal), and the literary effect achieved by the form of the expression. Jakobson (1960, pp. 356–357) illustrates the effect of euphony: we tend to say *Joan and Marjory* rather than *Marjory and Joan*. The former sequence sounds smoother and so we opt for it, usually without being aware of making a choice.[2]

The above discussion suggests that the performance model includes a component of communicative considerations (or "rhetorical component," Katz, 1972, pp. 417–434). These direct the application of realization rules, an operation we shall call SHUNTING. Shunting may be conceived of as follows: Whenever there are two realization rules for an I-marker relation or a protoverbal element, each has a SHUNTING MARKER indicating with which communicative consideration it accords. Thus, a word in the lexicon may have the shunting marker 'polite', while its synonym, entered under the same protoverbal element, has the shunting marker 'vulgar'. When there is a communicative consideration to be 'polite', a shunting operation determines that lexicalization is to be by means of the word marked 'polite'. Similarly, the relation rule applicable to GOAL–ACTION in the I-marker will include Examples (4.3) and (4.4), and the relation rules applicable to AGENT–ACTION will include Examples (4.5) and (4.6).[3] Shunting markers

---

[2] Further, the speaker may formulate his utterance so as to avoid ambiguity. However, this he presumably does by a revision after production has already taken place mentally, by taking the place of the hearer and "comprehending" the product in a way which differs from his original intention. Often, of course, this is done too late, since he has already uttered the sentence.

[3] Example (4.6) should be supplemented by a selection restriction to the effect that this realization is possible only when preceded by the first term of the goal relation. Even so, I am not sure whether Examples (4.4) and (4.6) are the best way of representing these rules. However, this does not affect the presentation below.

are indicated here by square brackets:

(4.3) $(\text{GOAL--ACTION } a, b) \rightarrow (\text{GOAL } b^V + a^N)^V$
[agent in focus]

(4.4) $(\text{GOAL--ACTION } a, b) \rightarrow (\text{GOAL } a + be + b^V + en)$
[goal in focus]

(4.5) $(\text{AGENT--ACTION } a, b) \rightarrow (\text{AGENT } a^N + b^V)^S$
[agent in focus]

(4.6) $(\text{AGENT--ACTION } a, b) \rightarrow (\text{AGENT } be + b^V + \text{participle} + by + a^N)$
[goal in focus]

When communicative considerations determine that the goal is to be focused on, a shunting operation selects Examples (4.4) and (4.6) and a passive sentence is uttered as a result. Conversely, when the agent is to be focused on, shunting selects Examples (4.3) and (4.5) and the sentence uttered is in the active form. It will be noted that the introduction of shunting markers entails an interdependence of realization rules (see Section 2C).

In addition to the shunting markers in Examples (4.3)–(4.6) there may be others for the agent and goal relations, corresponding to other communicative considerations. Some communicative considerations may be expressed by means of paralinguistic features, such as intonation, facial mimicry, etc. When no specific communicative considerations apply (roughly speaking, when the speaker is indifferent as to the way he expresses himself) the choice between relation rules and between lexicalizations is not determined by shunting operations but by response sets (discussed in Section 4D).

In the examples given above, the distinction between the "material" belonging to the I-markers and that which has been assigned to the communicative considerations component accords with intuition. The differentiation appeared to be largely that between "what" and "how," the gist of the message being left with the I-marker and stylistic factors, like emphasis and focus, being assigned to the communicative considerations component. Matters are not always as simple as that, however. In the two sections below we discuss notions which, though they are much more closely associated with the meaning of the message, should nevertheless be viewed as appertaining to communicative considerations.

4B.   ILLOCUTIONARY ACTS

Promising, asserting, threatening and other so-called illocutionary acts may affect the form of sentences uttered. These are therefore communicative considerations. There are certain illocutionary acts, however, whose status may seem at first to be less clear. According to Searle (1969), a question like *Does John smoke?* is composed of a propositional content (John smokes) and the illocutionary act of questioning; and commanding is likewise an illocutionary act. In current versions of transformational grammar, on the other hand, interrogative and imperative elements are incorporated in the base structure. And, indeed, one would intuitively ascribe to them a more central role in the meaning of the utterance than, say, focus, emphasis, or the illocutionary acts of threatening and promising.

However, a pretheoretical notion such as "meaning" constitutes too meager a support for a systematic distinction between two components of the model. The decisive consideration here ought to be: what is the function of questioning and commanding in the operation of the production mechanism? Whether a question is asked or a statement is made or a command is given determines the way a given relation is realized. The relations between *turn on* and *the heat* and *you* are the same in the following three sentences; and yet they differ in the realization rules applied.

(4.7)   1.   You turned the heat on.
        2.   Did you turn the heat on?
        3.   Turn the heat on!

This was of course the reason why in Chomsky's (1957) early version of transformational grammar interrogatives and imperatives were regarded as transformations of the corresponding declarative sentences. It is proposed therefore that questioning and commanding be allocated to the component of communicative considerations. Only the propositional content in Searle's (1969) terms will thus be left in the I-marker[4] (see, however, Section 4C).

Regarding questioning, it should be remembered that in addition to yes–no questions there are *wh-* questions asking about the agent, the goal, the action (*What did X do?*) and so on. The I-marker may here be viewed as containing a dummy element for the agent, goal or action term, respectively, and for each such question there will be a different communicative consideration.

Moreover, there is no unitary communicative consideration responsible even for all yes–no questions; nor is there a single communicative consideration of

---

[4] However, this would not be identical in all respects with Searle's (1969) propositional content. According to Searle (1969, p. 31, note 1), *Down with Caesar!* has no propositional content but only an illocutionary act and a referring expression. The latter concept has no function in the model developed here. It seems reasonable to accord to this utterance an I-marker with the propositional content corresponding roughly to that of *Caesar will fall* and a communicative consideration of wishing and exhorting. The case is less clear with *Ouch!* and *hurrah!* which Searle quotes as representing merely an illocutionary act. As for the negative, I am not certain whether it, too, should be ascribed to the communicative considerations component. This would be in line with the criterion adopted here, since the negative selects among alternative realizations of relations. On the other hand, an affirmative and the corresponding negative refer to different states of affairs; their propositional content differs, and their I-markers should differ accordingly.

"commanding." A subdivision is necessary here, as becomes clear from the following observation. In making a request, one has various syntactic forms at one's disposal: imperatives (*Give me my book back*), declaratives, (*I would rather you give me my book back*), and interrogatives (*May I have my book back?*). Similarly, there are various ways of expressing a question. In accordance with the principle advanced in Section 4A that two alternative forms of expressing the same content originate from two different communicative considerations, we conclude that there is a communicative consideration of polite requesting, another one of indirectly requesting, and so on, as there are likewise various communicative considerations of "questioning." While the structure of the communicative considerations component is still entirely unexplored, it seems reasonable to postulate that to each communicative consideration, or perhaps to each combination of communicative considerations, corresponds a shunting operation influencing the form of the utterance.

4C. PREDICATION AND ATTRIBUTION

Communicative considerations determine which part of the utterance is to be the focus. As we have seen in Section 4A, the choice between active and passive is partly determined by the desired focus. In addition, there are various constructions which permit focusing on different sentence parts. For example:

(4.8) Phyllis cuts roses in the garden.

(4.9) It is roses which Phyllis cuts in the garden.

(4.10) It is in the garden that Phyllis cuts roses.

(4.11) The garden is where Phyllis cuts roses.

These sentences differ in the way words are allocated to the subject and predicate of the sentence. The proposition is that the I-markers are nevertheless identical, just as the I-markers of active and passive sentences are identical (see Fillmore, 1968, for a treatment of subjectivalization from which the discussion below has borrowed much), and that the subject–predicate division is introduced by a shunting operation which selects relation rules appropriate to the intended focus.

Consider descriptions of a simple situation elicited in an experiment by Osgood (1971). Subjects gave descriptions like Example (4.12) when the ball had been seen and described previously, whereas when it was presented for the first time, Example (4.12) never occurred and the typical response was something like Example (4.13):

(4.12) The black ball is on the table.

(4.13) The ball on the table is black.

Whether *black* is realized as attribution or as part of the predicate is dependent on the context. The state of affairs described is identical in both cases (if we ignore the preceding context). The relations holding in the I-marker are identical, since 'black' is the attribute of 'ball' in both Examples (4.12) and (4.13).

In current linguistic theory these sentences have different base structures, the attributive structure being derived from an embedded sentence (see also Bolinger, 1967, who demonstrates the infeasibility of deriving attributions from predications as writers of transformational grammar have suggested). However, in a performance model a distinction ought to be made between what is talked about and how one talks about it. The former is the domain of the I-marker, and the latter is that of communicative considerations. As far as linguistic description is concerned, the cogency of this distinction may be overshadowed by such factors as simplicity and generality of the overall system, and consequently the base structures of the linguist contain information as to what is the predicate and whether the sentence is active or passive. But, as Watt (1970) observes, the linguist's criterion of economy may differ from that applicable to a performance model (see Section 2A). In the previous section it was argued that the illocutionary acts of questioning and commanding do not belong to the I-marker, and now it is even contended that not everything that Searle calls propositional content belongs to the I-marker. Any two propositional contents which, if realized as utterances of sentences in the declarative form, have the same truth value belong to the same I-marker. Thus, the propositions expressed by Examples (4.8)–(4.11) are correlated with one I-marker, as are those expressed by Examples (4.12) and (4.13). Which part of the I-marker is to be expressed as attribute and which as predicate is determined by a shunting operation.[5]

An I-marker may be realized without any predication. Such is the case, for example, with names of plays, books, and headlines:

(4.14) The Man Who Came to Dinner

(4.15) Syntactic Structures

(4.16) Earthquake in Boston Area

It is alright for the linguist to decide by fiat that these are not complete sentences because they have no predicate, but this does not make them any less acceptable as utterances than their counterparts; see Examples (4.17)–(4.19), which are endowed with full sentencehood. In fact, as titles and headlines the latter are rather awkward, if not odd:

(4.17) The man came to dinner.

(4.18) (The) structures are syntactic.

(4.19) There was (is) an earthquake in the Boston area.

---

[5] In fact, there seem to be at least two different kinds of attribution, as suggested by the difference between *the man responsible* and *the responsible man, the stars visible* and *the visible stars* (see Bolinger, 1967).

Predicates are introduced into Examples (4.17) and (4.18) by shunting operations, whereas in Examples (4.14) and (4.15) the same content is expressed in the form of attributes, introduced by a different kind of shunting operation. Similarly, Example (4.16) lacks the verbal expression of the predicate, which appears in Example (4.19).

In each of the following pairs, sentences differ in the way predication is introduced:

(4.20) Dick sold Paul a horse.

(4.21) Paul bought a horse from Dick.

(4.22) The children are with Mary.

(4.23) Mary has the children with her.

(4.24) The book belongs to Roy.

(4.25) Roy has the book.

One way of looking at the two sentences of each pair is as follows. The sentences have identical I-markers and the difference between them is due to different shunting operations which operate to select (1) different sets of relation rules, which determine, among other things, the predicate; and (2) different lexicalizations (*sold* versus *bought,* etc.). (Another possibility is discussed in Section 5B.)

A language provides its speakers with ways of realizing I-markers in accordance with at least the more common communicative considerations. The speaker can choose from alternative realization rules so that a given aspect can be focused on; when he wants to be formal and aloof rather than informal and friendly he will usually have the linguistic means at his disposal, and so on. But not every choice between alternative realizations is actuated by the communicative considerations component. Instead, the speaker may take whatever route to the utterance first presents itself, without any motive for preferring it to its alternatives. When this occurs one may speak of a response set.

4D. RESPONSE SETS

Linguists of the transformationalist school are not concerned with relative frequencies and sequential probabilities. When the upsurge of interest in psycholinguistics started under the influence of transformational grammar, much of the research was marked by a disregard of such jejune variables as frequency and probability (not to mention semantic variables, research on which appeared much too hazardous). Unadvisedly so, because these are performance factors with which psycholinguists ought to deal. But apparently these notions were felt to be unfit for psycholinguistic research; psycholinguists were meant for higher pursuits. This neglect seems to have been detrimental to some early studies, in which experimentation with concepts newly introduced from transformational grammar was confounded with such threadbare variables as sentence length and frequency (see Schlesinger, 1968, pp. 19–21, 45–56).

When there are two alternative ways of realizing a given I-marker and none of them is chosen by communicative considerations, its realization may be assumed to be determined by response sets. While truly synonymous expressions may be rarer than is usually assumed (Chafe, 1971), there may be situations where two expressions carry the same information, and communicative considerations do not indicate preference for any one of them. In these cases the response set determines which utterance is made.

Among the response sets that presumably operate is the relative difficulty of producing the utterance. This may be due either to the complexity of the realization rules or to the complexity of the surface string. In either case, a "principle of least effort" may lead the speaker to prefer the less difficult form. Further, of the two different realizations the one which comes to mind first may be applied. A factor of frequency may be operative here; but there may also be a recency effect, the word or structure most recently experienced being preferred.

Now, these response sets may be assumed to influence production not only in the absence of communicative considerations which prefer one realization over the other. When there is a conflict between response set and communicative considerations, the latter will presumably gain the upper hand, unless the response set is unusually strong (for instance, when difficulty of processing is very great, or the structure is hard to remember). Such conflict situations are probably quite common, and their outcome will of course also depend on the individual speaker and his motivation in a given situation.

The production of passive sentences apparently involves more complex relation rules than those required for the production of active ones. Compare Examples (4.4) and (4.6) with Examples (4.3) and (4.5).[6] Consequently a tendency should be expected to prefer the active over the passive. In an analysis of several speech samples, Goldman-Eisler and Cohen (1970) indeed found active sentences to outnumber passive ones by a ratio of about eight to one (see also Svartvik, 1966, especially p. 46). Moreover, most of the passives found in the samples were agentless passives, such as

(4.26) The manuscript was written in the twelfth century.

To reformulate these as active sentences would require either the addition of information about the agent, which may be unavailable, or else the awkward

---

[6] A number of findings evidence the greater difficulty of producing passive sentences (Tannenbaum & Williams, 1968). The finding of Miller and McKean (1964) on sentence matching, in which the passive transformation took longer than the negative transformation, might have been due to greater difficulty of carrying out the transformation. See, however, Schlesinger (1968, pp. 54–56) for a discussion of a possible confounding factor.

addition of words like *somebody*:

(4.27)   Somebody wrote the manuscript in the twelfth century.

Other passives accounted for only about 2% of the sentences in the sample. These authors also found negative sentences to be much less frequent than affirmative ones. But this can obviously be accounted for by pragmatic factors, since it is not always possible to express a given content in the negative form. An explanation in terms of response strength is more plausible for the low occurrence of passives. However, communicative considerations may also have been a contributory factor: possibly the goal is less frequently focused on than the agent, resulting in passives being less frequently produced.

No such communicative considerations were presumably operative in a laboratory experiment by Mehler (1963). In Mehler's study subjects were required to recall eight sentences presented in eight different syntactic forms. Four of the sentences were in the active voice and four others in the passive voice. During recall, the total number of sentences formulated by the subject in the active voice was far higher than that of those formulated in the passive voice, and, as shown in Table 4.1, this was true for affirmative as well as negative and for declarative as well as interrogative sentences. The explanation seems to be that subjects tend to produce fewer passive sentences, because these are more difficult to process. What is remarkable in these results is that, in spite of the subjects being presented in the experiment with as many passive as active sentences, this balance is not maintained in recall. Apparently, laziness gains the upper hand.

No similar response sets seem to have been operative to make subjects avoid negative or interrogative sentences. Recalculating the data of Table 4.1 for negative versus affirmative sentences, one finds 1,339 negative responses versus 1,372 affirmative ones; for interrogatives and declaratives there were 1,347 and 1,364 responses, respectively. It should be noted that in Mehler's experiment all sentences were in the present perfect tense, in which the negative differs from the affirmative merely by the addition of *not,* and the interrogative from the declarative in a change of the position of *has.*

TABLE 4.1
Frequencies of Active and Passive Response Sentences
in Mehler's Experiment

	Active	Passive
Affirmative declarative	460	325
Negative declarative	338	241
Affirmative interrogative	336	251
Negative interrogative	434	326
Total:	1,568	1,143

In 1963 Mehler disregarded, as did many writers of that time, such factors as response set and relative frequency. He interpreted his findings to the effect that sentences are stored in the form of a kernel, containing its semantic components, plus a tag indicating its syntactic form. The tags are conceived of as those that give rise to the following constructions:

1. N: *n*egative, active, declarative;
2. P: affirmative, *p*assive, declarative;
3. Q: affirmative, active, interrogative (*Q*uestion);
4. NP: *n*egative, *p*assive, declarative;
5. NQ: *n*egative, active, interrogative;
6. QP: affirmative, *p*assive, interrogative;
7. NPQ: *n*egative, *p*assive, interrogative

The kernel, K, is an affirmative, active, declarative sentence, following the then current *Syntactic Structures* model (Chomsky, 1957). Mehler noted that there were many more errors in the direction of the kernel than away from it. This he regarded as evidence that syntactic tags are more likely to get lost in memory than the semantic core, or kernel.

There are, in fact, considerably more errors of recall involving simplification — errors in the direction of the kernel — in Mehler's data. But a closer look at the data shows that the directionality effect noticed by Mehler occurs only for the passive transformation (as is also suggested by Table 4.1). Table 4.2 gives a breakdown of errors in Mehler's experiment according to the transformation involved (passive, negative, and interrogative) and according to whether they are in the direction of the kernel or away from it. The table shows clearly that only in the case of the passive transformation do errors in direction of the kernel outnumber those away from it.[7] This confirms the explanation given above that the passive (P, QP, NP, and NPQ in Table 4.2) causes difficulty, which makes subjects recall active sentences instead. No directionality of confusions is found for negatives and interrogatives. This in itself argues against Mehler's explanation in terms of forgetting of tags, because it leaves the question open why only the passive tag should get lost.

This conclusion is further strengthened by an analysis of those errors which involve changes both in the direction of the kernel and away from it. These

[7] Table 4.2 does not include errors involving more than one transformation. These are in part dealt with in Table 4.3. Another 14 types of error — of which there were 125 cases — involve more than one transformation in the same direction (for example, a change of Q to NPQ involves both converting an affirmative sentence into a negative one and an active into a passive one. Of these 125 cases, 82 were in the direction of the kernel and 43 away from it. Confusions involving both the negative and interrogative transformations (but not the passive) are those between K and NQ and between P and NPQ. Of those there were 45 in the direction of the kernel and 21 away from it. However, even if these numbers are added to either the negative or interrogative transformation in Table 4.2, the balance would not be tipped in favor of the directionality hypothesis.

TABLE 4.2

Number of Syntactic Confusions in Mehler's Experiment in Direction of the
Kernel and away from It, According to Transformation

| Transformation | Confusion between | Direction | |
		To kernel	Away from kernel
Passive	K and P	43	14
	Q and QP	32	8
	N and NP	49	11
	NQ and NPQ	44	23
	Total:	168	56
Negative	K and N	36	14
	Q and NQ	31	72
	P and NP	18	10
	QP and NPQ	38	60
	Total:	123	156
Interrogative	K and Q	31	12
	N and NQ	15	29
	P and QP	27	30
	NP and NPQ	5	31
	Total:	78	102

errors are presented in Table 4.3. The first row of this table pertains to the error
of recalling a P-sentence as an N-sentence. There were three cases of this error,
which represent three instances of turning a passive into an active sentence and
at the same time three instances of turning an affirmative into a negative
sentence; and so on for the following rows.

In this experimental task the negative tag which distinguishes N from the
kernel is evidently more likely to be added in recall than to get lost, and the
same holds true for the interrogative tag. It seems almost as if subjects were
trying to redress the balance and to make up for having simplified the passive
sentences, by turning other sentences into negative and interrogative forms.[8] But
whatever the explanation for this phenomenon, the data clearly do not square
with the hypothesis that syntactic tags of sentences get lost. Rather, there seems
to be a response set to choose the less difficult syntactic form, as evidenced by
the conversion of passive sentences into active ones in recall.

---

[8] Concerning the greater tendency of turning declaratives into interrogatives than vice versa,
one may also speculate that the subject notices that negative and affirmative sentences are
about equally represented, and when he cannot remember whether a certain proposition was
affirmed or negated, he settles for the more "neutral" interrogative form as a kind of
compromise. All this is done without deliberation, of course.

The tendency for passive sentences to be recalled in the active form was also found with a different experimental technique by Schlesinger (1968, pp. 58–61). In a recognition experiment, however, in which the sentences were in part the same as those used in the recall experiment, passives were not more often incorrectly "recognized" when presented in the active form than active sentences when presented in the passive form (Schlesinger, 1968, pp. 63–67). The same lack of directionality effect for passives and actives appears in other recognition experiments (Clifton, Kurcz, & Jenkins, 1965; Weisberg, 1971). In the series of experiments reported by Clifton and Odom (1966) the differences are small and vary in direction from experiment to experiment. If the direction-ality effect obtained in recall experiments was due to forgetting of the syntactic tag, one should expect forgetting to make itself felt also in a recognition task. The fact that such a result failed to show up in several experiments is additional evidence against the loss-of-tag hypothesis. On the other hand, response sets of the kind discussed above may be assumed to operate only in recall and not in

TABLE 4.3

Confusion Errors in Mehler's Experiment Involving Both Changes Towards the Kernel and away from It

Stimulus sentence	Response sentence	From: To:	Passive active	Active passive	Negative positive	Positive negative	Interrogative declarative	Declarative interrogative
			\multicolumn{6}{c}{Confusion errors}					
P	N		3	–	–	3	–	–
N	P		–	3	3	–	–	–
P	Q		8	–	–	–	–	8
Q	P		–	1	–	–	1	–
N	Q		–	–	20	–	–	20
Q	N		–	–	–	16	16	–
PQ	NQ		29	–	–	29	–	–
NQ	PQ		–	7	7	–	–	–
NP	NQ		16	–	–	–	–	16
NQ	NP		–	3	–	–	3	–
NP	PQ		–	–	16	–	–	16
PQ	NP		–	–	–	15	15	–
N	QP		–	6	6	–	–	6
QP	N		5	–	–	5	5	–
Q	NP		–	2	–	2	2	–
NP	Q		9	–	9	–	–	9
NQ	P		–	3	3	–	3	–
P	NQ		15	–	–	15	–	15
			85	25	64	85	45	90
Confusions of Table 4.2			168	56	123	156	78	102
Total:			253	81	187	241	123	192

recognition, because the latter requires a simple yes–no decision. Thus these results, too, support the explanation in terms of response set proposed above.

Experiments on recall (Mehler, 1963; Schlesinger, 1968) thus show that, because of their lesser degree of difficulty, active sentences are preferred in recall to passive ones. This tendency apparently operates without the subjects' awareness. One may assume that they intended to comply with the experimenter's instructions, and reconstruct the sentences as they were heard.

Sentence difficulty also affects production in a situation in which the subject is free to choose between constructions. This is shown in an experiment by Noizet, Deyts and Deyts (1972), who presented subjects with two sentences one after another and asked them to convert each pair into a single sentence with a relative clause. Analysis of the sentence form chosen as well as of errors made showed a bias towards easier-to-produce constructions. Another response set found was that the sentence presented first was more likely to be produced as the matrix sentence, for example, the italicized part of Example (4.28), in which the second sentence was embedded rather than vice versa, unless this led to a more difficult construction:

(4.28) *Le clown* que le musicien frappe *regarde la danseuse.*
'The clown whom the musician hits looks at the dancer.'

The difficulty of a construction will of course not invariably deter a speaker from uttering it: the effort to effect the communicative considerations requiring this construction may be worthwhile for him. Further, there may be other response sets which prove stronger. In an experiment on the learning of active and passive sentences, Prentice (1966) manipulated response strength of the initial word of a sentence by presenting the sentence after prompt words with different association values. For instance, Example (4.29) was presented after either one of the following words: *lion, man,* or *music.*

(4.29) A tiger frightened the woman.

The initial word, *tiger,* is elicited by *lion* as a primary associate; the final word, *woman,* is elicited by *man* as primary associate; neither one of these words is a frequent response to *music.* Prentice used a paired-associate learning task: subjects were to reproduce the sentence in response to the stimulus word. She found that a sentence was learned better when it began with a noun of high response strength; for instance, Example (4.29) was easier to learn as a response to *lion* than as a response to *man* or *music.* This result was obtained both for active and for passive sentences. By inference, argues Prentice, in a natural speaking situation there is a tendency to begin the utterance with the noun with the highest response strength. If this noun refers to the agent the sentence will be active, whereas if it refers to the goal it will be passive.

SUMMARY

There are two aspects to the message conveyed by a speaker:

1 . The propositional content, containing protoverbal elements and the relations between them; these are included in the I-marker component.

2. Communicative considerations, including illocutionary force, and those determining the desired emphasis, focus and other stylistic aspects.

Often there will be several alternative lexicalizations for a given protoverbal element and alternative relation rules for a given I-marker relation and alternative intonation rules. The choice between these alternatives is made by the communicative considerations component by means of shunting markers. Whenever this component does not select between two alternatives, response sets determine which of them is chosen.

5
Cognitive Structures

A thought may be compared to a
cloud shedding a shower of words
[Vygotsky, 1962, p. 151]

5A. I-MARKERS AND COGNITIVE STRUCTURES

The production process has been described in the preceding chapters as a mapping of underlying structures into utterances. These underlying structures have been assumed to be semantic in nature: notions such as "agent," "instrument," and "attribute" are closely related to the way we perceive the world. It might seem to be a natural consequence of this approach to regard I-markers as identical with the perceptual and cognitive organization of the world around us; that is, whenever we utter a sentence, the I-marker underlying it represents the way we view the situation about which we speak (where "situation" is used loosely for anything spoken about, whether present or not, and concrete or not). Such an equation between semantic structures underlying language and cognitive structures has indeed been implied by several writers (Antinucci & Parisi, 1973; Osgood, unpublished; Schank, 1972, 1973).

Against this view it is contended here that the production process originates at a "deeper" nonlinguistic level, the level of COGNITIVE STRUCTURES, and not in I-markers. The existence of such a level has already been intimated in Section 1A and I-markers were claimed to mediate between it and utterances. This chapter further explores the implications of this view, which seems to be in line with that of some writers (e.g. Chafe, 1971, who distinguishes between semantic structure and meaning, the latter being nonlinguistic). We see below how I-markers and cognitive structures differ and what motivates the distinction between them.

What argues against the possibility that the I-marker is the starting point of the production process? First, such a view would seem to imply that whenever there is something to speak about, I-markers present themselves to a speaker ready-made. This is evidently not so. When perceiving a situation to be talked about, we usually have several options regarding what to say about it. Usually, the choice between these options requires little or no deliberation, and hence we are only occasionally aware of it. Vygotsky (1962) gives the example of someone seeing 'a barefoot boy in a blue shirt running down the street', and argues that the whole situation may be perceived simultaneously, whereas linguistically it must be expressed item by item, linearly. In addition to this sequencing discussed by Vygotsky, the speaker may choose to omit certain aspects of the situation entirely; for instance, he may abstain from mentioning the way the boy was dressed, the fact that he was running, or any other aspect of the situation. In general, the speaker has to select from any given cognitive structure — from what he is aware of and intends to talk about — to what is to be included in the message conveyed. The production model must therefore include a component making this selection: the I-MARKER SELECTOR. The I-marker selector formulates an I-marker for a given cognitive structure.

What determines the choice made by the I-marker selector is little understood. Apparently, conversational implicatures in the Gricean sense (Katz, 1972, pp. 444–450), and the intended perlocutionary force of the utterance play important roles here. Further, Olson (1970) has shown that a speaker chooses the attribute of an object he describes so as to contrast it with other objects from which it is distinguished. For instance, a white circle would be referred to as *white* if it is contrasted with a black circle, but as *round* if contrasted with a white square. Thus, messages are decided on as required by the situation.

Usually the speaker has an option between the varying degrees of precision. *My mother's brother* is more precise than *my uncle*, as is *my father's sister's husband.* The speaker decides which expression to use (although he may be unaware of the "ambiguity" involved in an expression like *my uncle*). In the above example by Vygotsky he either may or may not mention that the boy's shirt was blue, and even if he does he may omit (as Vygotsky did) to mention what shade of blue it was. In addition to the choice between active and passive — which is determined by communicative considerations (see Section 4A) — we have the option of not mentioning the agent, by using, for example, the truncated passive (as in *The manuscript was written.*).[1] An informal experi-

---

[1] Watt (1970, p. 189) shows that the full and truncated passives are not transformationally related as far as the mental grammar is concerned. To account for the intuitive knowledge of the native speaker that these two constructions are related, he postulates an "archival competence faculty" in which this knowledge is stored. It seems, however, that no such component is needed if it is assumed that a given cognitive structure may be related in various ways to other cognitive structures. If a statement expressed as a full passive is true, we may reason that a corresponding statement expressed as a truncated passive is true as well, just as we deduce from two premises a logical conclusion (without the use of rules of grammar in the narrower sense).

ment by Osgood illustrates how different degrees of specificity may be aimed at by different speakers. In his experiment subjects were presented with simple situations that they had to describe. Osgood (1971) concludes from his observations that "... the form as well as the content of sentences can be influenced by manipulating the perceptual context in which they are produced [p. 498]." When the influence is on form this is due to the communicative considerations discussed in Section 4A, but when content is affected, different I-markers must be involved. Thus, when subjects saw a black ball rolling and hitting a blue ball, Examples (5.1)–(5.3) were produced, among others (by different subjects):

(5.1)   A rolling black ball hits a blue ball.
(5.2)   Black ball hitting larger blue ball.
(5.3)   A small black ball rolls into a larger blue one.

Both Examples (5.2) and (5.3) are more specific than Example (5.1) in that they refer to the relative sizes of the balls. Here speakers differed in the options taken by the I-marker selector.

After the production process has started, a speaker may change his mind as to the selection and the degree of specificity desired. In small children learning to speak their native language one can frequently witness different selections being tried out. This is how Bloom's (1973) little Allison struggles to make her meaning clear: "up up . . . neck up . . . neck . . . zip zip up [p. 51]." In Section 3C some changes of mind were shown not to involve merely a change in the tactics of realization but rather a change in the I-marker itself. Changes like these may occasionally result in speech errors. Suppose a speaker intends to talk about a given situation: an I-marker is formed and subsequently changed so as to yield what appears to the speaker to be a more appropriate description of this situation. There must then be a level deeper than the I-marker at which this change is decided on.

The above considerations lead to the conclusion that I-markers can not be the level where production of utterances begins. A level of cognitive structures must be postulated out of which I-markers are formed.

As stated, not all that is contained in a cognitive structure is included in the I-marker; a selection is usually made. One might conclude from this that there is a simple part–whole relationship between the I-marker and the cognitive structure from which it derives. But this is not so: I-markers differ from cognitive structures not only in extent but also qualitatively, in respect to the relations and elements they are constituted of (see Section 5E).

5B. PARAPHRASES

In the above section it was shown that the I-marker selector selects from the cognitive structure those aspects that are to constitute the message. I propose here that the I-marker selector does more than that: it chooses among alternative

I-markers that are appropriate for a given message. The availability of such alternatives is indicated by the existence of paraphrases. To substantiate this, let us examine various kinds of paraphrases and their implications for a production model.

Paraphrases have been the basis of much of recent theorizing in linguistics. The regularities involved in such paraphrases have typically been accounted for by postulating more abstract, or "deeper," deep structures. This occurred in the much debated case of the instrumental, when Lakoff (1968) argued that Examples (5.4) and (5.5) must have identical deep structures:

(5.4) Seymour used a knife to slice the salami.
(5.5) Seymour sliced the salami with a knife.

Likewise, one might make a case for ascribing identical deep structures — and I-markers — to Examples (5.6) and (5.7), and to Examples (5.8) and (5.9), the choice between the alternatives being dictated by communicative considerations:

(5.6) John bought the book from Peter.
(5.7) Peter sold the book to John.
(5.8) The play pleased Carl.
(5.9) Carl liked the play.

However, the attempt to accord identical deep structures to paraphrastic constructions becomes questionable when the phenomenon is of restricted regularity. Thus Examples (5.10) and (5.11) are synonymous, but few other verbs, (mainly *snow* and *hail*) enter into constructions which are similarly paraphrastic.

(5.10) It is raining.
(5.11) Rain is coming down (is falling).

Bennett (1968) gives the example of Example (5.12) which is synonymous with Example (5.13).

(5.12) At this moment he's on a train going to London.
(5.13) At this moment he's in a train going to London.

In most other linguistic contexts *on* and *in* cannot be substituted for each other without changing the meaning. Bennett argues that in the present case such mutual substitutability does not result from identical deep structures but from the fact that the two situations described are coextensive (see also Chafe, 1970, pp. 88–90). This argument seems to be compelling. If they were derived from the same I-marker it would be necessary to introduce additional realization rules, which would be required only for very specific kinds of sentences (those about riding on trains). Both sentences, then, should be viewed as derived from identical cognitive structures, which are converted into slightly different I-markers. A similar argument can be made for Examples (5.10) and (5.11).[2] We will use the term COAGULATION for the conversion of cognitive structures into I-markers by the I-marker selector and say that the cognitive structures underlying Examples (5.10) and (5.11) were coagulated into different I-markers, as were those underlying Examples (5.12) and (5.13).

These two pairs, then, show that synonymy is not a sufficient condition for assigning identical I-markers to utterances. On the other hand, there are paraphrases which are best viewed as different realizations of the same I-marker; for instance, an active sentence and the corresponding passive, or Examples (4.1) and (4.2). But what about pairs like Examples (5.4) and (5.5), (5.6) and (5.7), or (5.8) and (5.9)? The linguist may consider it his task to account for the regularities involved here. However, the question is in which cases do the rules internalized by the speaker make use of these regularities?

Consider, for instance, Example (5.4). One possibility is to view the I-marker of this sentence as including – just like that of Example (5.5) – the instrumental relation between 'slice' and 'knife'. This would be in line with Lakoff's (1968) approach, and would accommodate the fact that these two utterances can be used to refer to the same event. Alternatively, one might argue that Examples (5.4) and (5.5) only have identical cognitive structures, and that these are coagulated into different I-markers. In Example (5.4) *used a knife* could be viewed as a realization of the GOAL–ACTION relation, just like, for example, *took a knife* (see Figure 5.1). Then *slice the salami* might be the realization of an I-marker constituent which stands in the PURPOSE–ACTION relation to that underlying *used a knife* (see *sold his car to buy a new one*). Notice that while the former solution would entail an additional realization rule for the instrumental relation – one which results in its being expressed as in Example (5.4) – the latter solution requires only rules needed anyway to express the GOAL–ACTION and the PURPOSE–ACTION relation, and might be preferable for this reason.

The question is, therefore, where one draws the line between paraphrases having identical I-markers and those which result from different coagulations of identical cognitive structures. To answer this question many more detailed analyses of such paraphrases may be required, so as to arrive at an overall picture of the system of realization rules. But perhaps the problem could also be approached experimentally? Anderson and Bower (1973, pp. 222–234) discuss

---

[2] Some readers will by now have got the impression that what has been done here is belabor the hoary distinction between reference and sense. What is being dealt with here, however, is not any philosophical issue but the process of speaking. It is true, but only in a general way, that utterances about the same referent–situation spring from the same cognitive structure; and those having the same sense from the same I-marker. But it is best not to confuse the exposition here with a terminology appropriate to an entirely different problem area. The same goes for similar distinctions made by philosophers, such as extension and intension.

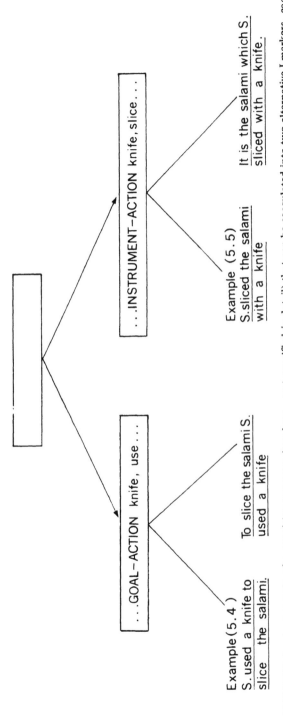

FIGURE 5.1. An example of a cognitive structure (top box – not specified in detail) that can be coagulated into two alternative I-markers, each of which can be realized in various ways according to communicative considerations. Note that in each of the boxes for I-markers only one of the constituents has been specified here.

...GOAL–ACTION knife, use...

Example (5.4)
S. used a knife to slice the salami.

To slice the salami S. used a knife

...INSTRUMENT–ACTION knife, slice...

Example (5.5)
S. sliced the salami with a knife

It is the salami which S. sliced with a knife.

the problem of how to decide when two sentences which are paraphrases of each other have identical underlying structures. They suggest that confusion errors may provide relevant experimental evidence. When a subject is presented with a sentence and later falsely recognizes a paraphrase of this sentence, this shows that the two sentences have the same underlying structure. For instance, Shafto (1973) found that sentences with complementary verbs – like *buy* and *sell* (see Examples 5.6 and 5.7) *give* and *get, lead* and *follow* – tend to be confused in memory. Note, however, that since we must postulate two underlying levels, such experiments cannot decide at which of these the two sentences are represented in identical form. The confusion may have occurred because the two sentences have the same underlying I-marker, or else because they originate from the same cognitive structure.[3] The question of where precisely to draw the line between different coagulations of identical cognitive structures and different realizations of identical I-markers can therefore not be settled by such experiments. In general, how these two possibilities differ operationally is not clear. The solution will probably be arrived at eventually by considerations of simplicity of the overall model.

At any rate, we have seen that the existence of certain paraphrases is evidence for a level of cognitive structure, because they cannot be accorded identical I-markers without unduly burdening thereby the apparatus of realization rules. The only alternative way of dealing with paraphrases would be that suggested by Simmons (1973, p. 81), who introduces into his model "paraphrase rules" specially designed to state equivalences of cases like Examples (5.6) and (5.7). Whatever the merit of this solution, it is inapplicable to two varieties of paraphrases: those based on knowledge of the world and situation-dependent paraphrases.

Observe first that Examples (5.14) and (5.15) for all intents and purposes entail each other:

(5.14) The cow behind the barn has only three legs.
(5.15) The cow behind the barn lacks one leg.

If speakers normally regard these two sentences as referring to the same situation, this is because they have certain information about cows. By contrast, the following pair of sentences need not be similarly regarded as "meaning the same," because there is no parallel information about planes available to every-

---

[3] This has been realized by Johnson-Laird and Stevenson (1970). In a memory task involving sentences with *bought* and *sold, liked* and *pleased* (see Examples 5.6–5.9) he showed that unless told that they would be given a memory test, subjects tended to forget the syntactic form of the sentence, while preserving the meaning. Johnson-Laird suggests two alternative conclusions: (1) the deep structure (I-marker) is forgotten and only the meaning (cognitive structure) is retained; or (2) deep structures should be formulated so as to be more close to meaning; that is, Examples (5.6) and (5.7) should have the same deep structure (or I-markers).

body: the plane may have had only two engines to begin with:

(5.16)   The plane in the hangar has only one engine in good working condition.

(5.17)   The plane in the hangar has three engines out of order.

Clearly, then, Examples (5.14) and (5.15) are not derived from identical I-markers, although they may well have derived from identical cognitive structures. Only factual knowledge shared by most speakers of the community makes them interchangeable. Any attempt to accord identical I-markers to sentences like these would entail that realization rules are so formulated that one and the same I-marker can result in either Example (5.14) or (5.15), but that the I-marker expressed by Example (5.16) can not be realized as Example (5.17). In other words, realization rules would have to incorporate information about cows' legs and planes' engines, the number of feet of humans, tables, grasshoppers, and centipedes, the number of wings of airplanes, birds, dragons, and insects, and in general, much of our knowledge of the world.

The absurdity does not end here. Consider that what makes sentences mutually substitutable is not only the factual knowledge shared by speakers of the community. If a particular speaker in a particular speech situation assumes, correctly or incorrectly, that the hearer has some information available, he may opt for a quite different sentence than when no such assumption is made. Thus, Examples (5.16) and (5.17) may be mutually substitutable, when both the speaker and the hearer know that there are only four-engined planes around. Similarly, in Osgood's (1971) experiment quoted above it seems to have been taken for granted by subjects that the balls were rolled on the table, and thus *hit* was intended by the speaker of Example (5.2) in the same way as *roll into* by the speaker of Example (5.3). If there had been any question of balls being thrown in the air rather than rolled, the speakers might have tried to be more specific. There is the possibility, then, of one message being understood as implying another one, at least by a given audience. When this occurs there may be one and the same cognitive structure.[4]

There is obviously no way to formulate realization rules of the kind discussed in Chapter 2 in such a way that they take into account such situation-dependent and speaker-dependent paraphrases. Production of utterances should therefore be viewed as a two-stage process. The first stage is the coagulation of an I-marker, and in performing this operation the I-marker selector is guided by

---

[4] In discussion a decoding model, Trabasso (1972, pp. 123–5) hypothesizes that when presented with 'A is not red', the subject recodes this into the affirmative 'A is blue', if there is no alternative besides red and blue. Since red and blue are in general not mutually exclusive, such recoding cannot make use of linguistic rules. These recodings can be equivalent only in the subject's cognitive structure.

knowledge of the world and a multitude of motivational factors. Only after this step has been taken can realization rules take over. It is their job to take into account various communicative considerations in producing an utterance.

But let us assume for the sake of the argument that one could disregard situation-dependent and speaker-dependent paraphrases like those above and that one were only faced with the task of accounting for paraphrases like Examples (5.14) and (5.15) which depend on factual knowledge. Even then, one-stage rules converting cognitive structures directly into utterances would be quite out of the question. It is not only the sheer amount of information which would have to be accommodated by these rules. No less serious is the fact that a one-stage mapping would entail an endless duplication of rules: all the variation in utterances taken care of by realization rules would have to be stated separately for each of those alternatives which are viewed in the present proposal as resulting from different coagulations of a cognitive structure. This extravagancy can be avoided only by introducing an intermediate level of I-markers. Production, then, comprises at least two stages: a one-to-many mapping of cognitive structures into I-markers and a one-to-many mapping of I-markers into utterances. (see Figure 5.1). Situation-dependent and speaker-dependent paraphrases must be due to alternative I-markers coagulated from identical cognitive structures. We are, of course, far from understanding the regularities in the mapping of cognitive structures into I-markers, just as we are far indeed from understanding most other regularities in cognitive processes. Figure 5.2 shows the components of the production model and the two rule systems operating therein.

From the standpoint of a performance model, then, the postulation of identical I-markers for all mutually substitutable utterances would lead to chaos in the system of realization rules. There also seems to be some linguistic evidence that at least some paraphrases can not have the same deep structures. Consider Examples (5.18) and (5.19), which seem to mean the same for all intents and purposes and would therefore have to be derived from the same deep structure (and it is immaterial for our present purpose whether or not we can spell out this deep structure):

(5.18)   Neal finished the job at the cost of many sleepless nights.
(5.19)   Neal had to go without sleep for many nights to finish the job.

But now we run into difficulties. Consider Example (5.20), which is structurally similar to Example (5.18) and hence must have a very similar deep structure:

(5.20)   Neal acquired the house at the cost of a small fortune.

However, one cannot rephrase Example (5.20) in a way similar to the rephrasing of Example (5.18) as Example (5.19): the fact that one spends a small fortune does not entail that one has to go without money. But if there are rules by which Example (5.19) can be derived from the deep structure underlying

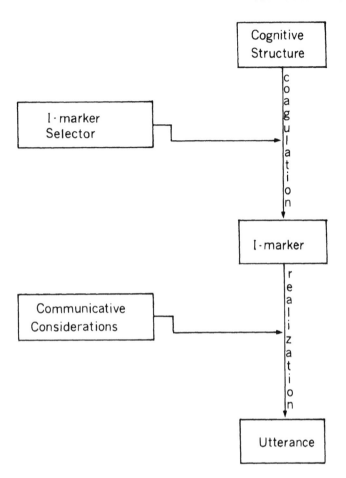

FIGURE 5.2. Components of the production model.

Example (5.18), the same rules should enable us to derive Example (5.21) from the deep structure underlying Example (5.20).

(5.21)   Neal had to go without a small fortune to acquire the house.

To avoid this difficulty one might conclude that Examples (5.18) and (5.20) do not have similar deep structures at all; that there are differences between their deep structures which block the application of the transformation involved in Example (5.18) to the deep structure of Example (5.20). Such an ad hoc measure seems to have little merit for linguistic explanation. It also seems incorrect as far as a production model is concerned. The explanation of the facts from the viewpoint of performance is intuitively clear: Examples (5.18) and (5.19) do not derive from the same I-markers. Rather, they are the result of two coagulations of the same cognitive structure by the I-marker selector. A different cognitive structure underlies Example (5.20), and because of our knowledge of the world we are barred from applying a coagulation which would result in Example (5.21): to spend much does not necessarily lead to penury. Only when it is deemed appropriate in view of what is known about the financial condition of Neal will it be possible to substitute Example (5.21) for Example (5.20). In this respect, then, the situation is similar to that in Examples (5.16) and (5.17).

Comparing Example (5.18) with Example (5.19) we note that coagulation determines which protoverbal elements are to be included in the I-marker as well as what relations are to hold between them. In the I-marker underlying Example (5.18) there is the protoverbal element lexicalized as *at the cost of,* whereas in the I-marker underlying Example (5.19) there is the protoverbal element lexicalized as *go without.* That these two are not identical is proved by the difference in meaning between Examples (5.20) and (5.21). Further, there is no parallel in Example (5.18) to the I-marker relation holding in Example (5.19) between the protoverbal element for *go without* and that for *sleep* (presumably the goal relation, though a detailed study of realization rules may show that this is not so).

As stated, there is little systematic knowledge concerning the determinants of our choice between alternative coagulations. Some studies have been made of the functions of presuppositions in the choice of negative as opposed to affirmative sentences. The work of Wason (1965) suggests that the negative formulation is chosen when it is intended to correct a mistaken expectancy, and Greene (1970a, b) has provided experimental results showing that the speaker chooses the negative form when he wishes not merely to state something but to do so in relation to a prior assertion or an unstated presupposition.

Let us review now the conclusions arrived at so far. The need for a level of cognitive structures in a production model becomes apparent from considering various phenomena, such as speech errors, changes of mind, and paraphrases. I-markers are coagulated from these cognitive structures by the I-marker selector (see Figure 5.2). The latter takes into account various considerations, only very few of which have so far been studied. The I-marker selector not only decides what part of the cognitive structure is to be included in the I-marker (see Section 5A), but also in what form it is to be included. In other words, it selects protoverbal elements and the I-marker relations holding between them. When paraphrases are available there will be two or more alternative sets of protoverbal elements and I-marker relations between which the I-marker selector has to choose.

One of the consequences of introducing a level of cognitive structures (which should have become apparent from our discussion of paraphrases) is that coagulations can take over part of the task of producing utterances and the operation of realization rules is thereby simplified. I-markers are thus much closer to the surface than the underlying representations postulated in generative semantics and in those recently proposed performance models which have been influenced by generative semantics, like Norman and Rumelhart (1975). (In Section 5E the differences between cognitive structures in those models will be discussed at greater length.)

If a given cognitive structure can be coagulated into two different I-markers, as has been shown above, then the relations in the cognitive structure can not be like either one of these I-marker relations. Instead, the cognitive structure relations must be somewhere in between: they must be "neutral" between these two sets of I-marker relations – in the sense that they can be coagulated into either one of them. Therefore cognitive structure relations must be viewed as different in kind from I-marker relations (see Section 5E).

That there is often more than one alternative available to the speaker for coagulating a cognitive structure explains why production occasionally seems to be a laborious process. Groping for the right way to express an idea may be a search for an appropriate lexicalization or relation rule, but it may also stem from an indecision as to which I-marker best expresses the cognitive structure. Such an indecision is all the more likely to occur in view of the different nature of cognitive structures and I-markers. Introspectively, the former seem to be more vague and formless than I-markers; this is perhaps what Vygotsky was alluding to in the quotation heading this chapter, in which he compares thought to a cloud. But characterizing cognitive structures as vague and formless unfortunately does not give us much leverage, so perhaps Vygotsky's metaphor should be construed as referring to the inscrutability of our thoughts from the point of view of the investigator.

This issue of the nature of cognitive structures is taken up again in Section 5E. Meanwhile, we will try to get a hold on the problem by a discussion of crosslinguistic comparisons.

5C. THE LANGUAGE SPECIFICITY OF I-MARKERS

I-markers have been defined as containing only linguistically relevant relations, and their formulation is intimately tied to that of realization rules. As pointed out before (see Section 1A), this means that I-markers are language specific. The motivation for this approach will now be discussed.

It is well known that languages differ in the relations they express by such grammatical means as word order, function words, and affixation. (Remember that by "relations" here, as elsewhere, we refer also to single-argument relations; see Section 1A.) Examples of this are legion; here a very small sample will suffice and the reader is referred to Cassirer (1953) for a useful review. Not all tenses in English have a parallel in the syntax of other languages. German has no progressive tenses, modern Hebrew has no past perfect, and the distinction between past and present perfect is rapidly fading in American English. On the other hand, in Italian there are more tenses than in English. Some languages have no tenses at all, but express grammatically certain aspects of the action, such as duration and repetition, for which English has no grammatical means of expression. Even a distinction which seems to us as "basic" as the singular—plural distinction is lacking in many languages. In general, as Jespersen (1964) has remarked, so called "primitive" languages may express "a multiplicity of *nuances* which in other languages must be expressed by clumsy circumlocutions [p. 427]."

Such clumsy circumlocutions may enable the speaker of any language to express any one distinction expressible by speakers of any other language by means of grammar.[5] This means that any cognitive structure operative in the speakers of one language may also be operative in those of another language, even if the latter provides no ready-made syntactic means of expressing it. It follows that a relation appearing in the cognitive structures of a speaker may be lacking in the I-markers of his language.[6] A moment's reflection should suffice to show why this should be so. There are indefinitely many ways of looking at the world around us. The I-markers of any given language, on the other hand, can accommodate only a limited number of relations, because otherwise the system of realization rules would become too complex for speakers of the language to handle.

An extreme example of lack of syntactic means to signal a common semantic relation is provided by the Israeli sign language. In investigating this language we found to our amazement that its syntax does not distinguish between the agent and goal of an action (Schlesinger, 1971c). Sign language has no inflections, and unlike English and other poorly inflected languages, word order does not distinguish between 'man bites dog' and 'dog bites man'. Needless to say, the deaf, even those who know no other language, are perfectly aware of this difference; we have no cause to suspect any deficiency in their cognitive structure. But they have no separate realization rules for these two relations, and hence the I-markers of this language, by definition, do not differentiate between these two relations.

[5] Often simple, rather than clumsy, means may be available. The word for 'this' is frequently resorted to by speakers of Lithuanian (a language which has no articles) to attain the effect of the definite article. On the other hand, sometimes the way to make up for a missing grammatical device is more tortuous. The lack of inflections to express certain aspects of verbs may reduce the speaker of English to use whole phrases instead ('I have heard that . . . ', 'I understand that . . . '). The situation here is quite similar to that encountered when a word for a concept is missing and a description for it must be substituted. Much inventiveness may be displayed in such cases by children, for instance by the little boy who was searching for a word for 'knee' and improvised *elbow of the leg.*

[6] Note that here and in the following the term cognitive structures is used somewhat ambiguously as referring to those structures potentially available to the speaker as well as to those from which an utterance actually originates at a given instance (as the term is used in Section 5A). This ambiguity is here indulged in for convenience, and it does not affect any of the following arguments.

The conclusion that I-markers are language specific can be evaded only by assuming that any relation expressed in any language appears ipso facto in the I-markers of all languages. I-markers would consequently contain all the relations the speaker is aware of (to the extent that these are expressed in at least one language), and not only those operated on by the realization rules in his language. The latter would be language specific: to many of the relations of the I-marker, realization rules would be inapplicable and these relations would thus be left unexpressed (as least as far as grammatical means of expression go).

It seems that this approach has little to recommend itself, considering that, for reasons discussed in the preceding sections, I-markers and cognitive structures can in no way be collapsed into one. Moreover, certain crosslinguistic comparisons provide grounds for rejecting this solution. There is good evidence that languages differ in the way they coagulate a given cognitive structure into I-markers. Waismann's (1962) example of Greenlandic has already been quoted above. Where in English we say *I shoot the arrow* the Eskimo can only say *the arrow is flying away from me.* 'The arrow' is thus the goal in the I-marker of the English speaker and the agent (or, perhaps, the object in Fillmore's, 1971, sense) in that of the Eskimo. There is no evidence that the latter conceives of the arrow in a different way; his cognitive structures when telling about his shooting the arrow may very well be like that of the English speaker, but their I-markers certainly differ. Nor is there any need to postulate different cognitive structures to account for the Irish English usage about which Burgess (1973) writes: "A locative is sometimes used instead of, or as reinforcement for, a possessive adjective [p. 37]" (see Greenfield & Smith, 1976, who observe that location and possession are collapsed for the child at the one-word stage). Whorf reports that speakers of Nootka do not refer to a boat grounded on the beach as an object but by means of a construction which we may paraphrase as something like "is on the beach moving canoewise [Carroll, 1956, p. 236]." Here again different relations are used by two languages, English and Nootka, to refer to the same event. It would be unreasonable, however, to follow the path of linguistic determinism to the end and assume that the speaker of Nootka fails to recognize that the canoe is an object. His cognitive structure need not differ in this case from that of the English speaker. In Section 2B it was suggested that sentences like *I see a tree* are the result of the experiencer being assimilated into the agent case. The Japanese resort to a quite different realization: their language expresses seeing as residing in the object seen (Weisgerber, 1962b, Volume 2, p. 311).

Apparently speakers of two languages may treat a given situation in terms of different relations. But this difference does not necessarily extend to their cognitive structures; rather, it may be the result of different coagulations of the same cognitive structures. The situation here is analogous to that of paraphrases within one language which are also often the result of alternative coagulations of the same cognitive structure. Evidently, these phenomena can not be accommodated by the alternative explanation above, which would include in the I-marker any relation expressed in any language. What we are faced with here is not the lack of expression of a relation by the grammar of a language, but a different expression of a relation, and this is evidence that different I-markers must be involved.

To summarize the argument so far, crosslinguistic differences can not all be explained as stemming from differences in the speaker's cognitive structures. Such an extreme version of linguistic relativity is ruled out by the fact that a language may lack syntactic means for expressing such basic notions necessary for everyday give and take as agent and goal (the Israeli sign language) and number (some primitive languages). But I-markers must differ for speakers of different languages, as evidenced by the possibility of similar situations being coded by them in terms of quite different relations. It follows that there must be two distinct underlying levels: I-markers and cognitive structures. To insist that these can be collapsed into one would mean to adopt an untenably extreme Whorfian position.

Now, since notions like "agent," "instrument," and "plurality" correspond to something in the real world (see Section 1A), the language specificity of I-markers implies that, for the purpose of speaking, a given situation may be perceived differently by speakers of two languages. The qualification "for the purpose of speaking" is important because it enables us to avoid a contradiction of this statement with the claim that the cognitive structures of these speakers may be identical. What is claimed is that while the Nootka speaker may perceive canoes on the beach in essentially the same way as speakers of other languages, for the purpose of speaking about them he adopts a different point of view. This parallels the process of semantic assimilation (see Section 2B): for the purpose of speaking, the English speaker may view the instrument as a kind of agent. The case is similar for many paraphrases, where identical situations can be viewed, for the purpose of speaking, in different ways.[7]

In this section we have so far considered only evidence concerning the relations in I-markers. Evidently, similar claims can be made about the language specificity of I-marker elements. Thus, the system of protoverbal elements in one language can obviously not contain all the concepts expressible by words in any language of the world (and such a suggestion has probably never been made). But different languages not only employ different subsets of protoverbal elements; there is also ample evidence that the entities spoken about are often catagorized in different ways by two languages. German has different terms for

---

[7] Evidently these crosslinguistic comparisons lend additional support to the distinction made here between cognitive structures and I-markers. Insisting that there is only one underlying level would virtually commit oneself to an extreme Whorfian position: that speakers of two languages speak in terms of different relations would imply that they think differently. As stated, this conclusion becomes untenable in view of the fact that a language may lack very "basic" relations.

'use', depending on whether one uses raw materials, objects belonging to the speaker, resources of others, and so on, and the English classification of *use, employ, utilize,* and *avil oneself of* seems to be largely orthogonal to the former (Weisgerber 1962a, Volume 1, pp. 190–191). Of course, English speakers may be aware of the distinctions made by German speakers, but while these may be in their cognitive structures they are not represented by words, and hence not by protoverbal elements.

If the elements as well as the relations in I-markers are language specific, the question may be raised how they are acquired in the course of learning language.

5D. THE ACQUISITION OF I-MARKERS

Recently, much has been written about the cognitive prerequisites of native language learning. It has been argued that if the child is to learn how semantic relations are expressed in his mother tongue, he must first be able to conceive what goes on in his environment in terms of these relations. The nativist position is that the child is somehow preprogramed to perceive these relations in the world around him. Now, such a solution retains little plausibility in view of the crosslinguistic findings discussed in the above section. It is quite implausible that the child is born with the vast number of distinctions to be found in the world's languages, particularly since, as we have seen, a given event or situation may be codable by language in a variety of ways. At best, a certain subset of these distinctions could be claimed to be innate, leaving us with the problem how the child acquires those relations which are expressed in his language but are not included in this subset. The same problem is faced by the proponent of a Piagetian account, according to which relations are acquired through interacting with his environment. This can again be true of only a subset of all the relations encountered in the world's languages, and leaves us with the question how the child comes to perceive his environment in terms of the remaining relations expressed in his language.

The problem is a spurious one, however. It rests on the false assumption that the child comes to the task of learning a language with a set of ready-made relations and all he has to do is to observe how these are expressed grammatically. Instead, it should be clear that these relations are themselves largely acquired in the course of language learning (Schlesinger, 1974).

Obviously, there are cognitive prerequisites to language learning. For instance, unless the child has matured to the point of perceiving certain actions as instigated by a human actor, he will be unable to find out how the agent relation is realized in his language. But this ability to interpret the world around him does not imply that he has acquired the agent relation prior to learning about its realization. Any relation involves a grouping of disparate occurrences on the basis of similarity. Thus, to acquire the agent relation the child must realize that various, to some extent dissimilar, events have something in common. He must not only be able to interpret one situation as mummy handing him a bottle and another one as daddy picking him up, but must also classify these and similar events as involving agents performing actions. However, there is nothing which might prompt him to classify these different occurrences in such a way − except for language. The fact that certain kinds of situations are spoken about in the same way (for example, that the animate instigator is always named before the action) leads to the formation of, and similarly for the agent concept, and similarly for other relational concepts.

To see why this must be so consider that acquisition of a concept means that various instances of it are tied to the same response. Now, what could possibly be a common response of the child to all agents? Or to all possessors, or to all instruments? Before learning language, all events are unique for the child. True, he may note certain similarities between them, but similarity by itself is not enough to engender concepts, as long as no common response is required.[8] As soon as language comes into the picture there is such a common ·response: a certain way of speaking is required for all situations involving an agent, another way for all those involving possessors, and so on.

Relations, then, are not learned in preparation for language learning but in the course of the learning process. The acquisition of I-marker relations and of realization rules is interdependent. It now becomes obvious why I-markers are language specific, as shown in Section 5C. I-marker relations are not simply "there" independently of language: each language prescribes which relations have to be mastered by the child.

What has been said here about I-marker relations holds for protoverbal elements as well. When many different objects are called by the same name, as *chair*, the child acquires the concept chair, in our terminology: he acquires the ability to form an I-marker with a protoverbal element lexicalized as *chair*. There may be some such concepts which are acquired independently of language on the basis of similarity of function: what certain classes of objects may have in common is that they require the same response (for example, all chairs can be used by the child to sit on so as to reach the table). If this concept is acquired before the word *chair*, subsequent learning of the word will be facilitated. But the prelinguistic concept may fail to correspond to any word. This was apparent-

---

[8] It has been argued that these relational concepts may have been learned before their linguistic expression by the child noticing possibilities of substitution. Thus, the agent concept would be acquired by the child through observing that different persons can substitute for each other in bringing about a desired result (Veneziano, 1973). However, this can explain, at most, the acquisition of relations of a very limited scope. For instance, the child may observe substitutability of persons and attain thereby the concept of "one who fulfills my wish for a change in the environment," without generalizing from this to the full agent concept. Such generalization again presupposes a common response (similarity per se, not being sufficient for it to take place), and such a response can only be a linguistic one.

ly the case with a Swedish-speaking child who is reported by Segerstedt (1947) to have used a word ('cake') for any food which could be put in his mouth by the child himself and another one ('eat') for all other food (things to be eaten with a spoon or other utensil). For this child, then, learning the adult terminology must have required a reclassification. Words thus do not all match precisely the prelinguistic concepts of the child learning language. Language draws different dividing lines between objects, and the child's misapplications of words bear witness to the arduousness of the task of learning the categorization imposed by language.

To conclude, both the relations and the elements in I-markers are attained by the child by noticing how the language spoken by adults categorizes what goes on in his environment. This account of acquiring I-markers has important implications for the nature of cognitive structures.

5E. THE NATURE OF COGNITIVE STRUCTURES

As has been shown above, in learning the native language the child not only acquires realization rules, but, at the same time, masters the system of proto-verbal elements and relations by which the child's world is classified. Before the advent of language, the perception of objects, events and situations was largely uncategorized. I-markers now impose order on this motley world. But the child's cognitive structure still remains uncategorized: each object, each event, and each situation is unique.

The categorization imposed by I-markers may be expected to exert a certain amount of influence on cognitive structures, so that one is prone to perceive the world in terms of the categories provided by language (see Section 5C). This influence may increase as the child grows up. But even the adult's cognitive structures will consist largely of relations, each of which is unique to the situation or event spoken about ("relations" may even not be the right term for such a singular uncategorized connection perceived between aspects of the environment). This is because he will be able to step out of his linguistic shoes and view the world in all its multifariousness. The fact that a categorization has been arrived at does not compel us to refer to it invariably. In particular, it may be the case that a given categorization appears in a person's thinking in some instances, whereas on the occasion of speaking about an event to which this categorization is seemingly pertinent, it does not appear. That is, it does not show up in the speaker's cognitive structure (in the restricted sense of the term used here: the structure prior to speaking coagulated into an I-marker).

So much for the relations in cognitive structures. The case is somewhat different for the elements between which these relations hold. We have already noted in the preceding section that the child may form concepts independently of language. This process may continue into adult life: categorizations may be formed in response to the exigencies of living, and not for all the resulting concepts will there be a name in the language (an example which comes to mind is: "things to be done before going out," such as turning off the gas). Here again the fact that we have a certain concept available does not imply that prior to talking it will figure in our cognitive structure. But there will no doubt also be cases where such a nonlinguistic concept will occur in cognitive structure. Thus, many mothers will have had occasion to say something involving the Swedish child's concept of "food baby can safely be left alone with" (see Section 5D). The concept will have appeared in their cognitive structure, but since for some curious reason there is no name for it (in English, Swedish, and many other languages), coagulation will pose a problem. (What usually happens, of course, is that one settles for a surrogate term, or resorts to a circumlocution.)

But cases like the above are the exception rather than the rule. Those of our concepts which frequently are talked about are likely to be given a name; in other words, the elements in cognitive structures will typically have protoverbal elements corresponding to them. The system of protoverbal elements (like the system of I-marker relations) may in its turn influence the way we think. But here again we will not be at the mercy of this categorization: we are able to perceive each of the various objects going under the same name as something unique and notice how it differs from all others. Likewise, although we now and then form a concept independently of language, this does not restrain us from viewing the concrete reality behind it. As noted above, a categorization once arrived at may be employed in some instances while being disregarded in others.

It is proposed, then, that cognitive structures differ from I-markers in being constituted largely of unique relations and of unique occurrences of "things" (objects and other entities that might be referred to by words). I-marker relations, by contrast, involve categorization (see Section 5D) and protoverbal elements correspond to classes of "things." A concept formation experiment by Shafto (1973) is relevant here. He let subjects sort sentences into four categories according to the relations exhibited in them (in the sense of Fillmore's, 1971, case grammar): the agent, the experiencer, the instrumental, and the object. Subjects were fast in learning the agent category, and somewhat slower in learning the experiencer. The instrument concept, however, was difficult to learn and there was little evidence for learning of the object. Shafto suggests that the latter two categories may "encompass a variety of notionally distinct semantic relations, even though there may be syntactic criteria for combining them into just two deep cases [p. 561]." His "semantic relations" correspond to the relations in cognitive structures.

We note in passing the implications of this approach for the relationship between thought and language. Thinking can proceed on two levels. We can think at the level of I-markers, using implicit verbalizations, and then we impose on our thought the categorizations acquired in the course of learning language. Or we can free ourselves from these constraints by retreating to the deeper level of cognitive structures. At this level, "things" and relations can be unique. Presumably, much of the intuitive thinking which has not been verbally formulated goes on at this level. (Piaget, 1959, presents an illuminating comparison of intuitive and verbalized thinking.)

Our characterization of cognitive structures as consisting largely of uncategorized relations and elements is opposed to recent trends in modeling the way the contents of sentences are organized in our cognitions. Schank (1972, 1973) has developed a system of "conceptualizations," which the hearer extracts from utterances and which are employed in making inferences. He postulates only one such level which underlies utterances, and here we will therefore proceed to compare his conceptualizations both with our I-markers and our cognitive structures.

One of the principles followed by Schank is that concepts underlying the verbs in the utterance are decomposed into a small number of elementary concepts. For instance, the elementary concept "trans" (for "transfer") enters into the analysis of *get, give, take, sell,* and many other verbs. The concepts underlying other words in the utterance are then related to "trans" by conceptual cases like agent, recipient, object, etc. These decompositions are a central feature not only in Schank's system but in some other recent programs as well. They make it possible to assign the same underlying representation to sentences which are paraphrases of each other even when their surface structures are rather dissimilar, for instance, to Examples (5.6) and (5.7) (see Norman & Rumelhart, 1975). Thus, the same action of "trans" occurs both in *x buys y from z* and in *z sells y to x*; and since *y*, the thing bought, changes ownership in the same way in both cases, the same relations hold between *x, y, z,* and "trans." This is therefore one difference between conceptualization and other representations based on decomposition on the one hand and I-markers on the other: as shown in Section 5B, paraphrases do not always have identical I-markers. Our I-markers are much closer in this respect to Kintsch's (1974) propositions than to Schank's conceptualizations (though they differ from the former in some respects). Conceptualizations are therefore at a "deeper" level than I-markers (see also Simmons, 1973, p. 107, who notes that Schank's, 1972, conceptual structures are at a deeper level than the networks which in his own proposal are the outcome of the parsing process). Quite in line with this, Schank intends his conceptualizations to be interlingual; I-markers, by contrast, are language specific.

This conclusion is further supported by the fact that conceptualizations contain much more information than I-markers. An example given by Schank (1973, pp. 200–201) is

(5.22) John ate the ice cream with a spoon.

The conceptualization here contains the following information: John took a spoon containing ice cream, moved ("trans") the spoon to John's mouth, and by this means John ate the ice cream. If a structure in which all this is made explicit is regarded as input to the system of realization rules which produces Example (5.22), these rules would have to be very complex indeed. Consider, for instance, that "move x to the mouth" is expressed here by *with x*. In other contexts, quite different conceptualizations will have *with x* as a realization. Thus, if one talks about hitting a person, a conceptualization paraphrasable as "move x to the person forcefully" will be realized as *with x*. Still different conceptualizations will underly *with x* in the context of writing, watchmaking, climbing mountains, and, in fact, for an indefinitely large number of contexts. This means that for each of these conceptualizations there have to be different realization rules resulting in the expression *with x*. The system of realization rules applicable to I-markers is evidently much simpler. In all these contexts, x appears in the I-marker as the instrument by means of which the action was carried out, and *with x* is the result of one of the realization rules applicable to the instrumental relation. This difference in rule complexity is due to I-markers being much closer to the surface than conceptualizations (see also Section 2B). Despite their difference in cognitive structure, all of the above can be categorized as belonging to the instrumental relation in the I-marker. It appears, therefore, that if utterances are to be generated from conceptualizations like those proposed by Schank, the rules will have to comprise more than one stage, just as deriving utterances from our cognitive structures requires the two stages of coagulation and realization.

All this suggests that conceptualizations may be more like cognitive structures than like I-markers. But here again we notice wide divergence. Schank's decomposition is based on 14 primitive action categories (in addition to "trans," his list contains "ingest," "speak," "grasp," etc.) He claims that every action verb can be categorized as belonging to one of these concepts. The discussion in this and the above section should have made us wary of such categorizations as far as the structures which occur prior to speaking are concerned. The major problem here is how such a categorization can possibly be validated. The categorization of relations in I-markers can be based on linguistic data: as pointed out in Section 1A, I-marker relations are those which make a difference linguistically. But once we move into the realm of cognitive structures, attempts at categorization no longer have a firm factual basis.

Is there any evidence that Schank's attempt at categorization is anything but a common-sense ontology? One of Schank's professed aims is to arrive at representations which permit computer simulation of inference making, and he points out that such simulation has indeed proved possible with his system of conceptualizations (Schank, 1973, p. 228; Schank & Rieger, 1973). But note that this is no guarantee that these conceptualizations have psychological reality. Just as the generative rules constructed by the linguist to account for the sentences of a language need not be identical with the rules used by the hearer–speaker, so Schank's system may be successful in making inferences, while it is still too early to say whether it also successfully models the inference-making process in humans. More important for our present concern is that even if Schank's conceptualizations are relevant to making inferences, this does not yet prove anything about the structures involved in utterance production. As noted above, the way information is structured in our minds may be task specific. For instance, Anderson and Bower (1973) have proposed a certain type of structure which forms the basis for predicting the outcomes of some experiments on retrieval from memory. This shows something about the organization of infor-mation in memory, but it does not follow that this information is coded in the same way when it is utilized, as in inference making. For this purpose their proposed organization may perhaps not be optimal and it may therefore first have to be transformed. Again, when we intend to talk about this information, we may need still a third type of structure into which it has to be converted. Thus, Kintsch (1974, Chapter 11) has concluded from the results of a number of experiments that, while it is possible to decompose upon demand a complex word like *attendant* 'someone who attends' or *accuse* 'say that . . . is guilty' – thus making possible various inferences – these words "are not necessarily decomposed either in comprehending or in memorizing sentences [p. 240]." There is, therefore, no foundation for the simplistic assumption, implicit in most recent work, that the same structures underlie such diverse mental operations as comprehending utterances, making inferences from them, storing the informa-tion in memory, and producing new utterances on the basis of this knowledge.

For the purpose of making inferences from an utterance it is important to extract from it the maximum information. But one may wonder whether all this information is also needed for cognitive structures which engender utterances that are not based on inferences. Take, for example, Schank's conceptualization for utterances about seeing, which includes the information that something is being transferred (mentally) from the eyes to the "conscious processor," and further that the person who sees something is aware of it as a result (Schank, 1973, p. 220). All this may be relevant for making certain kinds of inferences. But must all these aspects and implications of seeing be present in the cognitive structure when we mention having seen someone? Is it not more plausible that "see" appears as an unanalyzed notion in cognitive structure?[9] Admittedly, introspective evidence cannot settle questions like this, but the mere fact that people have the ability of extracting information from an utterance is certainly not sufficient justification for ascribing all this information to cognitive struc-tures. This is true for the cognitive structure from which speaking starts, as well as for those which have to be retrieved by the hearer from the heard utterance (see Chapter 7). Schank thus makes a tremendous leap when he assumes that

---

[9] That analysis of a concept does not always have to be complete is recognized by Norman and Rumelhart (1975, pp. 203–206). They discuss reasons for the assumption that there must also be a possibility of what they call "partial comprehension."

conceptualizations which contain all that is necessary for making inferences must be retrieved in the parsing process.

The question of what information does come within the scope of cognitive structures is of course difficult to settle. Presumably, the kind and amount of information varies from speaker to speaker and from situation to situation. Our ignorance of these determinants and their effects in no way can be diminished by investigations of inference making and of retrieval from memory. Nor are the latter likely to shed much light on the categories into which our cognitive structures are cast.

To conclude, Schank's conceptualizations are more detailed and specific than I-markers and to convert them into utterances, two-stage rules would be required. At the same time, they contain more categorization and in most cases presumably more information than those cognitive structures from which utterances originate.

To return to our account of cognitive structures, the recognition that these tend to comprise unique relations and elements make several previously discussed phenomena fall into place. These uncategorized relations and elements are categorized in the course of coagulation into I-marker relations and elements. Normally, there are various alternatives for carrying out the latter categorizations, and hence, there will be paraphrases. The uncategorized content of a cognitive structure can often also be dealt with by semantic assimilation. When talking about a knife cutting bread this may be viewed in cognitive structure as an event involving unique relations. For the purpose of speaking, this may be coagulated either so that the knife is viewed as an instrument of the action of cutting or else by treating it as the agent; but this is not true of every instrument or every action. It all depends on the particular event mirrored in cognitive structure (see Section 2B).

Coagulation, then, is like a prism which disperses the multifarious relations in the cognitive structure into qualitatively different I-marker relations. Let us consider here one additional example. The two events of a person riding on a horse and a person riding on a train seem, on cursory examination, to involve similar relations. In both cases, there is an object serving as vehicle and a person using this vehicle for locomotion. Note, however, that in the first case, *ride on a horse,* a realization of the locative relation, may be uttered, or else *ride a horse,* which presumably expresses the goal relation. This event is viewed in the cognitive structure in a way which permits both these coagulations. Now, these relations are peculiar to this cognitive structure and differ from those in the similar train-traveling event. For in the latter one can say *ride on a train* (or *ride in a train*), but not *ride a train.* Intuitively, the reason for this difference between utterances appropriate for horses and for trains is quite clear but a principled linguistic account of it does not seem to be in sight. Nor need there be one, because we are dealing here with coagulations, which are operations on nonlinguistic structures.

Earlier in this chapter, it was observed that relations in cognitive structures seem to be vague and formless. Assuming this intuition can be correct, we can now suggest an explanation for it, albeit a speculative one.

Consider first that coagulations differ among themselves in respect to difficulty. It is easy to find an appropriate protoverbal element for some notions, with the expression of which the speaker has had much previous experience; for others there is no such well-trod path. Again, there may be certain things a speaker has in mind for which there is no adequate word in his language, and hence, by definition, no protoverbal element (see Section 1B). A common experience is that some notion we want to express may lie somewhere between the various means of expression at our disposal: there are several words which come close to it, but none is quite adequate. There is only a partial overlap of intension.[10] All this may happen not only with the coagulation of cognitive structure elements into protoverbal elements but also with the coagulation of relations in cognitive structure into I-marker relations. As stated in Section 5C, there are relations which in a given language can be expressed only by clumsy circumlocutions.

The difficulty may be compounded in the case of sets of elements or relations in cognitive structure. A speaker's cognitive structure will contain a conjunctive set of elements when he intends to convey a message implicating all these elements in the same way, or a disjunctive set when he does not know — or when he does not deem it important — which of the set actually applies. Suppose now that for a given set in the speaker's cognitive structure there is no single corresponding protoverbal element. To communicate his intention exactly, he will have to include in the I-marker all the corresponding protoverbal elements (as a conjunction or a disjunction, as the case may be). But since finding an appropriate protoverbal element may often be difficult or even impossible, this may be a rather troublesome task. The final solution will often be a compromise between an exact rendering of his intention and conciseness.

A similar case obtains for relations in cognitive structures. While a single I-marker relation typically stands for a number of unique cognitive structure relations, each of which is coagulable into this I-marker relation, it is by no means the case that each set of cognitive structure relations is coagulable into a single I-marker relation. Rather, the relations in this set may pertain to different I-marker relations. Again, in coagulating such a cognitive structure, the speaker

---

[10] Note that the above is based on a distinction between (1) coagulating an element in cognitive structure into protoverbal elements; and (2) lexicalizing a protoverbal element. Difficulty may be experienced in either case; the "tip-of-the-tongue" phenomenon being characteristic of the latter difficulty. Further, the former may be precluded because of the lack of an appropriate protoverbal element, as we often note when casting about for a word to express our meaning (which is especially common in translating). On the other hand, for any protoverbal element there will be, by definition, a word, and hence the latter will always be possible in principle (though it may fail occasionally).

will presumably often settle for an I-marker relation which only partially overlaps with this set.

On perceiving that only a part of the set of elements (or relations) has been coagulated while another part has been left out, the speaker may feel that he has somehow missed his mark. There remains a vague and formless area in the cognitive structure in contrast to that area which has been coped with by the I-marker. Because I-marker relations and elements have been expressed verbally on countless previous occasions, they are bound to stand out as clear and well defined by comparison. As a result, the speaker will conclude either that thoughts are blurred unless verbally formulated, or else that language is woefully inadequate to express thought. Both these allegations, which have been made so often as to sound otiose, may spring from the same kind of experience.

In poetry, a resolution can occasionally be found for this lack of correspondence between sets of relations in cognitive structures and I-marker relations. As shown by Empson (1955), an ambiguity (a convergence of the realization of two or more I-markers on the same utterance) may be an adequate expression for the complex cognition from which the poem originated.

SUMMARY

In the first chapter of this book, semantic structures were postulated and it was shown in the succeeding chapters how utterances are derived from them. In this chapter we saw that a still deeper level of cognitive structures is necessary. I-markers typically do not contain all that is in the speaker's cognitive structure when he is about to speak. A selection from cognitive structures will therefore have to be made. Frequently, the speaker changes his mind in regard to what is to be included in the I-marker and what is to be left out. An additional component, the I-marker selector, which chooses among the various possibilities of coagulating cognitive structures into I-markers is therefore included in the model.

That cognitive structures and I-markers cannot be collapsed into one level is also shown by the existence of certain kinds of paraphrases, which cannot be explained as derived from the same linguistic deep structure by different realization rules. Crosslinguistic comparisons also demonstrate the possibility of coagulating a given cognitive structure in various ways. The same event may be coded into different I-markers by speakers of different languages. I-markers are thus language specific, whereas cognitive structures may be universal.

The evidence of paraphrases and crosslinguistic differences suggests that cognitive structures are qualitatively different from I-markers. An examination of the question how the child acquires I-markers leads to the conclusion that the elements and relations in cognitive structures are largely unique, in that they differ from situation to situation. Since separate realization rules for each situation is an impossibility, language imposes a categorization on the relations and elements in cognitive structures. This categorization is effected by the coagulation of cognitive structures into I-markers for the purpose of (external or internal) speech. When a cognitive structure contains a set of (disjunctive or conjunctive) relations, the speaker may experience difficulty in finding an appropriate I-marker relation and this may lead to a feeling of vagueness in respect to cognitive structures.

This chapter concludes the first part of this book. We have seen how the speaker's intentions (as embodied in cognitive structures, I-markers, and communicative considerations) are converted into utterances. The second part of this text deals with the reverse process, namely the retrieval of the speaker's intentions from the utterance.

Part II

From Utterance to Intention

Part II presents a sketch of a comprehension model. This follows the description of a production model in the first part. This sequence has been adopted not only for the trivial reason that for an utterance to be comprehended it must first be produced, but also for purposes of exposition. Comprehension, as is seen in the following, makes use of those rules which in Part I were shown to be operative in production, but it also relies on other kinds of information which may assist in the process: situational and linguistic context and knowledge of what normally happens in the world.

Chapters 6 and 7 abstract from the processes based on such information: comprehension is described as it occurs when the hearer or reader has no contextual cues to rely on, cannot be helped by expectations as to what is likely to happen in the world, but is dependent only on his knowledge of the language. Then in Chapters 8 and 9 I discuss the effect of this nonlinguistic information and the processes by which it is employed. The interaction of these two types of processes in comprehending a sentence is dealt with in the final chapter.

To comprehend, the listener retrieves the I-marker from which the speaker's utterance was derived. To what extent is this simply a retracing of the speaker's steps? This question will be treated in Chapter 6. In Chapter 7, I then discuss the retrieval of the speaker's communicative considerations and cognitive structures.

6
Retrieval of I-Markers

6A. REQUIREMENTS OF A COMPREHENSION MODEL
AND PREVIOUS APPROACHES

Considerably more work has been done on comprehension of utterances than on their production. Our discussion of a comprehension model will gain in perspective by viewing it against the background of previously proposed models. By examining these, much can be learned about the complexities of language which any model will have to deal with. Moreover, such an examination will reveal in what ways the previously suggested routines of comprehension differ from the processes one may assume go on when people understand an utterance. Which conditions have to be met by a theory of comprehension will thus become clear. The list of requirements drawn up in this review of previous work will serve as a take-off point for the sketch of a comprehension model.

One of the assumptions of much recent thinking on linguistic performance has been that production and comprehension of utterances are both carried out by means of the same set of rules (Chomsky 1957, p. 48). The opposite assumption that the hearer uses rules different from those used by the speaker appears to entail an unnecessary lack of economy. There must be of course a difference in the way rules of grammar are employed in speaking and listening, and regarding this several proposals have been made.

According to one proposal, comprehension is an "analysis-by-synthesis" process. The speaker produces output strings by those rules of grammar which generate sentences, and in analyzing utterances these rules are applied in the same direction, producing sentences—that is, synthesizing them—vicariously until a match of the input sentence is found. As soon as it had been proposed, it became clear that a human analysis-by-synthesis devise would be unable to function because of the formidable number of sentences the hearer might have to synthesize until a match could be found. It has been suggested, therefore, (Katz & Postal, 1964) that the analysis-by-synthesis procedure must be reinforced by various heuristics which would curtail the number of steps needed. These require a preanalysis of the input string. Exact details of such heuristics have never been spelled out, and it remains doubtful whether sufficient improvement can be achieved in this way. Discussions of the analysis-by-synthesis approach are to be found in Fodor, Bever and Garrett (1974, pp. 316–319) and in Wanner (1974, pp. 115–120).

Some of the shortcomings of the analysis-by-synthesis model are avoided by the "analysis only" model of Keyser and Petrick (1967). Essentially, their model involves the application of transformation rules "in reverse." The computer program written to implement this approach runs through the list of possible outputs of transformation rules until it finds one whose structure corresponds to that of the input sentence. Then the program retrieves that base structure which can be converted by this transformation rule into the input sentence. Provision is made for separate treatment of embedded clauses in the input sentence, so that the list of outputs of transformations does not grow indefinitely large. Applying this approach to human performance would entail that the comprehension mechanism run through a list of structures which are possible outputs of the production mechanism until a matching of the input utterance is found; thus retrieving the base structure (I-marker) responsible for this utterance. A similar proposal is discussed by Wanner (1974, pp. 120–124).

As pointed out by Wanner and by Fodor, Garrett and Bever (1974, pp. 313–316), the "analysis-by-analysis" approach is liable to lead into dead-end analyses, and it seems doubtful whether a comprehension model based on these principles is feasible. Moreover, there is one feature in the analysis-by-analysis process in which it differs from the human comprehension process. According to the former, the base structure is either retrieved in its entirety or not at all. This is quite unlike what we know from experience to occur in comprehension. We begin to understand an utterance before we have heard or read all of it. Often we are able to complete a sentence after hearing part of it and not too rarely are we indeed tempted to do so. Experiments on the eye–voice span suggest that we impose structure on an utterance before we have read to the end of it (Schlesinger, 1968). This suggests that understanding an utterance is not the saltatory process of Keyser and Petrick's computer program; it is, in fact, a much more loitering one.

The models discussed so far follow the principle that a sentence is analyzed by means of those rules which are specified in a transformational grammar. For some years now it has become clear that, as far as human language is concerned, this is not a plausible assumption. If it were, the difficulty of processing should be expected to increase with the number of additional steps required for its derivation by the grammar, and this, as has been shown by Fodor and Garrett (1967) is often not the case (see also Fodor, Bever, & Garrett, 1974, pp.

319–328; Watt, 1970). In a similar vein, Keyser and Petrick (1967) have pointed out that differences in processing complexity of sentences according to their computer program do not seem to correspond to differences of difficulty in human processing. They caution therefore against extrapolating from their model to human performance.

A different departure has recently been made by Thorne (1968; Thorne, Bratley & Dewar, 1968), who proposed a computer program that processes sentences from left to right. The grammar which, according to Thorne (1968), is a component of the model is used to make predictions about the structure of the sentence analyzed, and "each element of the sentence as it is read in is used to test certain predictions, those which prove correct forming the basis for further predictions about the next element [p. 381]." This model thus assumes a much greater difference between the way grammatical rules are employed in production and in comprehension than is assumed by the two models described above.

By means of the transformation rules of generative grammar base structures are mapped into surface structures. These rules are similarly employed in the first two models discussed above to map base structures into surface structures until a match to the input is found (in the analysis-by-synthesis model) or surface structures into base structures (in the "analysis only" model). By contrast, Thorne's comprehension model, while using a knowledge of these rules, does not employ them to convert one kind of structure into the other, but makes step-by-step predictions. Unlike the other two models, it gradually builds up the analysis as it scans the sentence. In this respect it seems to come closer to the way the human hearer understands the sentence. Another advantage of Thorne's approach is that it leaves room, in principle, for the incorporation of semantic processes involved in the analysis of sentence structure, as shown in Chapters 8–10. Thorne and his associates also make the assumption that in analyzing a sentence not every word has to be looked up in the lexicon; instead, the role of a content word in the sentence may be recognized by superficial cues. In this respect their proposal seems to come closer to human processing than some of the other computer models which have been proposed.

A further development came with Woods' (1970) augmented transition network grammar (see also Section 2C). The comprehension process in Woods' model is also viewed as progressing from left to right. At each step there are several options which are tested, and at each step a lower-order program can be called. For instance, at the first step of processing a sentence, the possibility is considered that it starts with a noun phrase. A lower-order program is called which specializes in noun phrases. This program examines the first word to see if it is a (definite or indefinite) article. If it is, it proceeds to the next word, and examines it to see if it is a noun, or else, an article; if the first word is not an article, it finds out whether it is an adjective or a noun. In this manner, the program analyzes the whole noun phrase and reenters the main program with the result that the sentence begins with a noun phrase (or else, that another possibility should be examined). Since noun phrases are followed by verb phrases, the program now tests for a verb phrase and here again it refers to a lower-order program, this time a specialist for verb phrases.

The outputs of Woods' model are deep structures of transformational grammar. It is possible, however, to reformulate his networks so that the output is given in semantic terms, as shown by Simmons (1973) and by Norman and Rumelhart (1975). Winograd (1972) has developed a comprehension model very much along the lines of that of Woods, except that his model operates within the framework of systemic grammar and the output is a semantic structure. Anderson and Bower (1973) have been working along similar lines and their model also constructs semantic representations. It should therefore be possible to develop an augmented transition network grammar for constructing I-markers from utterances.

There is one reason, however, why all these programs do not seem to model the human comprehension process correctly: their rigid adherence to left-to-right processing. The human hearer, of course, also receives the incoming utterance consecutively from left to right, but it would be rash to conclude that all processing must follow such an order. It is possible to hold the first incoming signals in memory and process them only after some of the succeeding ones have been dealt with. The situation here parallels that in production, where the utterance is emitted from left to right, but processing it may occur in different sequences (see Section 3A). Introspectively, this is precisely what seems to occur in comprehension. We may often understand the beginning of an utterance only after we are halfway through hearing the rest of it. In reading, where we are free to scan ahead, there is perhaps even more leeway for such deviation from left-to-right order. Presumably, the slow and inefficient reader is more dependent on a strict left-to-right sequence, whereas better readers have developed more efficient scanning habits. In rapid reading it can be shown that several words are taken in at one eye fixation, and the short time which elapses between fixations suggests that these words must be processed simultaneously.

Some evidence that the hearer may store part of the incoming utterance for subsequent processing comes from findings of Jarvella and Herman (1972), which seem to suggest that when a sentence begins with a subordinate clause, the listener stores it and delays processing.[1]

A further argument comes from an example discussed by Jackendoff and Culicover (1971). They present the following two sentences:

(6.1) I told the man that the dog bit a bandage.
(6.2) I gave the man that the dog bit a bandage.

---

[1] Jarvella (1970), however, found that when speech was interrupted, subjects would usually recall verbatim only the current syntactic clause. This and some other findings with ambiguous sentences (Bever, Garrett, & Hurtig, 1973) seem to suggest that the clause may serve as a unit of analysis, which is normally processed before a new clause is taken in.

While both are grammatical, Example (6.2) "sounds stranger," according to Jackendoff and Culicover, and certainly most native English speakers would agree, because there is a tendency to treat *bit a bandage* in the second sentence as a verb phrase, just as the same phrase is interpreted (correctly) in the first. Now notice that if in Example (6.2) the analysis of the preceding context had been completed, this incorrect interpretation would have been precluded, because then *that the dog bit* would have to be construed as the embedded clause it really is. And *the man* would already have been identified as goal of *bit*, which would rule out *bandage* as goal. It must be concluded therefore that the final phrase is analyzed before processing of the preceding material has been completed.

The evidence found by Moore (1972) in his experiment on grammaticality judgments that subjects first look for subject—verb—object relationships and only subsequently for modifiers of subject and object also implies that processing does not invariably proceed linearly from left to right. Herriot (1968) obtained results for "sentences" made up of nonsense words, which he interpreted similarly.

All this does not imply that there is no directionality in the comprehension process. A strong tendency — but only a tendency — to deal with words from left to right as they are heard or read is compatible with the above results. In fact, left-to-right processing has been found in some experiments, as in a study of the eye—voice span in reading (Schlesinger, 1968; although this result may be peculiar to the task of reading a text aloud, which obviates more efficient scanning practices). The point is that the human hearer—reader is free to diverge from a strict left-to-right order, and a computer program simulating human comprehension which cannot be adapted to make allowance for this element misses something essential. This, then, must be one of our requirements of a comprehension model: that it permits flexibility with respect to the order in which the utterance is processed.

Some further requirements will become clear by examining what is perhaps the most impressive simulation of comprehension proposed so far. Winograd's (1972) computer program uses knowledge of a small restricted "world" in understanding fairly complicated commands and questions, to carry out these commands and to answer these questions. The fact that this program employs knowledge of the world is in itself an important advance (this will be relevant to the issues dealt with in Chapters 8 and 9). As mentioned above, Winograd's program has many affinities with that of Woods. Among others, both strictly adhere to a left-to-right progression. In this respect, as we have seen, it is unlikely that the program models human comprehension. There are two additional features of Winograd's system, which may contribute to its efficiency in computer analyzing sentences but limit its value as a model of the human hearer. His program and those considered above seem to share these features, but since Winograd's treatment is more explicit and detailed on these points, it will be examined here.

Winograd's system is always prepared for all eventualities: at each step in processing a sentence it considers, one after the other, all alternatives. For instance, in dealing with the phrase *a big red block*, it looks for an adjective after the indefinite article; and after the adjective *big* is found it goes on to look for another adjective, which again is found: *red*. And since English has constructions with more than two adjectival modifiers (*big red wooden block*), the system goes on to check if there is a third adjective. This time it fails and, as a second choice, it goes on to look for a noun (Winograd, 1972, p. 101).

It is of course extremely implausible that humans look for a third adjective after two have already been found. Rather, one might expect them first to look for a noun, since this is the most probable continuation. However, serious as this discrepancy between the computer program and the human processor is, it can be remedied easily. The alternatives to be considered can be ordered so that the program checks first for those that are more probable, perhaps those that have previously occured more frequently. This has actually been proposed by Woods (1970) and by Kaplan (1971) for programs based on augmented transition networks. Ordering alternatives in this manner is a definite advantage for the program because of the saving of steps it entails in analyzing actually occurring utterances. In this case, then, what seems to be true of the human processor is also advantageous for the computer program. But there are issues in which their "interests" diverge.

Winograd's system is very conscientious. It checks on every detail of the incoming utterance to see whether it conforms to the grammar. For instance, the phrase *how many blocks* is checked for grammatical agreement in the noun phrase: *blocks* must be plural because of *how many* (Winograd, 1972, p. 103). No such agreement may be an indication that the analysis is wrong and the program will back up and attempt a different one. This makes for a foolproof program: except for ambiguities, Winograd's system will never go wrong, as long as the input conforms to the system's grammar—but only for such input. As soon as any deviance is encountered, there are no routines to deal with it. The human processor, on the other hand, actually hears, and usually understands, many ungrammatical utterances. Not only are grammatical mistakes made by speakers, but much of everyday conversation consists of interrupted utterances or elliptical ones. Humans can deal with this kind of "noise," and also with perceptual noise that prevents them from hearing clearly everything being said. Winograd's system is not flexible enough to deal with noise. If a sentence does not consist of a noun phrase and a verb phrase, or if grammatical agreement is not observed, it simply fails. This is the price it pays for being always successful with well-formed utterances within the purview of its grammar. By contrast, people, while being immune to noise to a striking degree, are not always successful. Misunderstandings abound and still more frequently, presumably, the hearer or reader corrects a previously made false analysis.

Unlike the computer systems developed so far, human hearers do not check for all available cues. We do not invariably consider all alternatives, but often only the more likely ones. Understanding an utterance involves taking shortcuts. As a consequence we often have to backtrack, and occasionally we make mistakes. This is the price we pay for jumping rashly to the conclusions, not at all like well-behaved computer programs. What we probably gain thereby is speed, and more importantly, the ability to cope with utterances which are not well formed. We have this ability because the cues in the utterance are redundant (see Section 6B). This redundancy combats noise: we can patch up what is lacking in the input with what is left of the cues. The task of dealing with noisy input is further facilitated by our tendency to prefer more probable alternatives, and this in two ways: first, in terms of the relative probabilities of syntactic construction, and second, in terms of what is probable in the light of the context and of our knowledge of the world. (The latter factor is discussed at length in Chapters 8–10.)

A comprehension model, then, must make use of redundant information in the utterance. Further, probabilistic strategies must be resorted to and consequently revisions will often be required in the course of processing.

Let us consider now a different approach developed by Fodor, Bever and Garrett (1974). These investigators have proposed a variety of "perceptual strategies" by means of which an utterance is interpreted. The perceptual strategy theory seems to avoid some of the shortcomings of the computer programs discussed above.

The first task in comprehending a sentence according to Fodor *et al.* (1974, pp. 344–348) is to group together surface elements into underlying clauses. A strategy applicable here is that a noun phrase immediately followed by a verb which is (optionally) immediately followed by a noun phrase is an underlying clause; and these phrases are the deep structure subject, verb, and object, respectively. There is experimental evidence that sentences for which this strategy does not work are more difficult than those for which it does (Bever, 1970, pp. 294–295, 298–299; Fodor *et al.*, 1974, pp. 344–348). Further, Fodor *et al.* argue that where the sentence does not have the noun phrase–verb–noun phrase form, the hearer tends to impose this form and to use this strategy. Moore's (1972) experiment, mentioned above, is interpretable in this way: subjects tend to look first for the subject, verb, and object of the sentence.

After deep structure clauses have been identified, they must be arranged relative to each other. This is achieved by looking up the lexicon. The lexicon lists syntactic features, particularly for verbs, which impose certain constraints on the deep structure. For instance, there are verbs like *decide,* which can have either a direct object or else receive a complement beginning with *that* or *to,* while other verbs, like *hit,* can have only a direct object. An experiment by Fodor, Garrett and Bever (1968) suggests that this difference actually affects the processing of sentences. (For additional experimental evidence see Fodor *et al.,* 1974, pp. 348–353; Wanner, 1974, pp. 124–139.)

After these lexical cues have been utilized, the surface structure must be consulted to decide which of the possible structures actually occurs in the sentence. One of the strategies here is to assume that the verb immediately following the initial noun of the sentence is the main verb. Evidence for this strategy comes, among other things, from an experiment showing that sentences in which the subordinate clause precedes the main clause are less well recalled than sentences in which the clauses appear in reverse order (Clark & Clark, 1968). Another strategy has been suggested by Bever (1970, p. 337) to account for the way center-embedded sentences like Example (6.3) are comprehended.

(6.3)   The boy the girl was seen by is here.

Bever's strategy specifies that in a noun phrase—noun phrase—verb phrase sequence the first noun phrase is the object of the verb in the "internal structure" and the second noun phrase is its subject. A further discussion of perceptual strategies in the comprehension of center-embedded sentences is to be found in Fodor and Garrett (1967; see Schlesinger, 1975b, for a different account). Additional strategies employed in sentence comprehension have been proposed by Bever (1970).

Unlike the computer programs discussed above, the perceptual strategies approach does not require strict adherence to left-to-right processing.[2] Cues for the interpretation of sentences may appear all over the sentence, and perceptual strategies can make use of them. Perceptual strategies are also different from computer programs in being probabilistic. In this respect a theory based on perceptual strategies comes closer to the way human hearers go about interpreting a sentence. Evidently, strategies like those discussed above only afford a good guess; there are many sentences in which the guess may be wrong. The list of strategies proposed by Fodor and his colleagues is certainly not exhaustive and much work remains to be done to show in detail how utterances are understood, particularly those utterances for which the proposed strategies fail. However, while they are not explicit on this point, Fodor and his co-workers seem to hold that a reasonably small number of strategies suffices to analyze a sentence or at least its global features. In the following sections, a case is made for a very large number of strategies (if that is not a misnomer for the processes suggested there), and for the redundancy of cues which make these possible. Fodor and his colleagues do not mention redundancy of cues, since they apparently do not regard it to be crucial for comprehension.

Our approach in Section 6B differs in another important way from that of Fodor and his collaborators. The latter assume that perceptual strategies retrieve the deep structures of transformational grammar. It seems, however, that the argument from language learning against the introduction of syntactic concepts

_____

[2] One may be tempted to say that this is because Fodor and his collaborators have not written a computer program: left-to-right processing seems to come naturally to a program, much more so than to a human hearer. Kaplan (1971), in fact, has proposed a way of formalizing some of Bever's (1970) strategies by augmented transition networks and his proposal involves strictly left-to-right processing.

into the production model (see Section 2C) holds also for the comprehension model. In the following sections it is shown how I-markers may be retrieved from the utterance directly, rather than via syntactic constructs.

The perceptual strategies proposed by Fodor and his colleagues are obviously quite unlike the rules which figure in transformational grammar. In fact, their approach was developed as a result of a growing awareness that the rules in a performance model can not be identical with those in a grammar (Fodor & Garrett, 1967). Their perceptual strategies, however, were inspired by grammar and make use of the information contained in it. In fact they make use of little else. Although Fodor and his colleagues recognize the contribution of our knowledge of the world to comprehension, they do not deal with the way this knowledge is put to use in analyzing sentences. This is clearly something a comprehension model must account for, and in Chapter 10 we see how information from the context and knowledge of the world can be made to dovetail with information from structural cues in the utterance. But since it is possible to understand utterances without the help of any extraneous information (an extreme case would be Lewis Carroll's "Jabberwocky"), the comprehension model must be able to stand on its structural feet alone. The question dealt with in this chapter is therefore how utterances are processed in isolation, without the help of knowledge of the world.

We can now summarize the requirements which must be met by a model of utterance comprehension:

1. *Flexibility.* While processing may be predominantly left to right, it is not limited to any one direction. Some of the incoming material may be stored and processed only after subsequent material has been dealt with. Just as there are several alternative ways for producing an utterance (see Section 3A) so there are several possible routes to comprehending it, and the exigencies of the situation and motivational factors determine which of these routes is taken.

2. *Redundancy.* To combat noise, the information available to the hearer should be redundant.

3. *Probabilistic strategies.* The hearer is not restricted to rules which lead invariably to the correct solution. Cues may be such that they point to an interpretation only with a certain probability. In following these cues the hearer risks an incorrect construal, which may require backtracking.

4. *Semantic concepts.* Only semantic notions should be resorted to in the retrieval of an I-marker, just as in production and for the same reason: syntactic concepts like "subject," "object," would pose problems for a theory of acquisition. An exception is grammatical categories like noun, verb, adjective, which present no such difficulty (see Section 2C).

5. *Context and the knowledge of the world.* Although the model must show how an utterance is interpreted in isolation, on the basis of our knowledge of

language alone, it must also account for the way this knowledge may interact with information about the context of the utterance and knowledge of the world.

6. *Economy.* This seems to be the least important requirement, which should be satisfied only to the extent that it does not conflict with the preceding ones. To minimize the number of rules which have to be learned and remembered, rules in comprehension should, as far as possible, be the rules of production applied in reverse.

None of the models discussed in this section meets all the requirements that seem to be essential for a theory giving a plausible account of human comprehension. The theory of perceptual strategies perhaps comes closest so such an account. It does involve probabilistic strategies and seems to allow for flexibility and redundancy. It has not yet been spelled out in enough detail to judge to what extent it can make use of the rules employed in production, and has not yet been developed to take into account knowledge of the world. The strategies proposed so far make use of syntactic concepts, but a reformulation in semantic terms seems feasible. Below, a comprehension model is sketched that does conform to the above requirements.

6B. STRUCTURAL CUES

Retrieval of the I-marker is made possible by various cues which the reader or hearer finds in the utterance. In this chapter we are concerned only with those cues that can be utilized on the basis of knowledge of the language, without recourse to knowledge of the word and contextual information. These are called STRUCTURAL CUES. Their properties are the topic of this section, and the strategies using these cues those of Section 6C.

The perception of a structural cue presupposes a phonological analysis of incoming sounds, which results in a string of words. Presumably, such an analysis involves the phonological rules which are also employed in production of utterances. There has been much work on phonological analysis (see Fodor, Bever & Garrett, 1974, pp. 279–313, for a useful review). There are indications that phonological analysis interacts with the interpretation of sentence structure. Here, however, nothing further will be said on this subject and instead we will just assume that phonological analysis has been performed and that the hearer deals with a string of words and the intonation contour imposed on them. To retrieve the I-marker from these, the hearer relies on structural cues.

The first thing to note about structural cues is that many of them figure in realization rules. Function words and affixes appear in the realizates of relation rules, and evidently these may serve as cues to the structure of the sentence (see Section 2C). Additional cues are supplied by word order, which is also determined by relation rules. The grammatical category of a word is also determined by relation rules and may serve as a structural cue. However, for grammatical category to serve as a cue, a certain amount of analysis has to be carried out first. Either the word has an affix which reveals its form class (like the ending *ence* which is characteristic of nouns) or else the word is looked up in the lexicon, which also lists its grammatical category (see Section 2D).[3] The result of intonation rules, intonation contour, furnishes cues as to the structure of the sentence. Concord rules are a further source of cues: grammatical agreement between a noun and a verb may signal that the AGENT—ACTION relation holds between them. The perceptual strategies proposed by Fodor *et al.* (1974; see Section 6A of this volume) make use of various structural cues, such as grammatical category and word order. One of their strategies requires information as to the kinds of complementation the verbs may receive. This information can also be obtained by looking up the lexicon, as noted in Section 2D.

As pointed out by Wanner (1974), many cues in the input are "ambiguous in the sense that they are related to different rules; others are unreliable, because they are not consistently present when the rule, to which they are related, is applied [p. 118]." The same ambiguity and unreliability of cues which Wanner notes in their association with rules, are found also in their association with semantic relations. Consequently, a strategy utilizing cues must be probabilistic. This is in line with one of our requirements of a comprehension model, as detailed at the end of Section 6A. A verb may often end with an affix characteristic of a noun (for example, *to influence*) and the affix is therefore an ambiguous cue. Looking up the lexicon may also fail to disclose the grammatical category of the word; compare $influence^N$ and $influence^V$; $adult^N$ and $adult^A$. If a word is suffixed by *s*, it may either be a noun with the monadic I-marker relation PLURALITY, or a verb with the relation HABITUAL (which moreover is associated with a third person singular agent). If a noun is followed by a verb, there is a reasonably high probability that the AGENT—ACTION relation holds between them, but this is by no means certain, as evidenced for instance by the two noun—verb sequences in

(6.4)   The linguist, challenged by the psychologist, dismissed this
         as due to performance factors.

The commas in Example (6.4) — or the intonation contour when the sentence is spoken — are structural cues contradicting the evidence of the word order cue. When grammatical agreement is violated, this may serve as a NEGATIVE CUE, the contribution of which is to block an inference from another cue.

---

[3] This look-up may retrieve only the category marker and not the protoverbal element, the latter being searched for at a later stage. That a look-up is not always indispensible has been noted by Thorne *et al.* (1968; see Section 6A). In addition to affixes, the written form of the word may provide a cue: when a word beginning with a capital letter is encountered in reading, one knows that it is a proper noun — unless the words appear at the beginning of a sentence.

Although most cues are ambiguous, the meaning of the sentence can usually be determined unequivocally with the help of the sum total of these cues, as shown in Sections 6C and 6D. The process is facilitated as the input string also contains cues which do not figure in the realizate of relation rules or in the output of other realization rules. For instance, Clark's (1965) findings on sentence completion suggest that animate nouns may more frequently be agents than goals, which seems to suggest that when a lexical look-up identifies a noun as animate, this may serve as a cue that, with a high probability, it is an agent. Active sentences are more frequent than passive ones (see Section 4D), hence, there is a high probability that the first noun in a sentence is the agent rather than the goal of the verb. Some paralinguistic features may also serve as cues.

Typically, many of the cues in an utterance will be redundant, that is, under perfect conditions of perception retrieval of the I-marker would be possible without these cues. This is in line with our requirement of a comprehension model posed at the end of the preceding section. Redundancy makes comprehension possible even when not all available structural cues are attended to. Considering that structural cues often reside in an inflectional ending or a punctuation mark, which may go unnoticed in rapid reading or in listening in noisy surroundings, redundancy of cues seems to be vital to comprehension.

6C. STRUCTURINGS

The retrieval of an I-marker involves finding the protoverbal elements expressed by the words in the utterance and ascertaining which relations hold between these protoverbal elements. The process by which this is achieved requires looking up the lexicon and utilizes structural cues. This process is here labeled STRUCTURING. Besides structuring there are other processes based on the context of the utterance and knowledge of the world; but these are abstracted from here, and the structuring will be discussed as if it proceeded in isolation.

The structuring process takes as its input a segment of the utterance and construes the relation or relations expressed in it. In doing so it often reverses the operation of relation rules: the latter take as their input an I-marker relation and its arguments and convert these into a realizate, which ultimately becomes an utterance segment.

To illustrate the operation of structuring, suppose the utterance segment *linguists described* is chosen for structuring; we say that this segment is the UNIT OF ANALYSIS. One way of structuring this unit is to look up the grammatical category of *linguist* and that of *describe* in the lexicon. For the sake of simplicity we assume here that the grammatical category is retrieved without the protoverbal element (this being one of the options mentioned in Section 6B). The structural cues at the hearer's disposal can now be summarized as *linguists*[N]

+ *described*^{V} (the plus sign indicating sequence). This fits one of the relation rules in English:

$$(6.5) \quad (\text{AGENT}-\text{ACTION } a,b) \rightarrow (\text{AGENT } a^N + b^V)^S$$

More precisely, *linguists*^{N} + *described*^{V} corresponds to $a^N + b^V$ in Rule (6.5); the category marker of the realizate as a whole – S, in this case – will usually not be utilized for structuring. This correspondence permits applying Relation Rule (6.5) in reverse, with the result

$$(6.6) \quad (\text{AGENT}-\text{ACTION } \textit{linguists, described})$$

The output of the structuring process – the above example – will also be called a STRUCTURING, since it seems that this process–product ambiguity is not likely to lead to misunderstanding.

Notice now that the structuring Example (6.6) has the form of an I-marker constituent. In this example it has the form of a constituent containing words (italicized) and not protoverbal elements (see Example 3.13 in Section 3B); if the protoverbal elements had been retrieved by a lexical look-up before structuring, protoverbal elements instead of words would appear in Example (6.6). By reconstructing an I-marker constituent the hearer has made the first step towards reconstructing the I-marker from which the utterance was derived.

Now, obviously Example (6.5) is not the only relation rule which fits *linguists*^{N} + *described*^{V}. The rule producing *the wine chosen by the host* . . . , for instance, with the goal relation between *wine* and *chosen*, fits equally well, and the structuring might therefore have been

$$(6.7) \quad (\text{GOAL}-\text{ACTION } \textit{linguists, described}).$$

If Example (6.6) is preferred over Example (6.7) this will probably be due to the relative frequency with which the corresponding relation rules are used in speaking. But this is, of course, no guarantee that this structuring is correct, and the comprehension mechanism must be ready to revise it. This can best be taken into account by postulating that each structuring has a subjective probability value attached to it. Typically this value will be less than unity,[4] but the hearer will often not be aware of this, the comprehension process being so fast that doubts and hesitations do not have time to appear. However, subjective probability values must be postulated so as to account for the comprehension process.

---

[4] A formulation in terms of response strength instead of subjective probabilities is also possible, and might indeed seem preferable to some. However, the impression a term like "response strength" might evoke of making contact with stimulus–response theories would be largely illusory, since we are dealing here with covert processes that are at present still rather far removed from direct experimental test.

Suppose that an incorrect structuring has been adopted. For instance, while Example (6.6) was structured on the basis of frequency, Example (6.7) may have actually been in the I-marker of the speaker. Although individual structurings are thus fallible, comprehension usually succeeds; for two reasons:

1. In the course of further analysis the structuring may be revised. A structuring is usually only one of the building blocks in arriving at a complete analysis of the utterance. As shown in Section 6D, several structurings may have to be combined to retrieve the full I-marker, and when this process of combination is blocked, the fault in structuring is detected.

2. Normally there are several structural cues for a given unit of analysis. These operate jointly, thus providing a system of mutual checks.

The latter statement needs to be explained and further amplified. There are two ways in which structural cues can relate to each other. First, it is possible that all cues found in a given unit of analysis converge on the same structuring. The subjective probability value of this structuring will then be influenced by the number and nature of structural cues which led to it. On the other hand, structural cues may lead to conflicting structurings. Suppose that on the basis of previously experienced frequency the hearer structured $linguists^N + described^V$ as in Example (6.6), but at the same time noticed the intonation contour (which is another structural cue) and arrived at Example (6.7). Each of these two structurings will have its subjective probability value. Then one of the following may happen: (1) both structurings are retained, each with its probability value; or (2) only the structuring with the greater probability value is retained, and the other rejected. In the case of the former, disambiguation will normally be achieved in the course of further processing (see Section 6D). When Case (2) occurs, the rejected structuring may have to be reverted to when the accepted structuring is proven wrong (or when its subjective probability becomes very low). This interplay of structurings is further complicated by their interaction with construals based on context and knowledge of the world, as is seen in the final chapter of this volume.

In the example discussed above, structural cues permitted the application of a relation rule in reverse. The inverse of concord rules can also operate in the structuring process. For instance, there is a concord rule requiring that if the agent relation holds between a noun in the singular and a verb in the present tense (more precisely, one to which HABITUAL or any relation realized as the present tense applies), then the verb is suffixed by s. This rule can be applied in reverse: the s after a verb serves as a structural cue suggesting the agent relation. Remember that reliance on the inverses of realization rules is our last requirement of a comprehension model (see Section 6A).

Absence of agreement between noun and verb (or in general, failure to conform to a realization rule) may serve as a negative structural cue (see Section 6B). Such a negative cue leads to a NEGATIVE STRUCTURING. The latter may lower the subjective probability of another structuring with which it conflicts or even cause its rejection. But, unlike Winograd's (1972) computer program (see Section 6A), our model does not require that grammatical agreement is always checked for. Due to the abundant supply of cues it can afford to neglect utilizing some of them.

That structural cues are abundant has been shown above. In addition to those cues which figure in realization rules, there will usually be others not provided for by these rules. Suppose that *linguists described* are the initial words in the utterance. Structuring may make use of the fact that, according to previous experience, the first word in the sentence is most frequently the lexicalization of an agent term. Further, if the protoverbal element expressed by *linguists* is retrieved from the lexicon, it will transpire that *linguists* refers to animate beings. Since agents are predominantly animate, this is another structural cue suggesting that this word is the agent term. The convergence of these cues on the same structuring tends to raise the subjective probability value of the latter. On the other hand, if some of these cues are not attended to, comprehension will still be possible because of their redundancy. As stated above, this redundancy is one of the requirements of a comprehension model.

The copious supply of structural cues makes it possible for these not only to reinforce but also to correct each other where necessary. The larger the number of cues, the less important it becomes for each individual cue to suggest the correct structuring: misleading cues will be held in check by others.

On the other hand, even very impoverished cues may justify a structuring. If this structure is erroneous, the error will be detected later in the process, when structurings are combined. Suppose, for instance, that for some reason the grammatical category of *described* has not been ascertained, and only the following cues are available: $linguists^N$ + *described.* Since, this, too, corresponds to part of the realizate of Rule (6.5), it is possible to apply Rule (6.5) in reverse with the result of Example (6.6). In this case, Example (6.6) may of course have a somewhat lower subjective probability than when $linguists^N$ + $described^V$ is available.

It is instructive to compare the above with one of the perceptual strategies proposed by Fodor, Bever and Garrett (1974, p. 356; see also Section 6A this volume), which specifies that a verb following a noun is construed as a main verb only if the noun is the initial noun in the sentence (and unless marked for embedding). Accordingly, $linguists^N$ + $described^V$ would be insufficient for arriving at a construal unless the hearer notes that *linguists* is the initial noun. This precaution obviates an erroneous construal for certain kinds of sentences. By contrast, our approach can afford to be much more tolerant of error, owing to the redundancy of structural cues. As noted in Section 6A, the proponents of the perceptual strategies approach seem to rest content with a limited number of strategies. This alternate approach, on the other hand, assumes a much larger number of structurings, which compensates for the probability often being much lower that each individual structuring is right. Instead of a few overall strategies, we thus propose a large arsenal of tactics.

Above, it was remarked that structuring may be based on cues not represented in realization rules. The comprehension process thus involves rules which do not correspond to any of the rules specified so far for the production process. But this raises an interesting question. One might argue that it would be wasteful not to employ the rules used in comprehension also in production. Accordingly, one might postulate for the production process additional and redundant relation rules, for example, one according to which the agent term is to come first. (Such a relation rule would of course have to be equipped with the appropriate shunting marker (see Section 4A) and with several safeguards, such as the proviso that articles and determiners may precede the agent term.)

But what would be gained by such redundancy in production? As we have seen, redundancy is vital for comprehension, because of the ambiguity of cues and the need to combat noise. In production, on the other hand, we incur far less danger of going wrong − in fact, realization rules are not probabilistic − and so redundancy is not required. It seems therefore likely that there are no redundant realization rules. This would mean that realization rules do not make use of all the regularities in language.

There is one reason, however, why there may be redundant rules in production as well. The child learning to speak induces rules from adult speech by matching it with the situation spoken about (Schlesinger, 1971b). Suppose that he forms a rule like "agent comes first," which he at once applies in producing utterances. (Such a rule has been proposed in Schlesinger, 1975a, to account for the agent−goal construction frequent in child speech.) If so, it is quite likely that he holds on to such a realization rule even after more explicit and "advanced" ones have been acquired, because there is nothing to reinforce him negatively for using it. The argument here is similar to that of Watt (1970) regarding the rule responsible for the truncated passive (see Section 2A). At present, therefore, this issue remains unsettled.

So far we have considered structurings involving an I-marker relation and all its arguments, as in Examples (6.6) and (6.7). Another type of structuring is one in which an argument is missing. Suppose, for instance, that instead of *linguists* and *described*, the first unit of analysis is *linguists*, which is the initial word in the utterance, and after a lexical look-up is recognized as a noun referring to an animate being. These structural cues lead to the conclusion that an agent of some action is expressed, without establishing, as yet, which word expresses the action:

(6.8) (AGENT−ACTION linguists, △)

Further processing must then COMPLEMENT Example (6.8) by retrieving the action term. Another example would be a word shown by lexical look-up to be an adjective, which suggests that this is an attribute of something − without establishing of what. We may call such structurings with missing arguments LACUNAL STRUCTURINGS. Lacunal structurings require complementation by the missing argument.

There is also the possibility of structurings which are more complex I-marker constituents than Example (6.6) or (6.7). Suppose there is a "perceptual strategy" à la Bever applying to noun-noun-verb sequences (see Section 6A) like

(6.9)   This is the lizard Alice kicked.

The structural cues, $lizard^N$ + $Alice^N$ + $kicked^V$, suggest the following structuring:

(6.10)   (AGENT–ACTION Alice, (GOAL–ACTION lizard, kicked))

Complex structurings like these may also be lacunal, for instance, when in Example (6.9) only *lizard* and *Alice,* and not *kicked,* form the unit of analysis and the structural cues suggest Example (6.10), but without the action argument 'kicked'.

The utterance segment for which a structuring is construed has been called here unit of analysis. A unit of analysis may comprise one word – the structuring will consequently contain a monadic relation (at least in English) – or it may contain two or more words, as in the above examples. The first unit of analysis to be processed may tend to comprise the first word or words of the utterance, but as mentioned earlier (see Section 6A) such left-to-right processing need not occur invariably. Occasionally, other words in the utterance may serve as the initial unit of the analysis.

The unit of analysis does not have to comprise consecutive words. For instance, a noun and a verb which are separated by several words may be focused on and structured as the agent and its action. Nonconsecutive words may be focused on because of the saliency of individual words, which attract the hearer's or reader's attention. In addition, there is the possibility that the hearer searches the utterance for certain elements or terms of I-marker relations. Moore's (1972) experiment, mentioned above (see Section 6A), suggests that the reader looks first for the agent, action, and goal terms. Schank (1972, p. 561) has suggested that the hearer first searches the input for the main noun and main verb. A directed search is also presupposed by Fodor, Bever and Garrett's (1974) strategy of grouping together the words belonging to an underlying clause (see Section 6A).

The above pertains to directed search leading to the initial unit of analysis. In the course of processing there may be structurings which indicate that certain elements in the utterance must be found. Thus, lacunal structurings require complementation. Further, an experiment by Mehler and Carey (1967) shows that a set for certain syntactic structures can be induced, and one might expect that such sets would also influence the formation of units of analysis. The extent to which a hearer or reader actively engages in such directed search or is steered by saliency may depend on various motivational factors as well as on subjective factors, such as the difficulty of linguistic material.

6D.   FROM STRUCTURING TO I-MARKER

To complete our account of the structuring process it must now be shown how various structurings are integrated into an I-marker. This is illustrated by means of an example of "Jabberwocky," that is, a text for the comprehension of which the reader can rely only on structural cues and not on context or any other factual information. When the latter factors are taken into account, some minor revisions in our description of the comprehension process will become necessary. These are dealt with in Chapter 10.

Suppose now that in perusing Jabberwocky the reader arrives at the segment *the slithy toves did gyre*. In this case lexical look-up will presumably draw a blank, unless the reader has been enlightened by Gardner's (1965) commentary. He will be left therefore with only a few structural cues. Assume that he notices the following:

1. *slithy* has *y* as its last letter; this is presumably a suffix, and the word is an adjective;
2. *toves* has *s* as its last letter, which presumably indicates the plural of a noun;
3. *gyre* is preceded by *did*, which indicates a verb with the relation **PAST**;
4. *slithy* precedes *toves*;
5. *toves* precedes *gyre*.

Let us summarize some of these cues as follows:

$slithy^A + (tove + s)^N$, by Observations 1, 2, and 4.
$(tove + s)^N + (gyre)^V$, by Observations 2, 3, and 5.

Obviously, these cues are ambiguous. Other words besides adjectives can end in *y* (*pry, by,* and *jelly,* for example); the final *s* in a word may indicate that it is a third person singular verb, and so on. But let us assume that the reader has been alerted to just these possibilities, whether because of previously experienced frequency or for other reasons. He may now arrive at the following three structurings:

(6.11)   (ATTRIBUTE *slithy, toves*)
(6.12)   (AGENT–ACTION *toves, gyre*)
(6.13)   (PAST *gyre*)

Now these structurings will be COALESCED, that is, combined into larger units. Coalescing is based on two structurings including identical words. In this case, the same occurrence of the word *toves* appears in both Examples (6.11) and (6.12). Consequently Examples (6.11) and (6.12) can coalesce into:

(6.14) (AGENT–ACTION (ATTRIBUTE *slithy, toves*), *gyre*).

The product of coalescing, Example (6.14), will be called a COALESCED STRUC-TURING. Coalesced structurings must coalesce further until the whole I-marker is retrieved. For instance, Example (6.14) can now coalesce with Example (6.13) by virtue of the common word *gyre*, with the result of:

(6.15) (AGENT–ACTION (ATTRIBUTE *slithy, toves*), (PAST *gyre*)).

Evidently, there must be some constraints under which coalescing operates. After all, for any two structurings $(R_1\ a, b)$ and $(R_2\ c, a)$ – where R_1 stands for any relation – there are two possible ways of embedding one within the other, namely, $(R_1 (R_2\ c,\ a),\ b)$ and $(R_2\ c,\ (R_1\ a,\ b)\ )$. However, the relations under consideration in the above example are such that Example (6.14) is the only possibility of coalescing Examples (6.11) and (6.12). Example (6.16) is not a possible I-marker constituent: an agent term can have an attribute (and so can several other terms) but an attribute of a complete AGENT–ACTION construc-tion doesn't "make sense." It is not one of the ways I-markers can ever be coagulated, and hence no such structuring will be construed.

(6.16) (ATTRIBUTE *slithy*, (AGENT–ACTION *toves, gyre*)

As noted, the cues in Observations 1–5 are ambiguous, and other structurings might be arrived at. Suppose, for instance, that a reader takes *slithy* as a verb (*y* being a frequent suffix of verbs). From $slithy^V$ + $toves^N$ he arrives at the structuring:

(6.17) (GOAL–ACTION *toves, slithy*)

But this structuring can not coalesce with Example (6.12), in spite of the common *toves*: one and the same word cannot be both the agent and the goal term. Hence, Example (6.17) will have to be rejected and another structuring will be tried instead. This example shows how the coalescing process detects incorrect structurings. As stated in Section 6C, one may reasonably rely on ambiguous cues and form structurings with low subjective probabilities: co-alescing is a safeguard against incorrect analyses.

Conversely, that two structurings can coalesce provides a certain degree of confirmation for these structurings. Construing *slithy* as an adjective and struc-turing *slithy toves* as in Example (6.11) has been vindicated ex post facto. The subjective probability value of both Examples (6.11) and (6.12) with which it coalesced will increase after coalescing, and the coalesced structuring itself, Example (6.14), will presumably have a higher subjective probability than those which went into its making. Further coalescing will again raise probability values, until the complete I-marker is retrieved. The latter may then have a probability value of unity or close to unity: the hearer or reader is usually quite confident that he has understood the utterance correctly, since all its parts fall into pattern.

Let us consider now a few varieties of coalescing. We have already seen that a coalesced structuring like Example (6.14) can in its turn coalesce with another structuring, like Example (6.13). It is also possible for two coalesced structurings to coalesce. Suppose for instance that after structuring Example (6.13) the reader has structured *did gyre in the wabe,* as expressing a locative relation,[5] and these two structurings coalesce into

(6.18)   (LOCATION–ACTION *wabe,* (PAST *gyre*))

This coalesced structuring can now coalesce with another coalesced structuring, Example (6.14), on the basis of the word *gyre* which they have in common. Alternatively, it can coalesce with Example (6.15). These different ways of coalescing are presented schematically in Figure 6.1.

At the end of the last section two special types of structuring were discussed: lacunal structurings and complex structurings. A complex structuring consists of an I-marker constituent in which there is more than one relation; they may have the form of Example (6.14) or (6.15) and it should be clear therefore that they can be coalesced by the same mechanism as the latter. Lacunal structurings may also coalesce, as can be seen if, for instance, *gyre* in Example (6.12) is replaced by the dummy symbol Δ. After coalescing with Example (6.11), the dummy symbol will appear also in Example (6.14). Complementing of a lacunal structuring may thus occur either before or after coalescing.

In the examples given so far the structurings which coalesced contained words. When the lexical look-up is performed before coalescing, these words may be converted into protoverbal elements. Coalescing will then proceed on the basis of protoverbal elements which were obtained from identical words.

One of our requirements of a comprehension model was flexibility. In Section 6C it was noted that any segment of the text may serve as initial unit of analysis and that sequence of structurings is free to vary. It should now be clear that both structurings and coalescings can occur in various sequences. Figure 6.1 shows one route of structuring and coalescing leading to a complex I-marker constituent. Another route to the same I-marker constituent and involving the same four simple structurings (but different coalesced structurings) is shown in Figure 6.2. The reader can easily prove that there are still other alternatives, made possible by the simple principle that structurings with a common word (or protoverbal element) can coalesce.

---

[5] Presumably, there are several locative relations, corresponding to the prepositions *in, on, at,* and so on. For convenience this will be disregarded here.

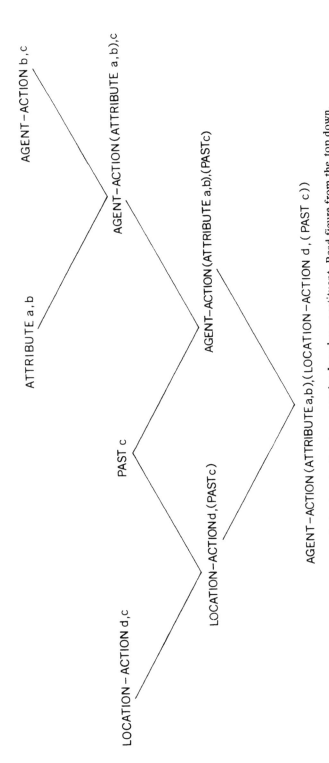

FIGURE 6.1. Coalescings leading to a complex I-marker constituent. Read figure from the top down.

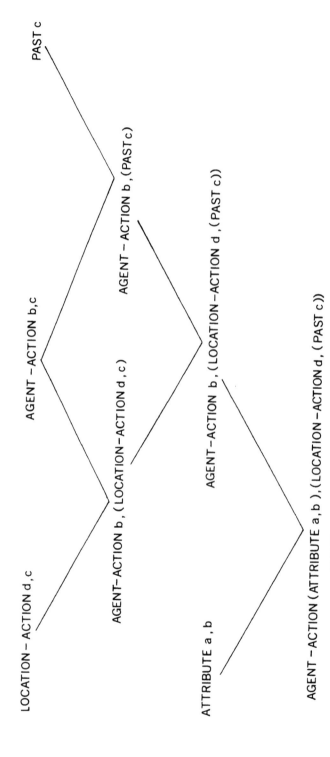

PAST c

AGENT – ACTION b, (PAST c)

AGENT – ACTION b,c

AGENT – ACTION b , (LOCATION–ACTION d , (PAST c))

LOCATION – ACTION d , c

AGENT–ACTION b , (LOCATION–ACTION d , c)

AGENT–ACTION b , (LOCATION –ACTION d , (PAST c))

ATTRIBUTE a , b

AGENT – ACTION (ATTRIBUTE a , b) , (LOCATION–ACTION d , (PAST c))

FIGURE 6. Another route of coalescing the I-marker constituent of Figure 6.1.

There also may be linguistic material within a structuring which can subsequently be structured. For instance, after Example (6.15) has been arrived at, the suffix of *toves* may give rise to the structuring (PLURALITY *tove*) which then coalesces with Example (6.15) by replacing *toves*. Several steps in structuring and coalescing may be performed simultaneously. Structural cues in different parts of the utterance may be processed simultaneously to arrive at two different structurings, and likewise, two coalesced structurings may be formed simultaneously. In this respect the structuring process is similar to the production process, where relation rules can be applied in any sequence whatsoever (see Section 3A). The similarity extends further, for just as lexicalization of two protoverbal elements can occur at any stage of production process, so the lexical look-up of a word which retrieves the corresponding protoverbal element can be carried out at any point in the structuring process.

Structuring does not necessarily follow the constituent structure of the sentence. Thus, in Figure 6.1 the ATTRIBUTE relation may be structured after the AGENT—ACTION relation. In coalescing, the former will then have to be embedded within the latter.

The coalescings described so far were based on a common word or protoverbal element in two structurings. Additional flexibility is introduced into the model by a different type of coalescing. A segment of the text can coalesce with a word (or with another segment) with which it has no word in common. This is made possible through the category marker of the structuring for this segment. This category marker must first be found by a process to be called CUE SUPPLEMENTATION. Let us explain this by means of an example.

Assumed above was that structural cues summarized as $slithy^A + toves^N$ led to a structuring with the ATTRIBUTE relation. The realizate of one of the relation rules for this relation is $(ATT\ a^A + b^N)^N$, which fits $slithy^A + toves^N$, and therefore this rule can be applied in reverse to yield Example (6.11). Now comes the crucial move. Since $slithy^A + toves^N$ has been recognized as corresponding to the realizate $(a^A + b^N)^N$, it can be viewed as a constituent with the category marker N: $(slithy^A + toves^N)^N$. The structural cues are thus supplemented by referring to the realizate. Suppose now that these words are succeeded by *gyre* which is a V (for convenience, we disregard *did*). Now $(slithy^A + toves^N)^N + gyre^V$ corresponds to $(AGENT\ a^N + b^V)^S$. Hence, the relation rule for the agent relation can be applied in reverse, and the result is Example (6.14). Note that there is no common word here on which coalescing could be based. Table 6.1 summarizes the above process. (Note that Steps 3 and 4 in the table are interchangeable or can be made simultaneously.)

A somewhat more complex example would be one in which, before Step 5, *gyre in the wabes* would be structured as in Example (6.18), the cues of this phrase are supplemented (the whole segment is a V), and then Steps 6–8 can be performed on the two strings, which are N and V respectively.

TABLE 6.1
Coalescing by Cue Supplementation

Step	Result
1	Find structural cues for a unit of analysis.	$slithy^A + toves^N$
2	Find a realizate which corresponds partially to result of Step 1.	$(ATTR\ a^A + b^N)N$
3	Supplement the structural cues in result of Step 1 by the result of Step 2.	$(slithy^A + toves^N)N$
4	Apply relation rule associated with Step 2 to the result of Step 1 in reverse.	$(ATTRIBUTE\ slithy, toves)$
5	Include result of Step 3 in a larger unit of analysis and find structural cues.	$(slithy^A + toves^N)N + gyre\ V$
6	Find a realizate which corresponds partially to result of Step 5 (as in Step 2).	$(AGENT\ a^N + b^V)S$
7	Apply relation rule associated with Step 6 to the result of Steps 5 in reverse (as in Step 4).	$(AGENT-ACTION(slithy^A + toves^N), gyre)$
8	Coalesce results of Steps 4 and 7.	$(AGENT-ACTION\ (ATTRIBUTE\ slithy, toves), gyre)$

At first sight, cue supplementation as presented in Table 6.1 might seem to be just another alternative to a simple structuring process for the same cues. Note that just as ($slithy^A$ + $toves^N$) is an N, so is $toves$ by itself. Step 6 could therefore have been performed on $toves^N$ + $gyre^V$ and the result could then coalesce with the ATTRIBUTE relation (see Step 4). But note that this way of arriving at the coalesced structuring in Step 6 would be barred if $toves$ had not been recognized as being a noun. Cue supplementation, on the other hand, is possible even with such impoverished cues: Steps 2–6 can be performed also on the basis of $slithy^A$ + $toves$ alone.

If structuring and coalescing can be carried out in so many alternative ways, what determines the route adopted by the hearer or reader in any given instance? There seem to be three main factors: (1) the relative saliency of words; (2) availability of structural cues; and (3) the expectations aroused in the course of structuring and coalescing. The effect of saliency has been briefly discussed at the end of Section 6C. As for availability, it stands to reason that there is a tendency to refer first to cues which are more easily accessible. Thus a function word like *with*, which marks the instrumental relation, may be more salient than a suffix like *'s*, which marks the possessive and, other things being equal, the former relation may be structured before the latter. A few more words must be said now about the expectations raised in the course of the analysis of the utterance.

One case of an expectation raised in the course of structuring has already been noted above in our discussion of lacunal structurings (see Section 6C). A lacunal structuring issues a DIRECTIVE, as we may call it, for complementation by a missing argument. Thus, the structuring in Example (6.8) results in a directive that the second argument, the action, is to be complemented. A further example of directives issued by a structuring may be found in a study by Rubenstein (1974). Discussing some unexpected results he obtained, Rubenstein suggested that when hearing an utterance beginning *the floor that the women*, the listener predicts that the women are alleged to have done something to the floor and that the next verb will say what they did. In other words, this unit of analysis gives rise to a lacunal structuring, which issues a directive for complementation by the missing action term. Rubenstein apparently believes this directive to be rather specific: it instigates a search for a word categorized as V.

A directive has two possible results. It either instigates an active search (in the above example: a search for the action term), or else it leads to an anticipation and, consequently, a greater alertness with respect to relevant cues and possibilities of structuring.

Directives are also produced by anaphoric terms. A pronoun like *he, she,* or *it* will be converted into a protoverbal element after the word is found to which it refers. Thus, in Example (6.19) the agent relation is found to hold between *Eve* and *read* (or between the corresponding protoverbal elements), instead of between *she* and *read:*

(6.19) Eve wanted to see the movie after she had read the book.

Further, as Fillmore (1968) has pointed out, verbs in English can be classified according to the case elements they require and those they may take optionally. This may give rise to directives. For instance, *give* must have an object and a recipient, and when this verb is encountered, either by itself or in a structuring, say (AGENT–ACTION *John, gave*), a directive will be issued to look for the missing terms. The agent term, on the other hand is optional for *give*. Nevertheless, a structuring containing *give* as one of its arguments may issue a directive to look for the agent term, perhaps because the hearer has learned from previous experience that the agent of giving is usually supplied. One of the possible reasons for such a directive may be the expectancies aroused by the situation which the utterance is about: the identity of the agent may be important in the particular circumstances. However, these considerations do not pertain to the structure of the utterance and therefore they are beyond the scope of this chapter (see Chapter 9).

In Section 6A we saw that one of the perceptual strategies postulated by Fodor and his associates is based on the information contained in the verb as to the types of complementation it may receive. This information, which is contained in the lexicon, serves as the basis for directives for further structuring.

Let us now examine once more what happens when two structurings fail to coalesce. As stated, such a failure may be expected to be quite common due to the probablistic nature of structuring: we admit structurings with a low probability because these are liable to be detected in coalescing the structuring with another one. Suppose, for example, that Example (6.20) is the first segment of an utterance, and the structurings for this segment have been coalesced into Example (6.21):

(6.20) The newly arrived ship loads

(6.21) (AGENT–ACTION (ATTRIBUTE newly arrived, ship), load).

Whether this coalesced structuring is correct or not depends on the rest of the utterance. This is because Example (6.20) is actually ambiguous, as becomes clear when we consider that it may be continued by something like *to their homeland.* The structuring involving this segment can not coalesce with Example (6.21), because *load to* is unacceptable. Hence Example (6.21) will have to be revised, and ultimately the following coalesced structuring will take its place:

(6.22) (AGENT–ACTION newly arrived, (GOAL–ACTION load, ship).

It may of course also happen that, since a lexical look-up shows that *ship* and *load* are each both a noun and a verb, Examples (6.21) and (6.22) are first produced as two alternatives, each with a subjective probability value. Revision then consists in eliminating Example (6.21) because of its failure to coalesce with structurings of the remaining segment.

Revisions of previous structurings will be part and parcel of the structuring process. Some will be far-reaching, as in the above example, and the hearer may become aware of having been misled by the "local" ambiguity in the utterance. Others may be effected after a smaller number of steps, and may perhaps not be noticed by the hearer.

It is important that revisions may have some measurable behavioral consequences. These include an increase in difficulty of processing the utterance, and a decrease in its judged acceptability. Processing difficulty is a variable well established in the experimental psycholinguistic literature, where it is known under several names, according to the various ways it can be measured (reading rate, errors in recall or recognition, and so on). Even where no measurable increase in difficulty is found, there may be a decrease in acceptability, the need for a revision engendering a feeling that the sentence is not formulated as it should be. Take, for instance, Bever's (1970) example:

(6.23)   The horse raced past the barn fell.

If, in line with one of the strategies proposed by Bever (see Section 6A), *horse* is structured as agent of *raced,* a revision will be subsequently required. Because of its local ambiguity, this sentence may therefore be judged as less acceptable than Example (6.24), in which the addition of function words obstructs this incorrect structuring (see also Fodor & Garrett (1967), who found that relative pronouns in center-embedded sentences aid comprehension):

(6.24)   The horse which was raced past the barn fell.

These behavioral effects make it possible, in principle, to test predictions based on the comprehension model. (Some very general suggestions concerning possibilities of deriving predictions from the present model are discussed in Section 10E.) The problem with obtaining empirical verification for the model is, of course, that experimental results are usually open to a variety of interpretations. There are other factors besides the need for revision (like the accessability of cues), which may affect processing difficulty and judged acceptability. Bever (1970) has discussed some factors influencing acceptability. Unfortunately, the native speaker–hearer is not always able to state the reasons for the unacceptability of a given sentence (Schlesinger, 1968, p. 125).

It has been assumed so far that the speaker's I-marker is retrieved by the hearer in its entirety. However, a certain degree of comprehension can be achieved without complete retrieval of the I-marker: due to motivational factors or load of processing, the hearer may restrict himself to retrieving only part of it. This will occur particularly often in reading, where we may distil the gist of the message and neglect other parts of it. Which parts will be retrieved may again be determined by differential saliency, either of various parts of the input string or of various aspects of the I-marker. Thus, the above mentioned findings of Moore (1972) make it plausible that, on certain occasions, after the agent and goal are retrieved the structuring process may terminate – and the attributes not be retrieved.

Alternatively, expectations raised in the course of analyzing an utterance may be so powerful that instead of issuing directives for complementing, the missing element is supplied by guesswork. Guessing and complementing by further analysis of the text are two extremes; processes combining both to differing degrees are also possible. Even larger portions of the I-marker may be supplied by guessing. This is presumably what often happens when one scans a line in reading: much of what fails to be taken in perceptually and processed may be filled in by the reader on the basis of his expectations. Eliptical utterances capitalize on this ability of the reader and hearer to obtain "closure."

Of course, one may guess wrong. Then there will be no identity between the speaker's and the hearer's I-markers. This will be a case of failure in comprehension, just like those which occur when, for some reason or other, an error is made in structuring or coalescing. Of greater interest than such errors is the possibility that the speaker's and hearer's I-markers may differ, but communication is not impeded, because their I-markers, while not identical, in some sense "mean" the same thing. In fact, it can be shown that there is no way of finding out whether the I-markers of the communicants are identical, because by every possible operational test the message may have been conveyed perfectly. Let us see why this is so.

Consider the lexical look-up of words (see Section 2E). A protoverbal element may be lexicalized either as a single word or, at times, as a string lexicalization, and for some I-marker constituents there are compact lexicalizations of one word. Where a compact lexicalization is possible, there will be no way to determine for a single word in the utterance whether it resulted from the lexicalization of a single protoverbal element or not. The same holds for string lexicalizations, where these are possible. It may therefore happen that the lexical look-up of, say, *youngster* retrieves a single protoverbal element whereas the speaker used this word to realize an I-marker constituent, (ATTRIBUTE young, man), or vice versa. On the other hand, *young man* may lead to the retrieval of this I-marker constituent, whereas for the speaker this was a string lexicalization of a single protoverbal element, or vice versa. Obviously, no misunderstanding can develop from such a change. But while for all intents and purposes the I-markers will stand for the same meanings, they are not identical.

Another reason why the I-markers of the hearer and the speaker need not be identical is that there may be some individual differences between hearer and speaker in the way they assign words to protoverbal elements. Differences in idiolects may lead to some residual ambiguity at the lexical level. This, however, is of little theoretical interest (and usually also of little practical import), unlike the structural "ambiguity" discussed below.

As pointed out in Section 1A, the boundaries of the uttered sentence do not necessarily coincide with the I-marker boundaries: an I-marker may at times be realizable either as a compound or complex sentence or as a number of sentences. Likewise, the boundaries of the I-marker(s) retrieved in the structuring process do not necessarily correspond to those underlying the input sentence. Hearing an utterance of a number of sentences may lead to their structurings being coalesced into one I-marker. Alternatively, the utterance of each sentence may be coalesced into a separate I-marker. In neither case is there a way of knowing whether the speaker started out with a complex I-marker or with a number of I-markers.

To illustrate, consider the following sentences, which were among those used in an experiment by Bransford and Franks (1971):

(6.25) The ants were in the kitchen.

(6.26) The jelly was on the table.

(6.27) The ants ate the sweet jelly.

(6.28) The ants in the kitchen ate the sweet jelly which was on the table.

These authors found that when subjects heard, among others, Examples (6.25)–(6.27) but not Example (6.28), they were likely to recognize the last sentence incorrectly as one already heard before. Bransford and Franks conclude from this that it is not the individual sentences which are stored in memory but "holistic" ideas. In terms of the present framework: on hearing Examples (6.25)–(6.27), structurings might have been coalesced until the complex I-marker underlying Example (6.28) was formed. When Example (6.28) was heard, its I-marker was retrieved and compared to the stored I-marker, and hence the sentence was incorrectly recognized.[6]

Extrapolating from this to a communicative situation, a person who utters Examples (6.25)–(6.27) in succession may have started out from three different I-markers. Alternatively, he may have had one I-marker in mind—the one underlying Example (6.28) – or perhaps an I-marker on which both Examples (6.25) and (6.26) are based and another one for Example (6.27), and so on. Hence, if the hearer retrieves from Examples (6.25)–(6.27) the I-marker which also underlies Example (6.28), he may arrive at an I-marker identical with that of the speaker, or else at one which means the same as two or three of his I-markers.

This description assumes that processing does not respect the sentence boundary. There is some experimental evidence to the contrary: that the sentence, and to some extent the clause, is a processing unit (Jarvella & Herman, 1972). To the

---

[6] This is not the whole story, however, because *The ants ate the jelly which was on the table* was also incorrectly recognized. Apparently the fact that a single complex I-marker may be retrieved from utterances of several sentences is taken into account by subjects, who therefore recognize any sentence derived from a constituent of the stored complex I-marker.

extent that this will prove to be a general phenomenon, an explanation of the above findings in terms of the cognitive structures retrieved by the hearer will be indicated. (Such a possibility is discussed in Section 7B.)

6E. THE ROLE OF SURFACE STRUCTURE

The structuring process described above does not assume that surface structures are retrieved. Instead, as assumed in the theory of perceptual strategies and in some computer programs, deep structure is inferred directly from cues in the input string. The possibility that phrase structure boundaries are disregarded is left open. For instance, one word of the main noun phrase and one word of the verb phrase may first be structured as agent and action, and other words belonging to the noun phrase enter only subsequently into structurings, which then coalesce with the AGENT–ACTION structuring (and similarly for the verb phrase).

On the other hand, there is nothing in the present view to preclude taking into account constituent structure in comprehension. For instance, in analyzing a sentence, intonation and pauses (punctuation in the written text) may first be attended to, and the division into two major constituents indicated thereby may be utilized in the subsequent structuring process. One way of viewing this procedure would be as of a (AGENT–ACTION a,b) structuring in which a and b are not words, as in Example (6.6), but whole segments of the input string to be replaced later by a fine-grain analysis. One can demonstrate that as the division of the sentence into constituents becomes more salient and easily accessible, comprehension is facilitated (see the studies quoted in Schlesinger, 1968, pp. 26–27, 43; Graf & Torrey, 1966). Phrase structure boundaries may thus serve as clues to deep structure relations. Note, however, that surface structure is not accorded thereby an independent status in the comprehension model: it is the I-marker relations and not the surface structure which is retrieved, and the surface string merely provides necessary clues to the former.

At first blush this approach appears to be refuted by the large bulk of psycholinguistic research allegedly demonstrating the "psychological reality" of surface structures. On closer examination, however, these findings turn out to be quite compatible with our proposal. In many of the experiments sentences were employed in which surface structure was congruent with deep structure. The investigators opted for what seemed at the time the more conservative interpretation, that their findings showed the behavioral effect of constituent structure. But in fact the effect could just as well have been due to deep structure. In a sense, therefore, the attempts, rampant in the sixties, to prove the psychological reality of constructs of transformational grammar were premature. A grammar is not in itself a performance model (though some psycholinguists at the time may have fondly hoped that in the end it would turn out to be one, thus sparing us the labor of model building). In the absence of a serious proposal for a performance model there were therefore no constructs whose psychological reality was actually worthwhile demonstrating.

Consider now those studies which show that a difference in surface structure affects comprehension even though the deep structures of the sentences involved are identical. Trabasso (1972), for instance, found such an effect on sentence classification; the subjects (agents) being identified faster in active sentences, and the object (goal) in passive ones.[7] What studies like this seem to show is that the arrangement of elements in the input strings may make a difference in comprehension. Naturally so, because certain arrangements make these elements more accessible to the structuring process than others. Thus, Example (6.29), which violates Rosenbaum's (1967) "minimal distance principle" — according to which the subject of the complement verb (here: *to leave*) is that noun phrase which most closely precedes it — may be expected to be in some way more difficult to structure than Example (6.30), which accords with this principle:

(6.29)   John promised Bill to leave.

(6.30)   John told Bill to leave.

As far as language acquisition is concerned, at least, complexity as predicted from the "minimal distance principle" has been shown to be an important factor (C. Chomsky, 1969). At times an arrangement of elements in the surface string may even lead to structurings which are incorrect and must later be revised (particularly when not all the relevant cues are attended to at the moment of processing). The importance of accessibility is dramatically illustrated in the case of multiply center-embedded sentences, like Example (6.31), in which the discontinuity of phrases is such that action terms cannot be easily matched with the agent terms to which they belong (Schlesinger, 1968, Chapters 5 and 6, 1975b).

(6.31)   This is the boy, that the man, whom the lady, which our
          friend saw, knows, hit.

As for storage in memory, there is experimental evidence that the sentence content or deep structure tends to be retained, and the surface form of the sentence to be discarded (Sachs, 1967). To the extent that the latter is also remembered, this does not imply that surface structure has been retrieved, but merely that the string of words has been partly remembered as such (James, Thompson, & Baldwin, 1973; but see Section 7A of this volume for an alternative explanation). Occasionally, word strings may be remembered even when I-marker relations are forgotten. This was found in an experiment by Roberts

---

[7] Note, however, that the deep structure of a passive sentence is held by some to differ from that of the corresponding active one (Katz & Postal, 1964).

(Martin, Roberts, & Collins, 1968) in which active and passive sentences had to be recalled. In some of the cases where subjects erroneously recalled an active sentence as a passive one or vice versa, the original position of the two noun phrases (those corresponding to the agent and goal terms) was retained. In other words, the meaning of these sentences was not recalled correctly, but some of their surface characteristics were.

Recent research findings on the effect of surface and deep structure are therefore compatible with the present approach, according to which I-marker relations are retrieved directly by means of structural cues without the mediation of surface structure. This is also in line with the findings of Martin (1970; see, however, Bond & Gray, 1973, for some reservations), that subjective constituents (those obtained by subjects' judgments) do not invariably coincide with grammatical constituents. Such judgments can obviously be made only after the utterance has been processed, and they may consequently be regarded as indicative of what occurs in processing.[8]

In apparent contradiction to the present position are findings by Olson and Filby (1972). These authors propose a model for the comparison of sentences and pictures. Their basic assumption is that in this task the surface forms of the sentences are compared, and not their deep structures. An alternative account of the comparison process is possible, however, which fits their findings equally well. This assumes that the more salient part of the I-marker is operative in the comparison process. As shown in Section 1D, there is independent support for the notion of differences between aspects of the I-marker in saliency, and hence availability for processing. The Olson—Filby model and my alternative proposal are discussed in Appendix A.

Olson and Filby also report on another experiment in which they measured the time it takes subjects to answer questions about the agent of an action (*Who hit?*) and its goal (*Who was hit?*). Each question was followed by a sentence containing the answer. They found questions about the agent to be answered more quickly when followed by an active sentence, whereas the reverse was true for questions about the goal of the action, which were answered more quickly when followed by passive sentences. Olson and Filby go on to argue that this finding is inexplicable on the assumption that comprehension involves retrieval of a subject—verb—object deep structure. Their finding can be explained, however, on the basis of the assumption made in their verification model that surface forms of the sentence are activated: when the surface structure of question and answer are similar, processing is facilitated. Like the results of their comparison

---

[8] Thorne (1968, p. 383) has remarked that in computer simulation it has been found inefficient to get first at surface structure and from there at deep structure. Recent computer models in fact reconstruct deep structures directly (Anderson & Bower, 1973; Winograd, 1972).

experiments, these findings have an alternative explanation based on differential saliency of various I-marker aspects. In an active sentence the agent is focused on (see Section 4A), and hence such a sentence provides a ready answer to the question about the agent. By contrast, the passive form serves to make the goal of the action salient, and hence sentences of this form provide a more easily available answer to questions about the goal of the action.

In their question–answer experiment Olson and Filby replicated a previous experiment by Wright (1969) with a somewhat different procedure. The explanation of Wright's findings may lie along similar lines (see however Wright, 1972, for a discussion of some other factors, which may have brought about her results).

SUMMARY

Just as production of an utterance cannot be the result of applying a rule to the I-marker as a whole, so comprehension is not the result of applying a rule to the utterance as a whole. Rather, comprehension results from a convergence of a number of operations carried out on segments of the utterance or units of analysis. The sequence in which these units are processed depends on their relative saliency and on the results of previous processing, which may instigate an active search.

Discussed in this chapter have been those operations which are based on our knowledge of the language, that is, structuring. Structuring employs the structural cues in the utterance – grammatical category (which may have to be retrieved by a lexical look-up), word order, function words, and so on – to retrieve I-marker relations. This may be done by applying realization rules in reverse, but other "rules" of the language may also be evoked (rules like "an animate noun at the beginning of the sentence is likely to be the agent"). Structuring is thus not constrained to retracing the speaker's steps. The result of the structuring process is also called structuring. A structuring may be either simple or complex, lacunal or not. Structurings coalesce into progressively larger units, until the complete I-marker may be retrieved. There can be no assurance that the I-marker retrieved from a given utterance is identical to that from which the speaker produced this utterance, even though for all intents and purposes the hearer may be said to have understood him correctly.

The structural cues on which this process is based are probabilistic, and each structuring has a subjective probability value attached to it. While it is usually far from certain that any individual structuring is correct, the concerted operation of all structurings normally leads to a high-probability construal. This results from the copious supply of structural cues, which makes a large number of structurings possible, and these may cancel or reinforce each other. Further, incorrect structurings are likely to be detected at some stage in the coalescing process.

The redundancy of cues may enable the hearer to comprehend an utterance under suboptimal conditions in which the cues available to him have been impoverished. Another important feature of the process which sets off the effects of (both external and internal) "noise" is its great flexibility: there are many different sequences of operations that can be employed.

7

Retrieval of Communicative Considerations and Cognitive Structures

7A. RETRIEVAL OF COMMUNICATIVE CONSIDERATIONS

Comprehension involves not only retrieving the speaker's I-markers but also his communicative considerations. The hearer is aware of whether the speaker is promising or threatening, asking a question or asserting, whether a given adjective is used for attribution or for predication (see Chapter 4), and so on. Evidence for the retention of communicative considerations in memory has been obtained by Jarvella and Collas (1974). They found that their subjects remembered not only the propositional content of a sentence like Example (7.1), but also whether it was said as an expression of thanks or sarcastically:

(7.1) How kind you are!

But how is the retrieval of communicative considerations achieved?

In Section 6C, we have seen that there are two kinds of structurings. One kind of structuring utilizes realization rules, applying them in reverse. Realization rules may have shunting markers associated with them, which indicate the communicative consideration they express (see Section 4A). When a structuring is effected by means of a realization rule, the shunting marker is registered, and the communicative consideration is thus retrieved. This applies to communicative considerations expressed by the choice of relation rules, intonation rules or by the choice of the appropriate lexicalization.

There are other structurings, however, which do not make use of structural cues provided by realization rules. Now, due to the redundancy in structural cues, it is possible, in principle, that the I-marker is retrieved without resorting to those realization rules that are furnished with the relevant shunting markers, and, hence, some communicative considerations may be missed. Such incomplete retrieval may occur. But there is still another possibility of procuring shunting markers. After the I-marker has been retrieved, the hearer may vicariously reproduce the utterance, utilizing, among other realization rules, also those which were circumvented in the comprehension process. By evoking the latter, the hearer finds the shunting marker and its corresponding communicative considerations.

There are also certain paralinguistic cues which serve as a clue to communicative considerations. Hesitations, halting speech, and the speaker's averting his eyes, for instance, although they are not the outcome of any realization rules, may give his intentions away. In fact, these paralinguistic cues may at times permit the retrieval of certain communicative considerations without retrieving the I-marker at all. The same can be said of the intonation contour (which is the result of applying a certain type of realization rules): one may, for instance, note that the speaker is asking a question or issuing a command without understanding the content of what he says.

The context in which an utterance is made may also serve as a clue to the speaker's communicative considerations. Thus, uttering a declarative sentence (*It's cold here.*) when the hearer is in a position to do something about the situation referred to (if he is near the open window) may be construed as a request; otherwise it may be taken as a complaint.

We have seen (Section 6E) that the surface form of a sentence occasionally may be remembered in addition to its content. Note now that this does not necessarily require that the surface form of the sentence itself is remembered: even when this is not the case, the surface form can be reconstructed by means of the retained I-marker and the communicative consideration, which together determine the utterance completely.

7B. RETRIEVAL OF COGNITIVE STRUCTURES

The hearer will retrieve not only the I-marker and communicative considerations but also, at least to some extent, the speaker's cognitive structure. We commonly do not rest content with understanding the literal meaning of an utterance but ask ourselves, "What did he mean by that?" And even when this question does not consciously come to mind, the answer may do so. Suppose someone says:

(7.2) I never eat Chinese food *with chopsticks.*

We will take this as meaning that he does eat Chinese food, though not with chopsticks. But note that this has not been stated explicitly. It is what Leech (1974, pp. 294–323), from whom this example is taken, calls an "expectation": the hearer is led to expect that the speaker sometimes eats Chinese food. Similarly in Example (7.3), another example by Leech, there is an expectation that some old-age pensioners do play football:

(7.3) Few old-age pensioners play football.

But this is not logically implied by Example (7.3). The speaker might add, for instance, *maybe none of them do* without contradicting himself. The expectation is not part of the I-marker but rather part of what was presumably in the speaker's cognitive structure.

A study by Kintsch and Monk (1972) reveals an effect of retrieving cognitive structures. In three experiments, subjects read either one of two parallel passages which conveyed the same meaning. Inspection of the examples quoted shows that the I-markers were not the same. Rather, the paraphrastic relationship between the sentences seems to have been due to their originating from identical or closely similar cognitive structures. The sentences differed in degree of complexity. In the complex version, the whole paragraph was formulated as one long sentence by means of subordination of clauses. After reading each paragraph, subjects were asked a question, the answer to which could be inferred from the paragraph. The questions on complex paragraphs did not take longer to respond to than questions on simple paragraphs. The reason seems to be that the cognitive structures retrieved by the subjects were identical for the two versions, and that the inferences were made from the cognitive structures.

Supplying missing links is another aspect of retrieval of cognitive structure. Consider the following newspaper story:

(7.4)   A burning cigarette was carelessly discarded. The fire destroyed
        many acres of virgin forest.

Reading this we immediately understand that the discarded cigarette started the fire. This is nowhere mentioned explicitly in Example (7.4), and was thus not in the writer's I-marker. But this information presumably did figure in the writer's cognitive structure, and it is crucial for getting the full import of the message that we obtain it. As Collins and Quillian (1972) remark, "How fully a person understands a sentence – or any experience he has – depends on how much stored information he applies to it [p. 119]." In this case, he must apply his knowledge of the fire-starting properties of burning cigarettes. (This subject matter is developed in the following chapters, which deal with the effect of our knowledge of the world on the comprehension process.)

In a study by Kintsch (1974, Chapter 8), from whom the above example is taken, it was found that after more than a 15-min delay, subjects could verify the implicit information (that the cigarette started the fire) as fast as explicitly stated information. After a shorter time interval, however, subjects reacted faster to explicitly presented information. Apparently, subjects stored the I-marker, or perhaps even certain aspects of the input string, for several minutes, and this facilitated the access to the explicitly presented information. Thereafter, memory for the I-marker and surface form deteriorates and only the cognitive structure (the "gist" of the passage) is retained. In the retained structure, the explicit and implicit information are stored in the same way, and this accounts for why they were responded to equally fast after 15 min.

In making such spontaneous inferences one is presumably assisted by the imagery evoked by the utterance. On hearing Example (7.5), an image of the spatial relationships between the turtles, the log and the fish may be evoked:

(7.5)   Three turtles rested on a floating log and a fish
        swam beneath them.

Bransford, Barclay and Franks (1972) found that subjects who were presented with sentences like Example (7.5) later falsely recognized sentences that were "potential inferences" from them, like

(7.6)   Three turtles rested on a floating log and a fish
        swam beneath it.

Several investigators have since obtained similar findings with sentences involving spatial relationships, both with adult subjects (Barclay, 1973; Potts, 1972) and with children (Paris & Carter, 1973; Paris & Mahoney, 1974). The "semantic integration" effect, as it has been called, has not only been demonstrated for material involving transitive relations, as was the case in the above studies, but for other relations as well. Bransford and Franks (1972) showed that if a passive sentence without an agent (without *by*-phrase) appears in a passage, and the identity of the agent is revealed elsewhere in it, the agent tends to be included in the sentence in recall. Similar results were obtained with children as subjects (Barclay & Reid, 1974). Olson (1972, pp. 156–164) discusses at length inferences made by children and adults in the performance of various tasks (such as, from "*A* is on top of *B*" to "*B* is under *A*"; but see also Appendix A).

In Section 6D, a study by Bransford and Franks (1971) was discussed in which several sentences bearing on a single event – like Examples (6.25) (6.27) – were presented. Subsequently, subjects falsely recognized a sentence in which the information in the individual sentences was combined, Example (6.28). The explanation proposed in Section 6D was that subjects retrieve a single I-marker from the several sentences. In the light of the above it seems also possible that the integration took place in the course of constructing the cognitive structure. In fact, Singer and Rosenberg (1973), who replicated these results, found evidence that the effect was partly due to the central idea of the text being better retained in memory. They conclude therefore that the hearer is ". . . not only integrating but also pruning or emphasizing portions of the received information [p. 283]."

Of special interest is a study by Honeck (1973), who found that recall of proverbs is facilitated when their interpretations are heard along with them, as when Example (7.7) is followed by Example (7.8):

(7.7)   Wealth is an oil which lubricates the machines of life.

(7.8)   Wealth is likely to contribute to the longevity and well-being
        of those who have it.

Honeck suggested that this was due to both being stored in a "common conceptual base." That the latter is apparently even more abstract than is indicated by the above studies is shown by there being much less lexical overlap between the proverb and its interpretation than between, for instance, Examples (7.5) and (7.6). In another study on semantic integration in children (Paris, 1975) there was also minimal lexical overlap between presented and inferred material.

There is a problem, however, in the interpretation of the above experiment. As pointed out in Section 5E, the form in which information is coded may be task dependent. Semantic integration could have been effected for the purpose of storage in memory and making inferences some time after comprehension has been achieved. In the case of Honeck's experiment, this explanation does not seem to be very plausible, but is there any concrete evidence that integration occurs at the time of comprehension? One of the findings in the above-mentioned experiment by Kintsch seems to point in this direction. Kintsch (1974, Chapter 8) found, as expected, a higher rate of error (response of "false" to a sentence which in fact was true) for implicit material, which had to be inferred from a text like Example (7.4), than for explicit material (which shows that retrieval from the I-marker is easier than subsequent inference from it). But unlike response latencies, which changed over time, error rates for both explicit and implicit material did not increase with delay interval, and after 30 sec, 20 min, and 48 hr they were not significantly higher than in the no-delay condition. This is regarded by Kintsch (1974) as evidence that the inference was made during reading rather than at the time of retrieval and "once that [inferred] proposition is stored in memory it is treated like all other propositions [p. 173]."

In order to go beyond the I-marker and reconstruct the speaker's cognitive structure, the hearer presumably tries to put himself into the speaker's place. The question 'What did he mean by that?' is turned into the question 'What would I have meant by that if I were in his place?' with the success of the venture depending on our ability to imagine what is hidden behind the phrase 'if I were in his place'. Often our search is made easier by rules-of-thumb learned by experience, like: 'If A says B in situation C, this shows that he . . .' or 'You know what Daddy means when he says . . .'. (The additional possibility of retrieving the speaker's cognitive structure directly and not via the I-marker is discussed in Sections 9A and 10D.)

But even with these strategies, it is unlikely that the hearer will always arrive at a cognitive structure which is the exact replica of the speaker's. Considering that there is a vast set of unique relations that can possibly figure in cognitive structures and that these are classified into a much smaller set of I-marker relations (see Section 5E), the recovery of the exact cognitive relations from the I-marker can often be problematic. For most purposes an approximate fit between the original cognitive structure and the one retrieved is all that is required. However, failure to arrive at a more faithful reproduction of cognitive structures seems to lie behind much of the talk about people who, though they succeed in conveying to each other the literal meaning of the message, do not "really" understand each other.

SUMMARY

The hearer retrieves from the utterance not only the I-marker but also the speaker's communicative considerations and cognitive structure. Communicative considerations may be retrieved by registering the shunting markers of the realization rules used to produce the utterance, and by attending to various paralinguistic and contextual clues. In retrieving cognitive structures we go beyond the utterance and make inferences as to what was presumably in the speaker's mind. These inferences do not make use of linguistic rules, but rather of knowledge of the world.

8
Factual Knowledge

In the two preceding chapters comprehension was treated as if it takes place in a semantic void. Our view of this process has been as if it were based entirely on structural cues inherent in the utterance, and no attention was paid to factors often loosely referred to as "semantic." The role of semantics in the comprehension of utterances is the subject of the remaining chapters.

8A. THE CHANGING PLACE OF SEMANTICS

Not so long ago psycholinguistic research was preoccupied with syntactic processes, with semantics falling into comparative neglect. Psycholinguists were in accord with the Zeitgeist then prevailing in linguistics, where semantics was regarded as a somewhat disreputable poor relative. The book which marked the advent of the transformationalist school, *Syntactic Structures* (Chomsky, 1957), similarly accorded to semantics a subsidiary role. Those concerned with sentence comprehension, largely under the influence of the transformationalists, followed suit and viewed the problem of decoding as one of specifying the operations by which the syntactic structure of sentences is computed from the input string. It seems to have been tacitly assumed, or hoped, that semantics plays only a minor role, which could be clarified, subsequently.

But time and again in the psycholinguistic lab, the processing of utterances reared its semantic head. Miller and Isard (1963) found that sentences that violated semantic constraints were less intelligible than normal sentences, when heard with masking noise. A similar effect has been obtained with a variety of learning tasks (Forster & Ryder, 1971; Marks & Miller, 1964; Slamecka, 1969; Wang, 1970; see also Tejirian, 1968). About the time these results began to be published, Chomsky revised his syntactic theory and incorporated into it much of what had up until then been regarded as falling outside the scope of syntax.

In the standard transformational theory, a component was postulated which provides the semantic interpretation of deep structure. Against this school of "interpretive semantics," the "generative semanticists" argued that deep structure is semantic in the first place. Another important semantic function is relegated in the Chomskyan model to selection restrictions. Whereas in *Syntactic Structures* the by now proverbial "colorless green ideas sleep furiously" was regarded as fully grammatical, the *Aspects* model (Chomsky, 1965) blocked the generation of such sentences by means of selection restrictions. The sentences employed in the above psycholinguistic studies were similarly "anomalous," and the obtained effect could therefore be accounted for, according to the new model, within the framework of grammar. The comprehension of sentences could be assumed to proceed along lines laid down by the grammar, with the consequence that anomalous sentences which violate selection restrictions were predicted to be more difficult to handle.

These changes in linguistic theory made it appear that comprehension of utterances might ultimately be explained entirely on the basis of the hearer's internalized knowledge of grammar. But this is not so. As shown below, there are processes in comprehension based on knowledge not formalizable by a grammar.

8B. KNOWLEDGE OF RULES AND FACTUAL KNOWLEDGE

Consider what usually happens when an experienced reader reads an easy text. Rather than perusing each word, he focuses on certain words which suggest the meaning. Thus, the following words might "stand out" in reading a sentence:

(8.1) girl − threatened − blazing − flames − enabled − firemen − escape − window

These words suggest a story, like that told in the following sentence from which they are taken:

(8.2) The girl was threatened by the blazing flames, but was enabled
       by the firemen to escape through the window.

Note now the following two types of information about relations between words which can be extracted from Example (8.2) and presumably also from Example (8.1):

(a) Flames threatened the girl (and not the girl threatened flames).

(b) The girl escaped through the window (and not the firemen).

Quite different relations seem to hold in a list which is similar to Example (8.1) in that it includes words of the same grammatical categories and in the same sequence:

(8.3) gangster – waved – blazing – torch – compelled – sheriff – escape – jail

We at once infer a different pattern of relations:

(a′) Unlike in Example (a) above, the gangster was waving the torch (and not the torch the gangster).

(b′) Unlike in Example (b) above, the gangster escaped from jail (and not the sheriff).

A sentence which Example (8.3) is culled from might be:

(8.4) The gangster waved a blazing torch, and compelled the sheriff to let him escape from jail.

There is a fundamental difference between (a) and (a′) on the one hand, and (b) and (b′), on the other. The incorrect interpretation that the girl threatened the flames is ruled out by selection restrictions in Example (8.2): the object of *threaten* must be animate. Likewise, in Example (8.4) the knowledge that a torch cannot wave a gangster is formalized by selection restrictions. While (a) and (a′) thus follow from rules of the grammar, things are different with (b) and (b′). We are inclined to believe that the fireman helped the trapped girl to escape rather than vice versa, and we expect gangsters, but not sheriffs, to escape from jail. Knowledge of the world thus builds up strong expectations which will serve us in the comprehension of utterances. On the other hand, once an utterance is comprehended it may add to our store of knowledge, which will be capable of feeding into subsequent attempts at comprehending utterances. When such a subsequent attempt takes place immediately, we say that comprehension is aided by the linguistic context.

The role of knowledge of the world in comprehension has long been recognized. Schleichert (1971) and Schank (1972, pp. 591–592) accord such knowledge a place in their comprehension models, and Winograd (1972; see Section 6A) incorporates knowledge of a miniature "world" in a computer simulation of comprehension. Schleichert and Winograd, however, treat knowledge of the world as if it operated on an all-or-none basis; certain occurrences are either possible or impossible. This is quite appropriate for a program like Winograd's which has the objective of dealing with a very limited "world" of blocks, where the constraints operating are few and well defined. In the real world, however, inferences have to be based on probabilistic knowledge. There is nothing inherently incorrect in a sentence which runs counter to this knowledge. Thus,

Example (8.1) must have been taken from Example (8.5), which, though somewhat improbable, is perfectly acceptable:

(8.5) The girl, though threatened by the blazing flames,
enabled the firemen to escape through the window.

It is quite conceivable that Example (8.5) may occur in a story (say, about unlucky trapped firemen) in which it does not sound in any way peculiar. Or we may know the girl in question to be such that Example (8.5) is not out of keeping with her character. Observe also how our expectations would change if in Example (8.2) the first few words would be:

(8.6) The girl was emboldened by her previous success . . .

The things we know affect the way we read.

Our knowledge of the world, then, and situational and contextual cues lead to inferences which influence the process of comprehension (see also Rommetveit, 1968). Knowledge of the world and the knowledge emanating from situational and contextual cues is referred to below as FACTUAL KNOWLEDGE. The problem to be dealt with here is how factual knowledge is employed in interpreting an utterance; in which form it is stored and by means of which rules it is employed in making inferences about the speaker's intentions. We note in passing that (as shown in Section 7B) such inference making is part of the retrieval of cognitive structure, not of the I-marker. The implications of this are developed in the next chapter.

If it were possible to formalize factual knowledge by means of grammatical rules, it might be feasible to explain its effects on comprehension by a modified account of the structuring process, in which provision would be made for structural cues based on selection restrictions. However, as inferred above, while some factual knowledge can be formalized by grammatical rules — more specifically, by selection restrictions — there is factual knowledge which is in principle not formalizable within a grammar.[1] As stated, there are certain expectations — like those giving rise to the inferences (b) and (b') above — which do not exclude an interpretation but only diminish its plausibility. Selection restrictions, by contrast, are currently formalized in deterministic terms.

One might propose to amend the format of selection restrictions and provide for probabilistic rules, which would include also expectations like the above. But

[1] It is important to note that the crucial distinction here is not between "syntactic" and "semantic" (in fact, the boundary line between these is becoming increasingly blurred in current linguistic theorizing), but rather between what is taken care of by the internalized grammar, and what is not. The reintroduction of semantics into the grammar in the more recent transformationalist models seems to have engendered some terminological confusion. In fact, psycholinguists have continued to use the term "semantic" indiscriminately both for what comes within the purview of the grammar as well as for what does not.

this would be precluded in any case because, as pointed out by Katz and Fodor (1963; see also Chafe, 1970, pp. 84–86), a grammar cannot aspire to formalize everything we know about the world, due to the sheer amount of information involved. Because of this problem, one of the most ambitious attempts to deal with the use of knowledge in making inferences about the information presented in the text also seems in danger of foundering. The attempt is by Schank, whose semantic representations ("conceptualizations") have been discussed in Section 5E. Here we will be concerned only with his proposal for an inference mechanism (Schank & Rieger, 1973).

In analyzing a sentence, Schank and Rieger's program extracts information which is only implicit in the text, regarding the cause and result of an action and the expected future and past actions of the persons involved. Evidently, these are the kinds of inferences which are useful in analyzing a text on the basis of partial cues – as in Examples (8.1) and (8.3). The authors make the important point that these inferences are probabilistic, and not necessarily true. As we have seen, this seems to hold for those inferences we continuously make in reading a text. Schank and Rieger discuss the following example:

(8.7)   John hit Mary.

From this the program extracts, among other things, the information that the instrument of hitting was John's hand, since no other instrument is mentioned. Knowledge of what normally occurs in the world is also brought to bear on the sentence: the probable result of what occurs in Example (8.7) is that Mary was hurt; the probable cause, that John was annoyed. Finally, the program makes predictions as to how Mary will react and what made John angry.

Schank and Rieger are the first to take these aspects into account in simulating human performance. However, while complimenting them for facing this problem squarely, one may entertain doubts as to whether they are really on the right track to solving it. Consider for instance what is required to infer the results of Example (8.7). If John is a baby, it certainly does not follow that Mary is hurt, and if John is three, five, or seven years old the probability of her getting hurt increases correspondingly. Now, differences of probability are taken into account by Schank and Rieger, who make provisions for different "strengths" of inference. But the really serious problem, which they do not discuss, is the amount of information that has to be stored. They do mention that the "measure of the amount of injury done is a function of the hardness, heaviness, sharpness, etc. of the propelled object [with which one hits], and of the particular body part hit (Schank & Rieger, 1973, p. 39)." But by granting this they conjure up a host of data, and one fails to see how they are going to cope with it.

The magnitude of the problem becomes even more apparent with the following consideration. To be really useful in constraining the range of choices in the comprehension process, the program must access information on all the elements involved in the situation which the utterance is about. What, for instance, would be likely candidates for the slot indicated in Example (8.8)?

(8.8) John shattered the ____ with his fist.

Consider only the following sample of candidates: *windowpane, table, wall, book, bike, mountain range.* What would be the probability of each of these? In addition, an indefinitely large set of actors would have to be taken into account: note what happens when one replaces *John* with, for example, *the baby.* And what if one replaces *with his fist* with *with a grenade, with an atom bomb,* or *with a pencil?* This information cannot be stored (as selection restrictions currently are) under individual words (*windowpane, table, wall,* and so on). Instead, it is necessary to state which phrases can occur in each other's vicinity. For each of the phrases: *shatter the dyke, dent the car, scratch the windowpane, cut the loaf, kill the elephant;* it would be necessary to state whether they can combine with each of the following: *with a rusty sword, with a toy grenade, with a plastic letter opener, with a sharp letter opener made of steel,* and so on.

The amount of relevant knowledge thus assumes such vast dimensions that one wonders how it can be dealt with by any sort of rules, whether these are rules of a grammar (selection restrictions) or rules incorporated in a computer program. There is simply not enough storage space for every single piece of information, and even if there were, a lifetime would not suffice to record each one and store it in memory.

And yet, humans do have access to all this information. Hardly anyone has probably ever had experience with a rusty sword scratching a windowpane, or with most of the other possible combinations indicated by the above phrases. But most of the time we have a fairly definite notion about the feasibility of perpetrating these or any other acts of aggression. Since such knowledge cannot have been stored, it must be computed — we do not know how — from other items of stored knowledge. If our understanding in this area is to make any progress, we must first rid ourselves of the view of knowledge being stored as if in a set of complex tables, perhaps with hierarchically arranged column headings, in which each piece of information has first to be entered in order to be later retrievable. We are perpetually called on to procure new information that we have had no occasion to store and, moreover, is much more finely graded than is suggested by the metaphor of the table. A more suitable simile would be that of a slide rule or a complicated nomogram which permit information to be read off from a continuous scale. Knowledge is available in analogue, not in digital, form.

No less formidable than the problem of storing and accessing information is that of ways this information is used in comprehension. Here a beginning has been made by Charniak (1972) in exploring the complexities of making inferences from factual knowledge. His research strategy is to concentrate on a small "microworld" of knowledge around one subject matter, like piggy banks, and to study the processes required for applying this knowledge in understanding children's stories. The body of knowledge about piggy banks which may be relevant in understanding such stories is relatively easy to state – Charniak takes 22 sentences to do so, and he is well aware that there are other areas where the organization of the requisite knowledge is bound to raise yet unsolved problems (Charniak 1972, p. 252).

Apparently, then, we are still very far from a formalization of the kind of inference making that goes on in the course of comprehension. Needless to say, this does not entitle us to rest content with taking care of structuring processes, like those in Chapter 6, in the hope that processes based on factual knowledge will take care of themselves. In the next chapter I discuss the little that can be said about the latter processes at the present stage, and in the final chapter I suggest how they may mesh with structuring processes. But first we must substantiate the claim that factual knowledge is indeed operative in comprehension. Examples (8.1)–(8.4) are, after all, only anecdotal. Experimental and other evidence for the effects of factual knowledge not formalizable by selection restrictions should be examined.

8C. THE EFFECTS OF FACTUAL KNOWLEDGE

Messages can be inferred from word strings having few structural cues, as, for instance, Examples (8.1) and (8.3) above. Even if no clue is provided by word sequence, it may be possible to "get the meaning":[2]

(8.9) careless give policeman driver ticket

On the basis of our knowledge of the world we immediately infer the relations which are not even hinted at by structural cues: the driver was careless, and not the policeman; and the policeman gave the driver a ticket, and not vice versa. Note that no selection restrictions would have been violated by a sentence exhibiting other relations, such as one which states that the driver gave the policeman a ticket, and not vice versa. If we do not spontaneously construe the sentence anagram Example (8.9) in this manner, this must be due to our knowledge of the world. Presumably, a process similar to the one which operates on the above word string also arises spontaneously upon reading a sentence.

Sentence anagrams are almost devoid of structural cues; but even in "normal" utterances where there are such cues they will often be insufficient by themselves to arrive at an unambiguous interpretation. Charniak (1972) discusses the

---

[2] Strictly speaking, even Example (8.9) is not devoid of all structural cues: the suffix *less* indicates an adjective, and the suffix *er,* a noun.

processes at work with the referents of pronouns, for instance,

> (8.10)   Mother made some cookies and left one out on a plate. She
> put the plate on the kitchen table, and went into the living
> room. "I am sure Janet will like it" thought Mother. [p. 72]

There is nothing in the structure of Example (8.10) which determines that *it* refers to the cookie rather than to the last-mentioned living room (or to the plate or to the kitchen table). But due to the expectations raised by our knowledge of the world we are not even aware of this ambiguity.

Ambiguities of reference, discussed by Charniak, are not the only kind of ambiguity which requires factual knowledge for disambiguation. Consider

> (8.11)   Efficient nurses and patients were seen in the ward.

One usually construes *efficient* as an attribute of *nurses* and not of *patients*. In contrast, in Example (8.12) the participle is taken to modify both nouns, although the structure is superficially similar to that of Example (8.11):

> (8.12)   Gaily conversing nurses and patients were seen in the ward.

Apparently, there is a process based on factual knowledge steering us towards only one of the possible interpretations (see also Garrett, 1970).

There are other cases, too, in which communication is successful although structural cues alone would be insufficient. The utterances of children learning to speak at first lack inflections and most function words. Whatever the structural cues in their utterances, these would hardly ensure their being comprehended; but on the basis of situational cues such utterances are usually understood by adults (see Bloom, 1970, pp. 9–10, for discussion of an instructive example). Conversely, as Bloom (1973, pp. 55–64, 1974) has argued persuasively, children understand utterances with the help of situational cues and with very little knowledge of linguistic rules. Later, children may resort to their knowledge of the world in comprehending utterances. De Villiers and de Villiers (1972) discovered that some two- and three-year-old children find nothing wrong with a sentence with incorrect word order, whereas they judge semantically anomalous sentences as unacceptable. Similarly, Wetstone and Friedlander (1973) found that in the earlier stages of linguistic development commands and questions with distorted word order were responded to as well as those with normal word order, suggesting that these children rely predominantly on situational context rather than on word order.

Paucity of structural cues is a characteristic which child language has in common with the sign languages of the deaf. In spite of the fact that it does not mark the subject or object of the sentence by either inflection or word order, this language provides an adequate vehicle for everyday communication, presumably because of situational cues and the communicants' knowledge of the world (Schlesinger, 1971c).

When adults communicate in unfavorable conditions, the message reaching the hearer may lack part of the usual structural cues. If in spite of this the message is understood, this may be due to the effect of factual knowledge, which combats noise.

So far we have discussed cases in which, due to insufficiency of structural cues, comprehension of utterances becomes possible only with the aid of factual knowledge. One should realize that even in the standard case, in which structural cues would be adequate for successful comprehension, factual knowledge has a role to play. Everyday experience shows that it is easier to attend to a lecture when we are familiar with its subject matter, and that a text reads faster when its content is expected than when it is not. There is experimental evidence that processing may be facilitated by factual knowledge.

Rosenberg and associates have compared "semantically well integrated" sentences, like Example (8.13), with "semantically poorly integrated" ones, like Example (8.14), in a variety of experimental tasks (summarized in Rosenberg & Jarvella, 1970), and have consistently found better performance with the former:

(8.13)   The maid cleaned the house.
(8.14)   The maid bought the chair.

This finding has been replicated by both Forster (1974), who ruled out the explanation that this result may be due to guessing or some other factor, and by Engelkamp, Merdian, and Hörmann (1972).

While the content of Example (8.13) is more "expected" than that of Example (8.14), both are perfectly commonplace as compared to a bizarre sentence like:

(8.15)   Mary chewed spears throughout the corrupt talk.

In an experiment in which words were projected one after another at the rate of 16 words per sec, Forster and Ryder (1971) found such bizarre sentences to be less well comprehended than normal ones like:

(8.16)   John smoked cigars throughout the dreary play.

Subjects also took longer to decide for these bizarre sentences whether they were sensible than for more plausible ones (Forster & Olbrei, 1973). Note that, unlike anomalous sentences, in which selection restrictions are violated, Example (8.15) is grammatical. No process utilizing internalized grammatical rules can therefore explain the above influence on comprehension.[3]

Constraints due to factual knowledge are responsible also for the reversibility effect reported by Slobin (1966). He found that while passive sentences were more difficult to comprehend than active ones and the logical subject and object

---

[3] That the effect of bizarreness is not quite as simple as suggested by this study is shown by Wearing's (1970) experiment, in which "predictability" interacted with retention interval. Wearing used bizarre (but not anomalous) and normal sentences, and found that after a retention interval the former were actually better recognized.

(the agent and goal terms) were reversible, this difference largely disappeared when reversal resulted in anomalous sentences. A similar finding for another syntactic construction was obtained by Waryas and Ruder (1973). Using sentences the reversal of which resulted in implausible statements, Herriot (1969) found that these took longer to respond to than sentences which accord with expectations based on previous experience. Forster and Olbrei (1973), however, failed to replicate these reversal effects when measuring the time it took subjects to decide if a sentence was meaningful.[4]

Difficulty in comprehension may make itself felt in hesitation phenomena. Interestingly, the number of pauses, both in retelling a story and reading it out loud, was found to be greater for improbable than for probable sentences (O'Connell, Kowal, & Hörmann, 1970).

Implausibility and bizarreness, then, affect comprehension adversely. This must be due to our knowledge of the world, which we draw on in analyzing an utterance. That contextual cues also influence the comprehension process has been shown by Dooling (1972), who found comprehension time to decrease as preceding context increases. Greeno and Noreen (1974) found that expectations built up in an earlier part of a paragraph led to a decrease in reading time of a sentence, and conversely, when the content of the sentence was contrary to expectations, reading was slowed down. Similarly, Bransford and Johnson (1972) found comprehensibility ratings to be higher when subjects were provided beforehand with a picture appropriate to the passage heard. In their experiment with ambiguous sentences, Carey, Mehler, and Bever (1970) have shown that an interpretation is more likely to be seen when it accords with a picture of which the sentence is a possible description.

Knowledge of the world may be crucial to the understanding of an utterance. Thus, Example (8.17) will be considered odd, but our reaction to Example (8.18) will depend on whether or not we know that old books can be had at Foyle's:

> (8.17) I will buy either a new book or one at a bookstore.
> (8.18) I will buy either a new book or one at Foyle's.

Sentences of very difficult structure may be comprehensible only with the help of our knowledge of the world. Thus, center-embedded sentences like Example (8.19) have been found to be quite well understood, whereas subjects usually failed to understand sentences of a similar structure but devoid of semantic cues, like Example (8.20) (Schlesinger, 1968; Stolz, 1967):

> (8.19) This is the hole, that the rat, which our cat, whom the
>   dog bit, caught, made.

---

[4]Forster (1974) argues that these negative results were obtained with techniques more representative of the comprehension process than those of Slobin and Herriot. All one may validly conclude from their negative findings, however, is that the reversibility effect does not make itself felt when their particular techniques are employed with the very short sentences used in their experiment, which are easy to process in any case.

(8.20)   This is the boy, that the man, whom the lady, which our
         friend saw, knows, hit.

Apparently, the construction in Example (8.20) is so difficult that structuring processes are carried out only in part or not at all and the subject relies mainly or entirely on factual knowledge. This conjecture is supported by the finding that when factual knowledge suggested an interpretation running counter to that required by the syntactic structure, subjects interpreted the sentence according to the former (Schlesinger, 1968, pp. 129–135). For instance:

(8.21)   This is the hole that the rat, which our cat, whom the dog bit,
         made, caught.

This sentence says that the rat caught the hole and the cat made the rat. That seven out of eight subjects were unaware of this absurdity and interpreted Example (8.21) in the same way as Example (8.19), suggests that instead of performing the structuring process in its entirety, they fell back on an interpretation according to factual knowledge. Herriot (1969) also found such a tendency to misunderstand sentences in accordance with expectations. We may call this SEMANTIC SHORT–CIRCUITING. Normally, however, the structuring process is carried out and semantic absurdities are recognized: when structure clashes with our expectations, structure wins. Hence, bizarre sentences are recognized as such. After all, bizarre things do happen in the world, and, furthermore, we are often invited to believe that they have happened. If there were no decoding contrary to semantic cues, fairy tales would remain unintelligible.

But the balance between structure and semantics often shifts. Primary reliance on factual knowledge has been found in children learning to read (Francis, 1972). Gleitman and Gleitman (1970) presented subjects with novel compounds and found a tendency to prefer sense over structure in their interpretation, especially among the less well-educated subjects. Here, as with multiply embedded sentences, the reader is faced with unusual difficulty. At the other extreme we have the case of the reader who finds the reading material so easy that he can afford to scan it rapidly, a process which presumably involves primary reliance on factual knowledge. Finally, Engelkamp (1972) has shown that semantic factors influence the way information is stored in memory, occasionally even in conflict with structural cues.

SUMMARY

In Chapter 7, the cognitive structure of speakers was shown to be retrievable among other things, by means of inferences from what is stated explicitly. This chapter makes the point that such inferences are liable to be made continually during processing and may affect it. These inferences are based on factual knowledge: our experience of what is likely to occur in the world, tempered by the information attained from contextual and situational cues. Factual knowledge may function in the resolution of ambiguities and may enable comprehension of utterances with reduced structural cues (as in child language). In semantic short circuiting factual knowledge takes the place of all structural cues. In other cases it may facilitate comprehension. Factual knowledge cannot be captured by a rule system; hence the structuring process described in Chapter 6 does not provide for factual knowledge. There must be an additional process dealing with such knowledge. After describing this process in Chapter 9, we demonstrate in Chapter 10 how its interaction with the structuring process can explain the effects described above.

9
Semantic Matching

9A. SEMANTIC MATCHING AND ITS VARIETIES

Suppose you are shown two pictures side by side, one of a cigarette, fresh from the pack, and one of a burning lighter. Presumably you will think of the lighter being used to light the cigarette; possibly, you will have an image of the lighter approaching the cigarette. This is something which is not in the pictures you are shown, but they suggest it to you. The lighter and the cigarette seem to belong together; you supply the missing relation between them.

Suppose now that instead of pictures, you see the two words, *cigarette* and *lighter* on a page. Most likely, you will have the same experience as with the pictures: as soon as the words have been understood – that is, as soon as the protoverbal elements have been retrieved – a relation suggests itself (and an image may also be evoked). As in the case of the pictures, this does not depend on your knowledge of language but is based solely on nonlinguistic knowledge (in this case, on previous experience). This is what occurs also when one construes out of the string of words in Example (8.3) a story about escaping gangsters: relations are found which match the words.[1]

We refer to this process as SEMANTIC MATCHING. The result of this process – the relationship established between the two protoverbal elements (as between "cigarette" and "lighter") – is called a MATCHING. The above is an introspective description of what happens in semantic matching. A formulation of the rules by which semantic matching proceeds is not yet in sight (see Section 8B). However, some plausible claims may be made about the nature of the process. But first a comment is in order on a matter of definition.

---

[1] More precisely, the relation is between the concepts (or protoverbal elements) the words stand for. But here and in the following I take leave to be less punctilious and use "words" instead. Similarly, "segment" may be used for the I-marker constituent which underlies it.

Semantic matching is based entirely on factual knowledge, as defined in the previous chapter: a knowledge of what one may expect to occur in the world and knowledge based on the context and the situation. In addition to factual knowledge, linguistic knowledge may be applicable to a given utterance. Thus, in Example (8.1) the suffix of *threatened* indicates that this word is a verb, and the relative position of this word may affect the construal of the story, but by definition it is a structuring process which makes use of such cues, and not semantic matching. These two processes may interact (as shown in Chapter 10), but for analytic purposes they have to be clearly distinguished.

What are the relations which figure in semantic matching? There is no reason why these should be confined to those relations which appear in I-markers. Since semantic matching is based on factual knowledge, it may be presumed to be responsive to the whole gamut of relations the human mind can conceive of. Any one of the unique relations which can appear in a speaker's cognitive structure may also appear in the matchings arrived at by the hearer. Moreover, a matching may comprise a set of such unique relations (just as sets of relations may figure in cognitive structures; see Section 5E). Suppose the reader sees the words *tie* and *shirt.* Semantic matching may construe a connection between these, which is not very specific: the tie may be lying near the shirt or on it, or be packed together with the shirt in a suitcase, or it may just go well with the shirt. All of these relations belong to the content of the matching. If the text then is found to contain *tie with a shirt,* a more specific relation will be established, which figures in the I-markers of English; but note that the latter is arrived at by means of structural cues, such as the function word *with,* and is therefore, by definition, a structuring. This particular structuring, then, carries more information than the matching, limiting the range of relations arrived at by semantic matching.

Or consider another example:

(9.1) Cleopatra, Egypt's renowned queen, and Marc Anthony met in Alexandria.

In hearing the first two words, one may expect *Cleopatra* and *Egypt* to be related in some way: Cleopatra may fulfill a function in Egypt, or live there, etc. In other words, the matching consists of a disjunctive set of uncategorized relations (see Section 5E), and only by processing the input further will this set be delimited. It may turn out, of course, that the matching for the first two words has to be revised; for instance, if they are part of:

(9.2) Cleopatra, Egypt's former ambassador to Phoenicia, and Marc Anthony met in Alexandria.

(Incidentally, both these sentences are structurally ambiguous, and the construal of Example 9.1 as a meeting of three is dependent on the hearer's factual knowledge — in this case, a knowledge of history.)

In the above example of *cigarette* and *lighter* the relation established may be some indeterminate kind of interaction between the two objects. The structuring which comes closest to the matching is a lacunal complex one:

(9.3) (AGENT–ACTION lighter, (GOAL–ACTION cigarette, Δ)).

However the matching itself need not necessarily be lacunal; rather it may involve a direct connection between the cigarette and the lighter. As Brown (1973) has remarked in a different context: "... the agent and object may themselves constitute a semantic relation. Consider a child kicking a ball or turning a key. The agent and object seem to be in direct interaction; a person initiates movement in a thing [p. 194]." Alternatively, the hearer may have had a clear idea of the action which is included in the matching. This would correspond to a complex structuring: Example (9.3) with the action term supplied.

At times, matchings may involve much more delimited relations than are found in structurings. *Egypt* and *queen* conjure up a very specific relation between these two words, much more specific than the possessive relation in the I-marker of Example (9.1). The latter may stand for a number of cognitive relations: alienable possession (John's shirt), unalienable possession (John's *brother*), nonmaterial possession (*John's latest book*), and so on (Charniak, 1972, pp. 240–242). Usually several relations appearing in cognitive structures can be coagulated into the same I-marker relation. Semantic matching construes the former kind of relations. In Example (9.4) it may establish that the knife is used as an instrument for cutting, even though in the I-marker of Example (9.4) the relation between *knife* and *cut* encompasses agents as well as instruments (see Section 2B):

(9.4) The knife cuts the bread.

In the marginal case, when semantic matching is carried out without the structuring process, it may constitute a leap directly into cognitive structure without the mediation of an I-marker. This is what happens in semantic short-circuiting (see Section 8C) and in the more artificial situation of reading the word string in Example (8.1). There, several matchings are arrived at, which MERGE with each other (the term "coalesce" is inappropriate here, since it pertains to the formally defined moves of Section 6D). Thus, after *threatened* and *flames* suggest a matching, a merging with *girl* may form a new, more complex matching. This merging continues till the hearer retrieves, on the basis of the remaining words, a cognitive structure, which to some extent may be identical with that which the speaker had in mind when he uttered Example (8.2), from which these words were taken.

It may thus be possible to reconstruct the speaker's cognitive structure without retrieving his I-marker. This may happen in some instances of rapid reading in which semantic short-circuiting occurs. In agrammatical texts, like some kinds of modern poetry, there may be no I-marker to retrieve, and therefore comprehension may involve merely a merging of matchings into successively more complex ones. Also, when trying to figure out the general meaning of an utterance in a language whose grammar we have not learned but whose vocabulary is somewhat familiar (as is Italian for the educated English speaker), the I-marker cannot be retrieved since no structural cues can operate. But some guesses based on knowledge of the world and contextual cues may afford glimpses of the writer's cognitive structure. In the normal case, however, semantic matching operates in conjunction with structuring (as is shown in detail in Chapter 10).

Semantic matching is a process which has no parallel in the production of utterances. Production employs only rules based on knowledge of the language, and this parallels the structuring process in comprehension.

In the above, only one major type of semantic matching has been dealt with: a lexical look-up retrieves protoverbal elements, and these suggest the relation holding between them. Another type of semantic matching occurs when a protoverbal element issues a directive (see Section 6D) to look for another one which stands in a given relation to it. For example, the hearer may focus on *threatened* and scan the sentence for the agent of this action or for its goal.

An interesting parallel to these two forms of semantic matching is to be found in the process of solving analogy tests (Shalom & Schlesinger, 1972). When presented with an item like

(9.5) shoes — leather
       house — ?

the testee performs in effect two tasks. First, he must infer a relation holding between the words in the first line. This is quite similar to the semantic matching engaged in when two words in an utterance are focused on. Next, he searches for a word standing in a given relation to the word in the second line. This has an analogue in the search for a word standing in a given relation to another word in the utterance. Both the solving of analogies and semantic matching might thus be viewed as variants of the same process. In line with Quillian (1967), one might regard analogy solving and matching as the tracing of paths in a semantic network. In Quillian's model, nodes (corresponding to words) are connected by a variety of relations. The meaning of each word consists of all the factual information pertaining to it which is stored in this network (see also Schleichert, 1971). What remains problematic, however, is the constitution of such a semantic network (see discussion in Section 8B).

When semantic matching involves the search for a word, the latter may at times have to be interpreted by semantic matching. The preceding context or our knowledge of the world may make clear what, for example, the goal of the action is; and when the missing term appears in the utterance as an unfamiliar word or phrase, we impose a meaning on it. This process is what is meant by understanding a word in context or guessing at its meaning. In fact, we learn the meaning of many words in this way.

Semantic matching may merely rule out a matching instead of construing one.

Thus, for *threatened* and *flames* the inference can be made that it is not the flames which are threatened. This NEGATIVE MATCHING may serve to cancel a structuring which has already been obtained (see Section 10B).

While the effects of bizarreness may be due, in part at least, to negative matchings, the greater facility of comprehending "semantically well-integrated" sentences, such as Example (8.13), relative to "semantically poorly-integrated" ones, like Example (8.14), cannot be explained in this manner, because there is nothing implausible in the latter which could be ruled out. The phenomenon must therefore be explained on the basis of positive semantic matching (see Section 10E for further discussion).

A negative matching may be followed by a positive one for the same segment. For instance, after determining that flames are not being threatened, *threatened* and *flames* may be construed differently: the flames threatened. Conversely, a positive matching may be replaced by a negative one when further semantic matching makes the former appear implausible.

The conflict revealed by a negative matching may instigate a search for a word or words with negative connotations. Suppose *teetotaler* and *intoxicated* are encountered in an utterance. There will presumably be a negative matching: the second word is not an attribute of the first one. When a word like *not, detest* or *refuse* etc. is then found, it will be assumed that this will bridge the gap, for instance, as in

(9.6) The teetotaler detested the guest of honor, who he saw
        intoxicated.

This would be a case of semantic matching for the second type mentioned above: a search for a word that stands in a given relation to another.

Semantic matching may pertain not only to words but also to larger utterance segments. The fact that a bizarre sentence is not as easy to comprehend as a more commonplace one can often be explained only on the basis of this assumption. For instance:

(9.7) Because she had to paint the room the tailors had been sewing
        in energetically, she was extremely callous.
(9.8) Because she had to clean the room the children had been playing
        in wildly, she was extremely angry.

There seems to be no difference between these sentences regarding the pairs of words which "go together": *tailors* goes with *sewing* as much as *children* with *playing*. If the rather bizarre Example (9.7) is more difficult to understand, this can be due only to the way phrases are related to each other. Being required to clean a room may reasonably be expected to make one angry, whereas being required to paint one would not normally result in one's becoming callous; and likewise. playing children, but not sewing tailors, may make it necessary to refurbish a room. The difficulty encountered will presumably be due to a negative matching which contradicts the results of previous processing.

The clues for semantic matching do not have to reside in the sentence analyzed; they may be found in previous utterances. Thus, the ambiguity of *visiting relatives* may be resolved by preceding context in:

(9.9) We usually stay home over the weekend. Visiting relatives can
        be a nuisance, because they often forget to leave.

The linguistic context of the first sentence results in a matching for *visiting relatives* according to which someone visits relatives. The subordinate clause beginning with *because* then adds to the hearer's factual knowledge, and this instigates a revision of the previous matching: it is now the relatives who visit (see also Garrett, 1970).

So far we have considered matchings pertaining to relations between proto-verbal elements. Semantic matching may also serve to determine the status of a single word. In Example (9.10) semantic matching suggests that *stings* refers to the result of the action of stinging and not to the action itself:

(9.10) Later, the stings began to bother him.

In Example (9.11) semantic matching may resolve the ambiguity, indicating that *pen* refers to an enclosure, and not to a writing instrument (see also Bar Hillel, 1964a):

(9.11) The baby is playing in the pen.

Note that in Example (9.10) the interpretation suggested by semantic matching can also be arrived at by structuring; not so in Example (9.11), where there are no structural cues which might serve to disambiguate *pen*.

Macnamara, Green, and O'Cleirigh (unpublished manuscript) found response times to Example (9.13) to be longer than those to Example (9.12):

(9.12) The act of courage saved the lady.
(9.13) The act of courage saved the theater.

This can only be explained by assuming that *theater* in Example (9.13) suggested an interpretation of *act* that is common in the context of 'theater' (division of a theatrical play), and this necessitated subsequent revision.

The nature of semantic matching is further clarified by a comparison of matchings and structurings.

9B. MATCHINGS AND STRUCTURINGS COMPARED

Semantic matching and structuring are two ways of arriving at the relations underlying an utterance. In Chapter 10 it is shown how both these processes converge in comprehension of the utterance. In order to understand how this occurs, the similarities and differences between matchings and structurings should be clarified.

An important characteristic common to matchings and structurings is that they are probabilistic. It will be remembered that most structural cues are ambiguous. The same is true for the cues leading to semantic matching. In Examples (8.1) and (8.2), for instance, the words *firemen* and *escape* may suggest the matching that the firemen escaped, for this is after all a conceivable course of action even for firemen. But, due to our expectations about their normal behavior, this matching will presumably have a subjective probability value lower than that for the matching of, for instance, *threatened* and *flames*.

The probability value of a matching – like that of a structuring – is subject to change in the course of the comprehension process. Suppose the word *girl* is found only after the matching 'the firemen escaped' has been formed. Then the probability value of the latter will presumably be lowered in view of the appearance on the scene of a more likely candidate for escaping. The process of merging, like the process of coalescing (see Section 6D), may increase the probability values of the merged matchings.

Negative matchings also have subjective probability values. Where selection restrictions apply, these values will be very high, perhaps unity.

Like structurings, matchings can issue directives. Consider

(9.14)   The mushroom that Alice was advised to ingest had some
         rather strange properties.

The reader may focus on *mushroom* and *Alice* and semantic matching may set in (at least if he has some minimal acquaintance with Lewis Carroll's works), suggesting that Alice did something to the mushroom. But what? A directive instigates further processing to find out which of the various possibilities apply: eat it, taste it, break off a piece of it, and so on. Or, assume that semantic matching indicates that the agent relation holds between, say, *John* and *hit*; a directive may be issued to search for a word which expresses what is hit.

It stands to reason that a directive may be followed in one of two ways: either by semantic matching which searches for a word standing in a certain relation to a given word, or by structuring. This is so whether the directive is issued by a structuring or by a matching. In other words, matching may be followed by matching and structuring by structuring, but matchings may also lead to structurings and vice versa. This is one of the ways in which the two comprehension processes may interpenetrate each other.

In Section 6C several kinds of structurings were discussed. Matchings, like structurings, may be either simple or complex. A complex matching would be one in which, for example, 'Alice' 'the mushroom' and 'ingest' in Example (9.14) are combined in one presentation. Of course, such a presentation can also be arrived at by merging. It is not clear whether such complex matchings and the result of merging should be viewed as hierarchical, like complex and coalesced structurings. Further, negative structurings have their counterpart in negative matchings.

The main difference between matchings and structurings lies in the relations which figure in them. Structurings involve I-marker relations whereas matchings are not so confined, as discussed at length in Section 9A. (The implications of this difference for the interaction between semantic matching and structuring are developed in Chapter 10.)

9C. THE STATUS OF SELECTION RESTRICTIONS

Some factual knowledge can be formalized by selection restrictions but, as we have seen in Section 8B, there is factual knowledge which resists such formalization. Section 9A demonstrated that both these kinds of factual knowledge may be utilized in semantic matching. The knowledge captured by selection restrictions may lead to high-probability negative semantic matchings, whereas other factual knowledge may lead to either negative or positive matchings with low to high probabilities. Once the process of semantic matching is incorporated into the comprehension model, there is no need for allocating to selection restrictions a place in the lexicon – as in the form of semantic markers – or, in fact, anywhere else in the model. One may suggest, therefore, that the concept of selection restriction has no independent status in the comprehension model, just as it has no such status in the production model (see Section 2D).

This is in accord with the opinion of both Bolinger (1965, pp. 568–569), who questions the distinction between "knowledge of language" formalized by semantic markers and "knowledge of the world," and Wilson (1967), who says: "There is no sharp line between what properly belongs in a dictionary and what properly belongs in an encyclopedia [p. 63]." Their views are vehemently opposed by Katz (1972), who argues that there is a radical difference, as between Examples (9.16) and (9.17), which are analytic – a fact captured by the semantic markers of *bachelor* – and between Example (9.18), which is not analytic:

  (9.15) Bachelors are male.
  (9.16) Bachelors are not married.
  (9.17) Bachelors are over one inch tall.

The difference between Examples (9.15) and (9.16) on the one hand, and Example (9.17) on the other, seems indeed to be psychologically real. The negation of each of these sentences is rejected outright as false by anyone who understands the word *bachelor* in the same way as Katz does, but there is the following difference. On hearing a sentence which is the negation of Example (9.15) or (9.16) one may say: "This is false, because if he is female (married) he is not a bachelor." The negation of Example (9.17), however, does not evoke such a response, because whatever the reason of its falsity, we do not attribute this to the very fact of bachelorhood. But in order to determine the implications of this difference for the status of selection restrictions in a performance model, we must first answer the question what causes the different responses to these sentences. Saying that being male and unmarried is true of bachelors "by definition" is, of course, to beg the question. Saying with Katz that the difference resides in semantic markers is one way of answering it.

However, we can do without introducing additional constructs for this purpose. The above distinction is motivated by the possibility of imaging the false sentence obtained by the negation of Example (9.17). One can visualize a miniature bachelor or a small-scale elephant just as well as one can imagine a mile-high gypsy or a colossal flea, and at the same time entertain the firm belief that such monstrosities do not exist. By contrast, one cannot visualize a female bachelor or a married one.[2] If anyone would claim that he just visualized one, he would be disbelieved (or, in a charitable mood, we might say that he was trying to talk linguistics; or that he merely imagined that a certain person who was a bachelor had turned female or had married).

That bachelors are male and unmarried are "institutional facts" (Searle, 1969), but this is not a necessary condition for the inability to visualize the negation of "analytical" sentences. Also impossible is visualizing green tables that are red all over, yellow virtue, and, generally, contradictions of analytic statements. If somebody says he dreamed of a one-inch high bachelor, or a winged elephant, or a weeping table, we might be inclined to believe him. But we would dismiss as nonsense a claim to have dreamed about a metal thought, or John's sister who is no relative of John, or a green table that is red all over. From the psychological standpoint this may be all there is to analyticity. This certainly does not provide sufficient grounds for semantic markers or selection restrictions in the performance model. To postulate these in addition to factual knowledge would be a violation of parsimony (see also Olson, 1970).

Since a grammar formalizes the regularities of language, there may be justification for the inclusion of selection restrictions in it. It is true that *weep* can have only animate subjects, but there are exceptions: sentences about dreams, hallucinations, and metaphorical speech. These and similar cases are among the reasons given by Haas (1973a) for his proposal that semantic anomalies should not be ruled out by a grammar. Consider further that if a grammar aspires to explanatory adequacy, there seems to be no justification for selection restrictions. For all we know, the way a child learns the knowledge formulated by a selection restriction is through acquiring many bits and pieces of factual knowledge: tables don't weep, nor does a chair, nor does a wall, ... but Johnny may weep, and so may Billy, and auntie, and so on. These pieces of information, acquired in

---

[2] Savin (1973) also points out that selection restrictions are largely "the linguistic counterpart of conceptual impossibilities [p. 225]." He observes, however, that a few such restrictions are entirely arbitrary, for instance, that *addled* can be said only of eggs. Here we are not concerned with restrictions of the latter type. They do play a part in comprehension: the "stage direction" (see Section 2D) for *addled*, when found by a lexical look-up, will affect the hearer's expectations.

diverse circumstances, eventually enable the child to generalize to new instances so that he will know when the occasion arises, without being told so, that a broom does not weep. Experience has changed his cognitions, not his linguistic knowledge.

As far as the evidence in the psycholinguistic literature goes, selection restrictions seem to have essentially the same behavioral effects as factual knowledge which is not formalizable by selection restrictions. There is evidence that infringement of either disrupts the comprehension process (see Section 8C). Findings by Howe and Hillman (1973) on children's judgements of acceptability are also relevant here. They investigated responses made to violations of selection restrictions by children from kindergarten through the fourth grade. Howe and Hillman distinguish between selection restrictions which are represented in a grammar and "Special Restrictions," which are not. For instance, in Example (9.19) the restriction violated is that the verb *build* requires an animate subject. This is a selection restriction provided for by the grammar. On the other hand, Example (9.18) is unacceptable not because it violates a selection restriction (the subject of *sting* is animate, as required), but rather because it conflicts with our factual knowledge (it violates a "Special Restriction"). The experimental material included sentences with two kinds of selection restrictions: those pertaining to the verb and its subject, like Example (9.19) and those pertaining to the verb and its object, like Example (9.20).

(9.18)   The cow stung the bee.
(9.19)   The nest built the bird.
(9.20)   The children scared the fight.

In the experiment each child was presented with a list of sentences, half of which were acceptable and half of which violated one of the three kinds of restrictions exemplified in Examples (9.18)–(9.20). The child was asked: "What can you tell me about the sentence?" According to his description of the sentence – as "silly" or "make believe" – it was judged whether he recognized the unacceptability of the sentence violating a restriction. The proportion of correct responses to unacceptable sentences over all ages was as follows:

1. for violation of subject–verb selection restriction, as in Example (9.19): 94.2%;
2. for violation of verb–object selection restriction, as in Example (9.20): 79.7%; and
3. for violation of "Special Restriction," as in Example (9.18): 87.7%.

The difference between the first and second cases may have been due to the greater saliency of the agent relation (see Section 1C), which resulted in greater conspicuousness of an implausible agent–action combination. What concerns us here is the differential effect of selection restrictions – the above mentioned cases – and "Special Restrictions," (the last case). At first sight this might be interpreted as evidence for the independent status of the former. However, upon close examination the kind of semantic anomaly exhibited in "Special Restriction" sentences seem to differ from sentence to sentence. In some, like Example (9.18), the agent—action combination is implausible: cows do not sting. In others, the action—goal combination is anomalous: ice is not cooled, as is suggested in Example (9.21). Finally, in sentences like Example (9.22) both the agent—action combination and the action—goal combination are quite plausible, when taken each by itself, but the whole sentence is not.

(9.21)   The drink cooled the ice.
(9.22)   The girl lifted the lady.

When judgments of sentences with implausible agent—action combinations are treated separately, we find the mean percentage correct to be exactly as in the sentences violating subject—verb selection restrictions, like Example (9.19).[3] This shows that in judgements of acceptability — at least of children — it does not make any difference whether the implausibility is due to violation of a selection restriction or not. We tentatively conclude, therefore, that selection restrictions operate in the same way as other factual knowledge: by providing a basis for semantic matching.

SUMMARY

Semantic matching is the purpose of construing the meaning of an utterance by means of factual knowledge. It can take various forms: disambiguation of a word or determination of its grammatical category; establishment of a relation between two protoverbal elements; or the determination of a word whose proto-

---

[3] The data for the individual "Special Restriction" sentences were kindly supplied to me by Professor Howe. Since readers may differ in their opinion as to the locus of implausibility, I quote the sentences here, with mean percentage correct in parentheses. In the following the implausibility is due, in my judgment, to the agent—action combination: *The skirt cleaned the soap* (94.4%), *The cow stung the bee* (95.0%), *The window broke the stone* (97.2%), *The stove carried the truck* (91.6%), *The baby fed the mother* (93.3%), *The bread sliced the knife* (93.8%). The mean is 94.2% — precisely like that for violation of subject—verb selection restrictions. That the agent—action combination was implausible thus made the inacceptability easy to detect. (This explanation is not invalidated by the fact that in some of these sentences the action—goal combination may also have been implausible). In three sentences the locus of implausibility was in the action—goal combination: *The drink cooled the ice* (79.4%), *The grass dried the wind* (92.2%), and *The bag filled the sticks* (78.8%). The mean of these is 83.5%. The remaining sentences were like Example (9.22) in that both the agent—action and the action—goal combinations, each taken by itself, was plausible: *The boys punished the teacher* (91.6%), *The girl lifted the lady* (91.6%), *The farmer shot the soldier* (47.4%), *The floor covered the rug* (91.1%), *The tools held the box* (76.6%), *The baby dropped the man* (96.1%). The mean is 82.4%.

verbal element stands in a specified relation to a given element. Not only relations appearing in I-markers, but any kind of relation or set of relations can be construed by semantic matching; this is the main difference between the form of a matching (the result of the process) and that of a structuring. By merging matchings, the speaker's cognitive structure with all its multifarious relations may be reconstructed directly with greater or lesser fidelity. But usually matchings interact with structurings in retrieving the I-marker in a manner described in Chapter 10.

Various parallels between matchings and structurings may be noted. Matchings, like structurings, have subjective probabilities. Both can issue directives. Both matchings and structurings can be simple or complex, positive or negative. Negative matchings with very low subjective probabilities are often those constructions that are formulated in a grammar by selection restrictions. In a comprehension model, however, the latter apparently have no independent status.

10

The Interaction
between Semantic Matching
and Structuring Processes

In this final chapter we examine how semantic matching and the structuring process converge on the comprehension of an utterance. The first question discussed here concerns the temporal relationship between these processes. Semantic matching may come before or after the structuring process, or be carried out simultaneously with it. These should not be viewed as mutually exclusive alternatives. Rather, different strategies may be employed at one time or another, according to the exigencies of the situation. As argued repeatedly in the preceeding chapters, having a very flexible model of language performance is necessary, so as to enable the speaker–hearer to deal optimally with the task he is faced with at a given moment (see Sections 3A, 6A, and 6C).

The first strategy to be considered here is a sequential one: structuring is first carried out for the whole utterance and thereafter semantic matching sets in. We call this strategy SEMANTIC POSTMATCH. The function of this postmatch is to detect errors in the structuring process and lead to a revision of the initial interpretation, if necessary. Some of the effects of factual knowledge discussed in Section 8C might be explained as due to this strategy. For "semantically well-integrated" sentences the semantic postmatch is easier to carry out, and therefore faster, than for "semantically poorly integrated" ones, which might explain the obtained differences between these types of sentences. In the case of bizarre sentences the semantic postmatch may sound a warning, which leads to structurings being reviewed to see if an error has been made.

Other effects of factual knowledge are not as readily explained by this strategy. The influence of preceding context – as in Example (9.9) of Section 9A – might be explained only rather circuitously by assuming that the context is stored for subsequent use by the semantic postmatch. But furthermore the strategy fails to explain the reversibility effect (see Section 8C). It cannot therefore be the only available strategy; others will have to be resorted to in various cases.

Suppose now that the converse sequence is applied: semantic matching is first carried out for the whole utterance, and then followed up by structuring. Such a SEMANTIC PRESCAN   may serve as a preparation for the structuring process, directing it towards those structurings which are in accordance with semantic matching. Thus, when semantic matching suggests that a certain relation holds between two words, the structuring process may subsequently examine them in order to determine whether structural cues warrant a structuring in which this relation appears. The greater the success of the semantic prescan in finding matchings confirmable by structuring process, the easier the latter process will be. This may account for the greater facility of handling "semantically well-integrated" sentences (see Section 8C). Further, the special difficulty caused by bizarreness may be due to the semantic prescan arriving at matchings which mislead the structuring process and ultimately require revision.

That there must be other strategies besides semantic prescan can be shown by the following examples:

(10.1)   George insisted that Steve needed a rest after feeling his pulse.

(10.2)   George insisted that Steve needed a rest after exerting himself unduly.

These sentences are structurally ambiguous. No structural cues prescribe that the agent of 'feeling' in Example (10.1) is 'George', whereas that of 'exerting' in Example (10.2) is 'Steve'; rather, the plausibility of the content − factual knowledge − is responsible for these construals, which must therefore be made by semantic matching. Likewise, it is semantic matching which indicates that *his* and *himself* refer to *Steve* rather than to *George* (see Quirk, Greenbaum, Leech, & Svartvik, 1972, p. 678 on interpretation of proforms by context). But note that this construal can obviously not be obtained by a semantic matching carried out on pairs of words: *feeling* and *Steve* suggest just as acceptable a matching as *feeling* and *George* do. It is only after the whole clause *George . . . a rest* has been analyzed (and further, after the phrase *feeling his pulse* has been analyzed) that semantic matching can arrive at the conclusion that it was George who felt the pulse and not Steve. Moreover, it is only after this clause has been analyzed that semantic matching can determine that *his* refers to *Steve* rather than to *George*. But the former clause cannot be interpreted by means of semantic matching alone: structural cues − word order, in this case − are required to determine that George is the one who insisted on a rest for Steve, and Steve the one who needed it. Therefore, the output of the structuring process directed at analyzing the first clause (*George . . . a rest*) must be operated on by semantic matching, with the result that 'George' is construed as agent of 'feeling'.

Structuring and semantic matching may thus alternate. There are different ways in which such alternation may occur. In the above example, structuring of one segment of the utterance may have been followed by a semantic prescan for another segment. In other cases, both structuring and semantic matching may operate in one and the same segment in sequence. Here again there are at least two possibilities. Semantic matching may suggest certain relations, in the manner of a semantic prescan, and this is then followed by structuring. Alternatively, semantic matching may take the form of a postmatch, which checks the result of previously performed structuring. The latter is the possibility envisaged by Winograd (1972, p. 23). To illustrate this strategy, he discusses the following example:

(10.3) I rode down the street in a car.

The syntactic parser (Winograd's term for what is here called structuring) always operates first in his model, but it does not always have to parse the whole sentence before the semantic process sets in. Suppose that *the street in a car* has been parsed as a constituent. Then, Winograd (1972) claims, "the semantic analyzer will reject 'in a car' as a possible modifier of 'street' [p. 23] " since cars cannot contain streets. This sentence is therefore returned to the syntactic parser, which now tries to attach *in a car* to *rode*.

Other mixed strategies are available as well. A structuring may issue a directive, which is complied with by semantic matching, and the result of the latter may in its turn issue a directive requiring the operation of the structuring process (see Section 9B). Further, semantic matching may at certain points in the comprehension process serve to construe relations and at others to check on the relations established by structuring.

So far it has been assumed that semantic matching and structuring occur sequentially. This is, of course, not necessarily so: the two processes may operate simultaneously part of the time or throughout. The results of one process then presumably are available to the other so that wrong paths are avoided and the number of revisions required is reduced. Schank's (1972, 1973) theory apparently assumes such an interaction between syntactic and semantic processing. He holds that an initial syntactic analysis determines (in a manner which is not made clear in his articles) what are the main noun and the main verbs of the sentence and which items are syntactically dependent on each of these. Then the "conceptual processor" begins to operate, utilizing both structural cues and knowledge of the world (Schank, 1972, pp. 592–594, 1973, pp. 234–235). The following two sentences are therefore construed differently despite their superficial similarity:

(10.4) I hit the boy with a stick.
(10.5) I hit the boy with long hair.

The analysis here will be guided both by a structural cue — *with* may indicate either the instrumental or the possessive — and by knowledge of the world. The latter is accessed through the verb *hit* and partly also through the nouns in question (see Section 8B for the problems attendant on this). The entry for *hit* requires that the instrument of the action be a weapon. *Stick* qualifies for this, but not *hair*. Since the latter is listed as a body part, the hair is taken as belonging to the boy. But, as Schank points out, there is no absolute certainty that these interpretations are correct. In Example (10.4) it may be after all the boy who held the stick, and in Example (10.5) a whip of long hair may have been used to hit the boy. Schank thus recognizes the important point that knowledge of the world operates on a probabilistic basis (see Section 8B).

The syntactic and conceptual processors, then, work simultaneously and, as Schank (1972, p. 559) puts it, "talk together." One might wish to consider, as an alternative to such interaction, that semantic matching and structuring operate in parallel but independently of each other. However such a procedure seems to be wasteful and nothing is gained by postulating it. Moreover it is contradicted by findings of Forster and Ryder (1971), who varied both syntactic complexity and semantic plausibility and found that both these factors affect processing time. They argued that if the two processes were parallel and independent, processing time would be a function of only one of these factors, namely whichever one took longer, or (according to a possible alternative not considered by those authors) whichever one took less time.[1]

Apart from such independent processing, which as stated is implausible and conflicts with experimental findings, any of the above strategies, whether se-quential or simultaneous, may be resorted to at one time or another. Semantic matching and structuring may interleave in several alternative ways, depending on the material analyzed and on other momentary factors. In marginal cases, only semantic matching will take place: the strategy of semantic shortcircuiting is resorted to (as in rapid reading when only some of the key words are attended to, or when the structuring process presents unusual difficulties; see Section 8C). On the other hand, in the absence of semantic cues an utterance may be subjected only to structuring processes. Usually however the two processes interact with each other.

---

[1] In this experiment and in others (Forster & Olbrei, 1973) it has been shown that when sentences are projected very rapidly word by word, the size of the increase in processing time resulting from syntactic complexity is unaffected by degree of semantic plausibility. This is regarded by Forster and associates as evidence against the interaction strategy (see also Forster, 1974). However, as long as the interaction strategy is not spelled out in full detail (in fact in even greater detail than below), no predictions follow from it as to the relative contributions of syntactic and semantic factors to processing time. Therefore their findings cannot at the moment invalidate the interaction hypothesis, due to the weakness of the latter. Neither does their failure to replicate the reversibility effect seem to affect the credibility of the interaction strategy (see Section 8C, footnote 4). Forster proposes as the only alternative to the interaction strategy the hypothesis that semantic processes follow syntactic ones. This is essentially the semantic postmatch strategy discussed above, which as we have seen, may be resorted to at times, but is insufficient to account for all the phenomena known to us.

But to say that semantic matching and the structuring process interact is not very illuminating, unless the manner of their interaction is described.

10B. READINGS

In the preceding section, we examined the various ways semantic matching and structuring may work together in achieving comprehension of an utterance: how they may alternate or proceed simultaneously in dealing with various segments of an utterance. We must now narrow our focus and ask: What happens at the level of a single unit of analysis (see Section 6C) for which there is a structuring and also a matching? The structuring may have preceded the matching or follow it, or they may both have been arrived at simultaneously. When there is both a structuring and a matching for the same unit of analysis, they will interact.[2]

What happens when such an interaction takes place? Here we need a new term to refer to the result of the interaction between a structuring and a matching for the same unit of analysis. Let us call this result a READING. This section deals with the formation of readings and Section 10C with the way readings for various units of analysis combine to render a complete interpretation of the utterance. The presentation here is only a slight modification of the treatment of structurings and coalescing of structurings in Chapter 6, the modification being necessary so as to take into account the contribution of semantic matching.

What is the relation of a reading to the matching and structuring that produce it? The answer to this question depends on the relation between the interacting matching and structuring. When the matching is compatible with the structuring, the reading includes the information contained in both of them. On the other hand, when they are incompatible with each other, either one may win out and determine the reading, or else the decision between them may be deferred until later.

These general remarks must be discussed in greater detail. Consider first what it means for a matching and structuring to be compatible with each other. As shown in Section 9A, the relations which may figure in matchings, like the relations in cognitive structures, are not confined to those relations which appear in I-markers, and hence in structurings. The former relations are categorized into a limited number of I-marker relations, or in other words, there is a many-to-one mapping of the relations in matchings into the relations in structurings. A relation in a structuring will therefore usually correspond to a set of more than one relation figuring in matchings. Let us refer to the set of relations to which a structuring corresponds as S. A matching may also contain a set of relations (as in Example 9.1). Let M be the set of one or more relations in a matching. A matching and a structuring for the same unit of analysis will be compatible when

---

[2] It will be convenient here to speak of interactions of products – structurings and matchings – as well as of interactions of the processes resulting in these products.

one of the following holds:

1. M is identical with S;
2. M includes S as a proper subset;
3. S includes M as a proper subset;
4. M and S intersect; that is, S is only partly included in M, and M in S.

A matching and structuring will be incompatible when none of the above applies, that is

5. M and S do not overlap.

When a matching and a structuring interact it will be assumed that the result is a reading which includes what is agreed upon by both. In other words, we propose the general principle that the reading consists of the relations in the intersection of M and S. In the fifth instance, in which the intersection is zero, the matching and structuring are incompatible – they have no common ground – whereas in the first four cases they are compatible. In cases 2–4 the relations that M has in excess of S or S in excess of M are discarded. Let us now see what this implies in each of the above cases.

1. *M is identical with S.* The structuring contains the same information as the matching for the unit of analysis. For instance, semantic matching may have arrived at the result that the word *a* stands for the agent of the action expressed by the word *b*. In addition, the structuring (AGENT–ACTION *a, b*) is construed. The reading then also has the form (AGENT–ACTION *a, b*).[3] In the case of identity of matching and structuring, then, the reading *is* the structuring. Let us call this a TYPE 1 READING .

2. *M includes S as a proper subset.* The set of relations in the matching may be more indefinite than that in the structuring (examples can be found in Section 9A). In this case, too, the structuring will be adopted as the reading: the result is a Type 1 reading.

3. *S includes M as a proper subset.* This is the opposite of the above: the matching is more narrow and circumscribed than the structuring. A speaker who intends to express a cognitive structure containing the information in this matching might coagulate it into this less delimited structuring. For instance, the instrument of an action may be coagulated as an agent in the I-marker (see Section 2B). The matching according to which *a* expresses the instrument of the action and *b* expresses the action is thus compatible with the structuring

---

[3] As shown in Section 10D, this is not the only possibility. The construal of a matching may be dependent on that of the structuring for the same segment or vice versa. Readings, like structurings, may involve either words, as in the formula presented here, or – after a lexical look-up – protoverbal elements. As stated in Section 6C, the lexical look-up may be carried out at any stage in the comprehension process.

(AGENT–ACTION *a*, *b*). The matching, however, contains more information than this structuring. This excess information is not discarded; rather, the reading resulting from the interaction of such a matching and a structuring contains the information of both. This type of reading has the form of the structuring, but with an appended "footnote" to further circumscribe it (such as "the agent relation is of the instrument–action type"). Let us call this a TYPE 2 READING.

4. *M and S intersect.* Presumably, a matching may be both more inclusive and (in other respects) more circumscribed than a structuring; that is, the matching and structuring partly overlap. The relations which are specified by the matching in excess of those in the structuring will then be disregarded, and as for the rest the result will be as in the previous case: there will be a Type 2 reading (one with the form of the structuring) which will be provided with a "footnote" delimiting the relation in the structuring as prescribed by the matching.

In the above cases of compatible matchings and structurings the reading will always have a subjective probability value which is an (as yet unknown) function of those of the matching and structuring from which it results.

5. *M and S do not overlap.* In this case, the matching and the structuring are incompatible. There are several possible outcomes of such a situation. One is a stalemate: no reading results, other utterance segments are turned to for processing, and the one given up on is returned to later. Alternatively, the structuring may be so strong as to win the upper hand and constitute the reading by itself, the only effect of the matching being perhaps to lower the subjective probability value of the reading. The structuring process may thus overpower semantic matching. This occurs, for instance, when we read what we believe to be wrong or even nonsensical (see Section 8C). In other cases the matching may win out, the structuring merely lowering the probability value of the resulting reading. Thus, we may occasionally misread a text to make it accord with what we know or expect to be the case. Finally, incompatibility of matchings and structurings may result in two readings being retained, each with its own probability value: one containing the matching (as in the above case of no structuring); and another one, the structuring. This "local" ambiguity either is or is not resolved as a result of further processing.

This concludes the discussion of types of readings resulting from the interaction of a matching and a structuring. Often, however, there is no such interaction. Either only a structuring and no matching is obtained for an utterance segment (for instance, because of the absence of semantic clues), or else only a matching and no structuring is arrived at (perhaps due to the paucity of structural cues). It is convenient to introduce the convention that even in these cases there is a reading. When there is only a structuring, the reading is the structuring: it is a Type 1 reading. On the other hand, when there is only a matching, the reading is of a type different from those dealt with so far. It contains all the information of the matching. But since matchings do not have the same relations as structurings, it is not formalized like a structuring. Subsequently it may, however, be converted into such a form, as shown in Section 10C. This is called a TYPE 3 READING.

To summarize, we distinguish three types of readings:

1. Type 1: the reading for a unit of analysis has the form of the structuring for this unit of analysis.
2. Type 2: like Type 1, but the reading has a "footnote" appended to it containing the excess information in the matching for this unit of analysis.
3. Type 3: the reading contains all the information in the matching and does not have the form of a structuring. This type of reading can be converted into one of the above types (see Section 10C).

The type of reading obtained for a given utterance segment is determined by the relationship between the structuring and the matching for this segment. A Type 1 reading results when:

1. the structuring and matching contain the same information;
2. the matching is more inclusive than the structuring;
3. only a structuring and no matching is obtained; or
4. the structuring and matching are incompatible; the structuring proves stronger and hence is adopted for the reading.

A Type 2 reading results when:

5. the matching is more circumscribed than the structuring.

A Type 3 reading results when:

6. only a matching and no structuring is obtained; or
7. the structuring and matching are incompatible, and the matching proves stronger.

Two or more alternative readings for a given utterance segment will be the outcome when:

8. the structuring and matching are incompatible without either one displacing the other; or
9. two or more structurings and/or two or more matchings are obtained for the segment.

The structural cues of the segment *horse raced* (see Example 6.23), for instance, permits both the agent relation and, if this segment is the first one processed, the goal relation. Presumably, the latter structuring usually does not even occur to the reader, but if it does, the result may be two alternative readings for this segment, the ambiguity being resolved by further processing.[4] A similar process will take place when there are two different matchings for the same segment, none of which is contradicted by structural cues. Case 8 results in one Type 1 and one Type 3 reading (for the structuring and matching, respectively), whereas Case 9 will result in two or more Type 1 or two or more Type 3 readings (or both).

In the above, we have dealt primarily with the simple case of a matching and structuring pertaining to the same words and the relation between them. It should be realized, however, that the same principles hold for other cases in which one of the types of structurings described in Section 6C – regular, lacunal, or complex – interacts with any kind of matching (see Section 9B), provided that they pertain to at least one common element of the utterance.

10C. COALESCING OF READINGS

Readings are the stepping stones to the complete interpretation of an utterance. For such an interpretation to be achieved, readings for the various units of analysis have to be combined. As far as Type 1 readings (readings of the form of structurings) are concerned, this is the process we are already familiar with: coalescing. We say that readings can coalesce when they have a protoverbal element or word in common, and the result is to be called a COALESCED READING. Schematically, the readings in the first two rows in Example (10.6) can coalesce, and the result is the coalesced reading in the third row.

(10.6)   (ATTRIBUTE a, b)
(AGENT–ACTION b, c)
(AGENT–ACTION (ATTRIBUTE a, b), c)

Note that this changes the formulation presented in Section 6D: there the process in Example (10.6) has been called coalescing of structurings and the result, a coalesced structuring. This is only a terminological change, of course, and an optional one at that, because in some contexts it may be convenient to continue using the previous terminology.

Coalesced readings coalesce further until the full I-marker is retrieved (see Section 6D).

A more substantive modification of the account of coalescing given in Section 6D is needed for Type 2 readings: readings which have the form of those in

---

[4] This is in line with one of the possible strategies of processing ambiguous sentences. According to the "garden path" strategy (Garrett, 1970), on the other hand, only one of the readings is retained for further processing, the other being resorted to only after revision is necessitated. This seems to involve the additional assumption that of two structurings, or readings, for the same unit of analysis, the one with the lower probability is deleted (see also Bever, Garrett & Hurtig, 1973; Carey, Mehler, & Bever, 1970; MacKay, 1970).

Example (10.6) but with an appended "footnote." When a Type 2 reading coalesces either with a Type 1 reading, or with another Type 2 reading, the "footnote" (or "footnotes") are carried along into the coalesced readings.

With Type 3 readings the situation is entirely different. One should remember that these readings are virtual matchings. Unlike readings of the other types, they do not have the form of a structuring. The process in Example (10.6) therefore cannot apply to them as long as they are not converted into the form of a structuring. We are already familiar with this process of conversion from the description of utterance production. The relations in matchings (and Type 3 readings) are those that figure in cognitive structures (see Section 9A), and the relations in structurings are those which appear in I-markers. The conversion of a Type 3 reading into a structuring is therefore analogous to the coagulation of a cognitive structure relation into an I-marker relation (see Section 5B). But there is one qualification to this: when the relation in the Type 3 reading is more definite and narrowly circumscribed than the relation into which it is converted, there may be a "footnote" appended to it which carries this extra information. In other words, before coalescing, a Type 3 reading has to be converted either into a Type 1 reading (without "footnote") or into a Type 2 reading (with "footnote"). The various ways in which readings may coalesce are described in Figure 10.1.

In describing the merging of matchings (Section 9A) it was pointed out that a cognitive structure can be retrieved by such merging into increasingly complex matchings. Accordingly, the above account must be supplemented by the statement that Type 3 readings (those having the form of matchings) can merge with each other. Obviously, for merging to take place no conversion into another form is necessary.

When only Type 3 readings are obtained, as in semantic short-circuiting (see Section 8C), the cognitive structure is retrieved directly, not via the I-marker. But note that merging of Type 3 readings is not the only way that information pertaining to cognitive structures may be recovered. In every Type 2 reading there is a "footnote" and, as stated, this is carried along in coalescing. Coalesced readings coalesce further, carrying along the "footnotes," and the hearer thus retrieves not only the I-marker but also the much more specific information contained in the "footnotes." Cognitive structures, then, are not necessarily reconstructed only after the I-marker has been retrieved: the hearer may already begin to recover them when he engages in coalescing, or else he may recover them directly through merging. Figure 10.2 describes these connections between readings, I-markers, and cognitive structures.

The comments made in Section 6D about the effect of coalescing on subjective probability values hold also for the coalescing and merging of readings. But another possible factor in failure to coalesce must now be added: semantic matching may exercise constraints on the coalescing process. Two readings, either of which is plausible by itself, may yield an implausibility when coalesced,

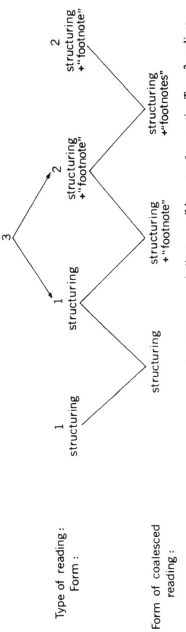

FIGURE 10.1. Coalescing of different types of readings. The arrows indicate possible ways of converting Type 3 readings.

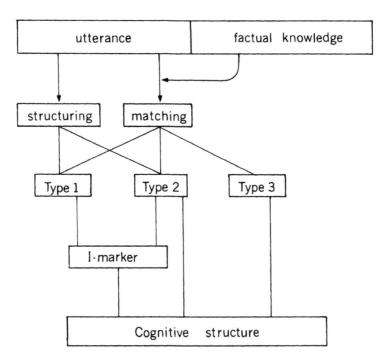

FIGURE 10.2. The contribution of structurings and matchings to the retrieval of the I-marker and cognitive structure. Note the simplification: that readings can coalesce and merge with each other is not in the diagram.

and then coalescing may be vetoed by semantic matching (or else the probability value of the coalesced reading may be lowered). As a consequence, it may be necessary to revise the readings which are to be coalesced. That bizarre utterances create difficulties in comprehension may be due to semantic matching detecting implausibilities at the stage of coalescing (see Example 9.7).

Failure to coalesce may resolve "local" ambiguity. When there are two alternative readings for the same utterance segment, one of these may subsequently fail to coalesce and hence be deleted (or its probability value lowered drastically).

A special case of ambiguity is one where partially overlapping utterance segments are each assigned a reading, and the two readings conflict with each other. Consider

(10.7) I threatened the boy with the rifle.

In Examples (10.4) and (10.5) we noticed how the ambiguity of the *with*-phrase might be resolved by semantic matching. In the present example the evidence of factual knowledge is less unequivocal. Two readings may arise: according to one, the boy has a rifle; according to the other, the rifle is the instrument of the action of threatening. These readings cannot coalesce. Either one of them gives way, because of its lesser strength (as indicated by their probability values), or both are retained. In the latter case, there will be two analyses of the sentence, that is, the sentence is perceived as ambiguous.

10D. PATTERNS OF INTERACTION

The results of the interaction of a matching and a structuring for a given unit of analysis have been discussed in Section 10B. Here we make some further (admittedly speculative) comments about the various ways in which this inter-action may come about. As pointed out above (see Section 3A), it seems to be good strategy to explore various alternative processes and to assume – until evidence to the contrary becomes available – that all of these may operate at one time or another.

For a given unit of analysis a matching and a reading may be arrived at independently of each other. These are then compared and the relations common to both of them are incorporated in the reading. This is the process discussed in Section 10B. Let us call this a CONFRONTING of a matching and a structuring.

One may assume, however, that matchings and structurings are not inevitably arrived at independently of each other. Possibly one of them steers the forma-tion of the other. For instance, semantic matching may be performed first on an utterance segment and restrict the set of possible structurings to be considered or affect the probability value attached to the structurings. Let us call this SEMANTIC STEERING. Similarly there may be STRUCTURAL STEERING: the structuring process influences semantic matching by drawing attention to certain possibilities while neglecting others. As for the rest, the rules of the game are as described in Section 10B: steering may at times fail to find a compatible matching or structuring.

Steering may be facilitating by narrowing down the amount of processing which has to be done, or dysfunctional by blinding us to certain possibilities, as the case may be.

Whether confronting or steering occurs in a given case may depend on the relative saliency for the hearer at the moment of structural cues, and on aspects of factual knowledge. For instance, when structural cues are more salient, structuring may be instigated first and steer semantic matching.

Suppose that for a certain utterance segment no positive matching is attained. Structural cues, on the other hand, are sufficient to arrive at a structuring, which however is implausible in view of factual knowledge. Since the unavailability of a positive matching precludes confronting and steering, there will be (normally) another process which brings factual knowledge to bear on the structuring. We may call this SEMANTIC CHECKING. Semantic checking ascertains whether any negative matching (see Section 9A) contradicts the structuring. When such a negative matching is found, the possible outcomes are as in the case of incompatible matchings and structurings confronting each other (see Section 10B): the matching may veto the structuring, or lower its probability; when the structuring has a high enough probability, the matching will be entirely disregarded. When there is no such negative matching, the structuring is confirmed by default and becomes the reading (see Section 10B).

Similarly, STRUCTURAL CHECKING may be resorted to when, because of insufficiency of structural cues, only a matching is found. The question asked by structural checking is: Does there exist a negative structuring contradicting the matching? To illustrate, suppose that for some reason factual knowledge (based on the preceding context) produces a matching for *doctor* and *argued* in Example (10.8), according to which it was the doctor who argued:

(10.8)   The doctor, argued John, was really a quack.

Evidently, there will be no positive structuring for these two words because, as shown by the comma, no I-marker relation holds between them. But the comma (or pause and intonation if the sentence is spoken) is a structural cue leading to a negative structuring: *doctor* is not related to *argued* as agent to action. The final result of structural checking will therefore be: no reading for *doctor, argued*. In those cases where no negative structuring is found, the matching becomes a Type 3 reading.

Checking should not be confused with the revision of a reading (see Section 10C). Checking may occur in the process of arriving at a reading, whereas a revision (but not checking) may be required after the hearer arrives at a reading through confronting, steering, or checking. The effect of checking is therefore merely negative: it may delete a construal, not produce one.

Occasionally, there may be a failure to carry out semantic checking due to inattention or other factors (for instance, we may understand what we hear but fail to notice its absurdity). In the absence of any positive or negative matching the structuring then becomes a Type 1 reading. Further processing may or may not lead to a revision of this reading. Likewise, failure to carry out structural checking results in a previously obtained matching being accepted as Type 3 reading.

In the two preceding sections, we discussed interactions between matchings and structurings for a single unit of analysis, which lead to the formation of readings. This account can be extended to apply to readings and coalesced readings as well. A reading is essentially either like a structuring or like a matching. It should be possible, therefore, for a reading to interact with another matching or structuring. To illustrate, let *s* be a segment of an utterance, and suppose that (perhaps through inattention) no matching is arrived at for it. The reading *r* then consists of the structuring (or structurings, in the case of a coalesced reading) for *s*. In the course of further processing it may occur that a matching (either a positive or a negative one) is construed for utterance segment *s*. The matching and the reading *r* then interacts either by confronting or through semantic checking on reading *r* (which is really a structuring). This may lead to a revision of the reading.[5] Alternatively, reading *r* will steer the subsequent construal of a matching for utterance segment *s*. This may occur even when semantic matching has already been carried out for utterance segment *s*, because in the course of the analysis additional factual knowledge may then become operative (for instance, by comprehending part of the sentence the available context has been increased). In short, that a structuring has attained the status of a reading does not prevent it from interacting with a matching, or with another reading having the form of a matching.

Likewise, a matching which has become a Type 3 reading can interact with a subsequently construed structuring (or a reading having the form of a structuring) and the interaction may take the form of semantic steering, confronting, or structural checking. This, again, may lead to a revision of the reading. Moreover, the material in the "footnote" of a Type 2 reading may influence and be influenced by the material in subsequently formed matchings and structurings.

These possibilities of interaction exist not only for readings but presumably also for coalesced readings and the results of mergings. In Section 10C we saw that coalescing of readings may be affected by semantic matching. In line with the preceding we may now add that after a coalesced reading has been obtained, additional structural or semantic cues may become operative and the coalescing process be revised, that is, the coalesced reading is deleted or its probability value changed. Ambiguities may be resolved by deleting coalesced readings or drastically lowering their probabilities.

It now becomes evident that the various strategies discussed in Section 10A may be viewed as special cases of the interaction strategy. Thus, a semantic prescan may construe Type 3 readings for an utterance segment, or even for the entire utterance, and these may subsequently interact with structurings (and, possibly, additional matchings). This may require revisions of the Type 3 readings. The semantic postmatch strategy, on the other hand, implies that Type 1 readings are first arrived at exclusively by structuring processes, but matchings are subsequently obtained that interact with these readings, and possibly lead to their revision.

The proliferation of possibilities which has been described here may seem bewildering indeed. It would be so much more comforting to have a concise, readable presentation (which perhaps could be made to fit snugly into a simple flow diagram). But, as stated repeatedly, the adverse circumstances in which hearers are able to piece together the speakers' meanings force us to assume great versatility in the comprehension mechanism. Simplicity is a virtue in a theory,

---

[5] We may speak of a revision whenever the probability value of a reading is changed: it may be increased or lowered (if lowered to zero, the reading is deleted).

but in this case to explain matters simply is to be simplistic. Note that the way in which an utterance is construed in any single instance is not assumed to be very complex; but the model as a whole is complex because it envisages many alternatives.

It should be realized, however, that by relinquishing simplicity serious obstacles are put in the way of testing the theory. Because of the great variety of alternative routes that are postulated, one can explain or explain away most empirical findings in a number of ways. But, evidently, trimming the theory into a simpler shape would mean shutting our eyes to alternatives which are plausible on a priori grounds. The empirical tests, however relevant to the theory tested, will then remain inconclusive, due to the alternatives left out of account. One should rather aspire to a well-thought-through theory, difficult as it may be to verify.

With these limitations in mind, we examine one of the ways in which the model presented here might be connected to empirical data, though this does not yet amount to a test of the theory.

10E. PROCESSING DIFFICULTY

In this final section some possible links are suggested between the foregoing account of comprehension and PROCESSING DIFFICULTY. Processing difficulty is viewed here as an intervening variable that may be operationally defined as, among other things:

1. the time it takes to process an utterance, as measured, for instance, by latency of response;
2. the judged difficulty of comprehending an utterance;
3. the acceptability of a sentence;
4. the probability of comprehension errors.

Most of the behavioral effects described in Section 8C refer to Measures 1 and 2. Acceptability judgments, Measure 3, presumably also reflect difficulties encountered in comprehension, and errors, Measure 4, may also be looked upon as occasioned by such difficulty.

One of the factors affecting processing difficulty is availability of structural cues. This variable has been briefly discussed in Section 6D and studies were quoted in which it is operationally defined and its relationship to processing difficulty explored.

To explain effects of factual knowledge on processing difficulty on the basis of the processes described in the preceding section, some further assumptions must be made. These are presented in the following as a set of principles linking the postulated constructs to processing difficulty. After suitable refinement, these principles may serve as research hypotheses liable to experimental corroboration or discomfirmation:

1. Principle A: processing difficulty increases as the probability values of readings decrease.

2. Principle B: revision of a reading increases processing difficulty.

3. Principle C: the contribution of a revision to processing difficulty increases with the number of steps intervening between the construal of the reading and its revision.

4. Principle D: the contribution of a revision to processing difficulty is greater, the higher the probability value of the discarded reading.

Principle A reflects the generalization, which can be made from findings in several areas in psychology, that the higher the probability of a response, the faster that response will be. Principle B seems almost self-evident, and Principles C and D are (not so self-evident) elaborations of it. Other things being equal, the effect of a revision may be presumed to be more far-reaching the greater the number of steps (construal of other readings, coalescings of readings) that have intervened since the construal of the reading. This is because the amount of processing that has to be overhauled, so to speak, grows with the number of steps (Principle C). Further, a repudiation of low-probability reading (by which not much store was set anyway) should not affect the comprehension process as much as that of a reading with a higher probability value (Principle D).

The effects of plausibility on comprehension can be accounted for by Principle A. "Semantically well-integrated" sentences will result in higher-probability matchings than "semantically poorly integrated" ones, and bizarre sentences will result in no matchings at all, the probability values of the readings decreasing accordingly. If a semantic prescan is carried out on bizarre sentences, the matchings arrived at may subsequently have to be revised, and the greater difficulty of these sentences will then be due to Principle B.

In ambiguous sentences alternative readings may be arrived at and, other things being equal, the probability value of each of these will be lower than it would be in the absence of a rival reading. This in itself may be conducive to an increase in processing difficulty, according to Principle A. In addition, ambiguity may lead to revisions (see Sections 6D and 10D), which increases processing difficulty, following Principle B.

Let us examine now how acceptability judgments may be influenced by the operation of the above principles. In an informal experiment I have found that native speakers tend to judge Example (10.9) as less acceptable than Example (10.10) (see Appendix B for a fuller account of experimental findings).

(10.9)   Mary was thrown the key by John.
(10.10) Mary was given the key by John.

Since exactly the same set of rules is employed in the generation of each of these sentences (the dative movement rules) the difference cannot be due to a difference in grammaticality (Jackendoff & Culicover, 1971). Instead, it seems to reflect some minor difficulty encountered in comprehending Example (10.9), which is not found in Example (10.10). Most of the judges were indeed able to pinpoint this difficulty: in Example (10.9) the interpretation occurred to them for a moment that "somebody threw Mary," and this interpretation had to be rejected subsequently. For Example (10.10) a similar interpretation is apparently quite unlikely, because people are not the kind of things one usually gives to anybody. If this introspective evidence is accepted at face value, it suggests that for the segment *Mary was thrown* a reading is construed according to which someone throws Mary. This reading fails to coalesce with the reading for *the key* because rules of the structuring process preclude construing both 'Mary' and 'the key' as goals of 'throw'. Consequently a revision is required. *Mary was thrown* is reanalyzed in the light of this failure to coalesce, and this time the correct reading is procured and coalescing can be carried out.[6] By contrast, in the case of Example (10.10) no need for revision arises due to the implausibility of one of the interpretations. Closer examination reveals the following three possibilities for *Mary was given*:

1. Only one structuring is construed, perhaps due to semantic matching steering the structuring process (possibly because a semantic prescan was carried out; see Section 10D). Hence, there will be only one, correct reading ('something was given to Mary') and no revision will be required. Following Principle B, processing difficulty should be expected to be smaller — and hence acceptability greater — than for Example (10.9).

2. Two structurings are construed for *Mary was given* ('Mary' as goal and as beneficiary of the action). Only one matching will be arrived at, however, and the structuring according to which 'Mary' is the goal will be ruled out by it. There will therefore be only one correct reading. As in Case 1, no revision of a reading will be required, and Principle B can explain the differential acceptability of Examples (10.9) and (10.10). Conceivably, deletion of a structuring operates like a revision in that it increases processing difficulty. Even so, it is still true that, by Principle C, such a "revision," following directly after the structuring and before the reading is construed, should have a slighter effect than the one required after a reading is construed, as is the case in Example (10.9).

3. Two structurings and two matchings are construed for *Mary was given*. According to one matching, 'Mary' is the beneficiary of 'give' and according to the other — the goal (after all, Mary may have been given, as in marriage, by her

---

[6]There are other possibilities as well. For instance, the problematic segment may be abandoned for the moment and the discontinuous segment *was thrown ... by John* attempted. The reading of the latter is then coalesced with that for *the key*. The resulting coalesced reading then steers the construal of 'Mary' as beneficiary. In any case a revision is required.

father, etc.). Of course, the latter matching has a much lower probability value than the former. The probability values of the two matchings will each be reflected in that of the reading corresponding to it. Coalescing with *the key* is possible only for the high-probability reading. The reading according to which 'Mary' is the goal is blocked in coalescing (for reasons pointed out above, in connection with *Mary was thrown*), and will therefore be deleted. As stated by Principle D, the revision of this low-probability reading will have a smaller effect than that of the high-probability reading in Example (10.9).[7]

It is possible, of course, that *Mary was thrown* also gives rise to two matchings, and consequently to two readings, that is, Example (10.9) may be "locally ambiguous" just as much as Example (10.10). However, since the incorrect reading in Example (10.9) – 'Mary' as goal – has a higher probability value than the corresponding one in Example (10.10), revision (deletion due to failure to coalesce) will have a greater effect on processing difficulty in the case of Example (10.9) than in that of Example (10.10), again according to Principle D. Moreover, the correct reading of Example (10.10) will have a higher probability value than that of Example (10.9) and Principle A, too, would predict a difference in favor of the former.

The differential acceptability of Examples (10.9) and (10.10) is, of course, not definite evidence for the principles proposed above. Other explanations may be possible (see, however, Appendix B, in which one of these is refuted). The differential acceptability can also be explained by assuming that only Case 1 applies and thus Principles C and D are unnecessary for the explanation of this phenomenon. In proposing the above principles I can claim no more than to have made a first step, to have merely provided some suggestion as to the direction which the development of a theory of comprehension might take.

SUMMARY

In the preceding chapters, it was shown that utterances are comprehended by means of two processes: structuring, which is based on structural cues in the utterance, and semantic matching which makes use of factual knowledge. In this chapter I discuss the interaction between these processes and introduce a new construct, the reading, which is the result of the interaction of a matching and a structuring for a given unit of analysis.

There are various patterns of interaction. When a matching is formed first for a given unit of analysis, it may point the way to a structuring which conforms to it; this is called semantic steering. Alternatively, a matching may subsequently be

---

[7] Another possible assumption would be that of two readings for the same utterance segment only the one with the higher probability value (or alternatively, only those whose probability value is above a given threshold) is carried along for further processing, the others being deleted. This would accord with the "garden path" strategy of processing ambiguous sentences (see note 4).

deleted by a negative structuring, a process called structural checking. Likewise, a structuring may either steer semantic matching or be checked by it, and we speak accordingly of structural steering and semantic checking. In addition to steering and checking there is the possibility of a matching and a structuring, for a given unit of analysis, confronting each other. When they are compatible, the reading will consist of their overlap; when they conflict, whichever has greater subjective probability will constitute the reading, or else there will be two readings.

A reading may have the form of a structuring (Type 1 reading), of a structuring to which a "footnote" is appended that contains the more precise information in the matching (Type 2 reading), or of a matching (Type 3 reading). The subjective probability value of a reading is a function of those of the matching and structuring from which it results.

The above pertains to matchings and structurings for the same unit of analysis. In addition, matchings and structurings obtained for one unit of analysis may influence those of others by means of the directives they issue.

Readings for different units of analysis coalesce into progressively more complex readings until the total I-marker is retrieved, the "footnotes" of Type 2 readings providing additional information pertaining to cognitive structure. Type 3 readings may either coalesce with other types of readings after being converted into Type 1 or Type 2 readings, or else they may merge with each other.

Readings and coalesced readings can also interact with matchings and with structurings, just as the latter can interact with each other. A segment of an utterance or the entire utterance may be processed first by semantic matching. This occurs in semantic shortcircuiting, in which these readings merge into a cognitive structure. Alternatively, structuring may be carried out first and the resulting Type 1 readings be subsequently submitted to a semantic postmatch.

To derive testable research hypotheses from this general model, certain assumptions have to be made regarding the behavioral consequences of, among other things, revisions at various points in the process and the subjective probability values of matchings and structurings.

A Kind of Epilogue

Science is angling in the mud.
    ALDOUS HUXLEY, *After Many a Summer Dies the Swan*

Science is self-conscious common sense.
    W. QUINE, *Word and Object*

Which is it to be?

Some readers will feel that I have failed to fulfill the expectations raised in this book. They may object that the links with empirical research are too tenuous and that, therefore, the theory presented is not yet testable. In this they are right, of course. But, their argument may go on, of what use is theorizing if it does not lead directly to experimental test? Can the frivolity of speculation be atoned for by anything but the honest toil of the laboratory?

In the Introduction, I have done my best to forestall such a criticism, but I do not delude myself into thinking that I have quite succeeded in overcoming all the misgivings which are liable to arise in some of my readers. All I can do now is to reiterate my belief that, though the proof of a theory is doubtlessly in its testing, we are still in need of much careful preparation for empirical work on language production and comprehension. Much experimental research will be pointless as long as it is not based on a much firmer theoretical basis. Such a basis can be provided only by careful consideration of the available data and by using common sense — "self-conscious common sense," in Quine's words — so as to arrive at a plausible model. To make progress we must first gain perspective and survey the ground ahead so that we know where we are going.

The Verification of Active and Passive Sentences

In an interesting paper entitled "On the Comprehension of Active and Passive Sentences," Olson and Filby (1972) report on a series of experiments concerning the time it takes to compare a sentence with a picture or to answer a question about a sentence. The experiment regarding question answering and its implications are discussed briefly in Section 6E. Here we will discuss three experiments concerning the use of sentences in verifying a picture, whose results lead Olson and Filby (1972) to conclude that ". . . the process of comprehending a sentence, whether that sentence is used for verifying a picture or answering a question, involves matching or bringing into correspondence the coding of two events . . . this correspondence is in terms of the surface structure coding of the compared events [p. 379]."

In Olson and Filby's experiments pictures were presented of either a car hitting a truck or a truck hitting a car, after a set had been induced in the subject – by various experimental manipulations which differed from experiment to experiment – to attend either to the agent of the action or to its goal. After the picture, an active or a passive sentence was presented and the subject had to respond whether it was "true" or "false" as a description of the picture. Olson and Filby present a model to account for their findings. They hypothesize the following steps in carrying out the verification task:

1. The picture is coded into verbal form, as an active sentence when the agent is focused on and as a passive sentence when the goal is focused on,

2. The surface subject of the presented sentence is compared with that of the sentence describing the picture,

3. The verb form of the presented sentence (*hit* or *was hit*) is compared to that of the sentence describing the picture.

Strictly speaking it is not the "surface structure" (as in the above quotation from Olson and Filby) but the surface form of the sentence which is used in the comparison process. The model outlined in Chapter 6 of this volume implies only that deep structure but no surface structure is retrieved. The input to the structuring process is the surface string, which conceivably may be available for purposes of comparison. Still, one would expect that the task of comparing involves the product of the comprehension process, which according to our model is the I-marker. Olson and Filby also state in their conclusions (quoted above) that comprehension involves surface strings only, and this contradicts the account given in Chapter 6. We shall therefore present an alternative to their model which is in keeping with Chapter 6. But first we must return to a description of the Olson—Filby model.

They assume that any mismatch between surface subjects or verbs demand a change of the "truth index," and this requires time and hence increases response latency. Latency is also increased by coding a picture in the form of a passive sentence and by reading a passive sentence (rather than an active one) and by a "false" response (rather than a "true" response). By comparing processing times for their eight experimental conditions (focusing on agent or goal X active or passive sentence X true or false sentence) parameter estimates were arrived at for each of the factors, and the results showed a remarkably close fit to predictions from these estimates.

To illustrate, suppose the agent is focused on in a picture of a car hitting a truck, and the sentence *the car was hit by the truck* is presented. According to the Olson—Filby model, the picture is coded as an active sentence; let us say this is *the car hit the truck*. The surface subject of this sentence (*car*) matches with the surface subject of the presented sentence. The verb forms, however, do not match (*was hit* versus *hit*) and this requires a change in "truth index" from *true* to *false,* and consequently a delay in processing. Latencies are further increased by the presented sentence being in the passive form, rather than in the active form, and by the response being "false" rather than "true."

Compare this now with another experimental condition where the same picture is presented and the agent is again focused on, but this time a true passive sentence is presented: *the truck was hit by the car.* The process here according to the model differs from the foregoing in that the surface subjects of the sentence verbalizing the picture and of the presented sentence do not match. This requires a change of "truth index" from *true* to *false,* which is later changed back to *true* when the mismatch of the verb forms is noted.

The response latency for verifying the latter true passive sentence may be predicted from the parameter estimates to be longer than the response latency for the former false passive sentence (in spite of the "false" response for the latter) and this result was indeed obtained in three experiments with slightly differing procedures. This result is taken by Olson and Filby to show that the passive sentences were not converted into their base structures. Their argument runs as follows: The base structure of passive sentences according to the current conceptions in transformational grammar is close to that of an active sentence (subject–verb–object). The false passive sentence, *the car was hit by the truck,* would accordingly be converted to a base form close to *the truck hit the car* with the result of a mismatch between subjects and an increase in latency. Conversely, the true passive sentence *the truck was hit by a car* would be converted into a base form close to the *car hit the truck* so that the compared subjects match. Therefore the false passive sentence would be predicted to take longer to verify than the true one, contrary to the obtained results. The reckoning from this is, according to Olson and Filby, that sentences are not decoded into their base structures, at least in this experimental task.

The alternative to their model, presented below, is based on the assumption that I-markers rather than surface strings are compared in the experimental task. Let us consider first the sentence presented after each picture, taking as an example

(A.1) *The car hit the truck.*

The I-marker underlying this sentence includes the goal relation between 'truck' and 'hit' and the agent relation between 'car' and 'hit'. As argued in Section 1D, I-marker relations differ in saliency and availability for processing. Since in active sentences the agent is usually focused on (see Section 4A), the latter relation will be more salient and, conversely, the goal relation will be more salient in passive sentences. The explanation below assumes that the more salient relation is resorted to first in the comparison process, and only if no comparison is possible thereby are other I-marker relations employed. Table A.1 shows the relation in the I-marker first activated, for each of the four sentences in Olson and Filby's experiment.

The pictures used in their experiment were of a truck hitting a car and of a car hitting a truck. If we assume with the authors that when the picture is shown its content is verbalized, it will again be the more salient I-marker relation which is activated in the comparison process. When the car is focused on, the result will be one of the structurings in the first two rows of Table A.1, and when the truck is focused on it will be one of those in the last two rows.[1] If, on the other hand, the content of the picture is not verbalized, some symbolic representation must be abstracted from it which has enough common ground with the semantic relations in the I-marker of the sentence to make the comparison possible (this is made explicit by Olson & Filby, 1972, p. 379; see also Chase & Clark, 1972). For the purpose of this exposition, we will assume that pictures are ultimately coded in the same form as sentences, as in Table A.1, although the comparison process may actually have to be carried out on a level beyond that of I-markers.

---

[1] A similar account is that of Chase and Clark (1972), in a verification experiment, that when viewing a picture of *A* above *B* (where the only other alternative is *B* above *A*), "Subjects in fact say they do not code the object so that the final structures look something like (*A above*) [p. 217]."

TABLE A.1
Relations in Olson and Filby's Sentences First Activated in
the Comparison Process

Sentence	Relation
(1) The car hit the truck.	(AGENT–ACTION car, hit)
(2) The car was hit by the truck.	(GOAL–ACTION car, hit)
(3) The truck hit the car.	(AGENT–ACTION truck, hit)
(4) The truck was hit by the car.	(GOAL–ACTION truck, hit)

Suppose now that the picture is of a car hitting a truck, and the car is focused on. The I-marker relation retrieved will therefore be (AGENT–ACTION car, hit). For "true" sentences two cases now must be distinguished:

1. The sentence presented after the picture also focuses on *the car*; the subject reads Sentence (1) of Table A.1. The arguments of the salient relations (car, hit) of the coding of the picture and those of the sentence are identical; the comparison is therefore straightforward.

2. The sentence presented after the picture does not focus on *the car,* that is, Sentence (4) of Table A.1 is presented. The salient relation is (GOAL–ACTION truck, hit); that is, arguments differ from those of the coding of the picture. Now, to make comparison possible, the less salient relation, namely (AGENT–ACTION car, hit), must be resorted to. Looking up the latter takes time and hence increases latency. In everyday language we may say that after focusing on the car in the picture, the subject is geared to a sentence concerning the car. When he then encounters a sentence beginning with *the truck,* he has to find out what this says about the car, which takes a small fraction of time.

Table A.2 presents the steps involved in "true" judgments, when the car in the picture is focused on. (Sentences in this Table are numbered as in Olson and Filby's paper so as to facilitate comparison). The factors contributing to increase in latency are:

1. in Step B, reading of a passive sentence (as compared to an active one);
2. in Step D, activating a less salient relation.

The factor in Step B is in line with what is known about the relative difficulty of passive sentences (see Section 4A) and is also postulated by Olson and Filby. An additional source of increase in latency assumed by the authors, verbalizing the picture as a passive sentence, is unnecessary for our explanation. The above two factors predict Sentence (4) of Table A.2 to have the largest latency, since both Step B and Step D take more time, and Sentence (1) the smallest latency. The empirically observed latencies in the Olson–Filby experiments (see their Figures 4, 5, and 6) were, in ascending order, Sentences (1), (7), (6), (4). Our prediction is thus sustained. Further, the results indicate that Step D contributes

TABLE A.2

Steps in the Verification of "True" Sentences

	Sentence			
Step	(1)	(4)	(6)	(7)
A Find salient relation in representation of picture (in which car is focused on).	(AGENT–ACTION car, hit)	(AGENT–ACTION car, hit)	(GOAL–ACTION car, hit)	(GOAL–ACTION car, hit)
B Read sentence.	*The car hit...*	*The truck was hit*	*The truck hit...*	*The car was hit...*
C Retrieve salient relation of sentence; if arguments are identical with those in A compare and proceed to E.	(AGENT–ACTION car, hit)	(GOAL–ACTION truck, hit)	(AGENT–ACTION truck, hit)	(GOAL–ACTION car, hit)
D (If arguments not identical) find less salient relation and compare with A.	—	(AGENT–ACTION car, hit)	(GOAL–ACTION car, hit)	—
E Respond according to match or mismatch in C or E.	"true"	"true"	"true"	"true"

more than Step B to latency: Sentence (7) took less time to respond to than Sentence (6) (although in one of their experiments — see their Figure 6 — the difference was negligible).

The steps for false sentences are described in Table A.3. Sentence (8) should take longest, because it is passive and requires activating the less salient relation, and Sentence (5) should take least time because it is active and requires only the salient relation. Moreover, in view of the empirical results for true sentences which show Step D to contribute more to latency than Step B, Sentence (2) should take longer than Sentence (3). In Olson and Filby's Experiment 1 (their Figure 4) this was indeed the rank order of latencies obtained. In Experiments 2 and 3 (their Figures 5 and 6) the latency for Sentence (5) was greater than those of either Sentence (2) or (3), a result which neither this proposal nor their model can explain. Also, in Experiment 3 the predicted order of Sentences (2) and (3) was reversed, but the difference was slight.

So far, then, our hypothesis that in verifying sentences subjects compare I-markers does no worse in predicting the result of either true or false sentences than Olson and Filby's hypothesis that surface structures are compared.[2] In their Experiment 1 (their Figure 4) sentences were ordered in respect to mean latencies from shortest to longest as follows: Sentence (1), (7), (5), (3), (2), (6), (8), (4). The ordering for Experiment 2 was the same except for Sentence (5), which was intermediate between Sentences (2) and (6), a result which both our model and Olson and Filby's fail to account for. In Experiment 3, Sentence (5) took still longer and there was little difference between Sentences (7), (3), (2), and (6). (Below we consider only Experiment 1.)

The rank order obtained in Experiment 1 suggests that the relative effects of the steps on latency are as follows:

1. The smallest effect is due to Step B (the sentence read being in the passive rather than in the active voice),
2. The effects of latency on the "false" response is a little larger,
3. The effect of Step D is larger than that of the two preceding effects combined.

---

[2] It has been assumed here that I-markers can be compared only if their arguments are identical. Alternatively, comparisons may be made if the same relations are involved and arguments differ. Consider, for instance, Sentence (2) of Table A.3. It appears intuitively, that after the picture of a car hitting, the subject hears the sentence beginning *the truck hit* . . . and immediately realizes that this is wrong: it was the car which hit, and not the truck. He may therefore respond "false" without first activating the less salient relation. Likewise, for Sentence (8) the goal relation is involved, as it is in the corresponding picture, and hence matching may be possible without activating the less salient relation. To account for the obtained order of sentence difficulty — Sentences (8), (2), (3), (5) — the additional assumption would then have to be introduced that comparison of arguments takes longer than comparison of relations. Even if this strategy was not universally adopted it may have been favored by some subjects (see below). Note that for the "true" sentences of Table A.2, one would still have to postulate that the less salient relations are invoked, because pictures and sentences differ in both the relation and the arguments.

TABLE A.3

Steps in the Verification of "False" Sentences

Step	Sentence			
	(2)	(3)	(5)	(8)
A Find salient relation in representation of picture in which car is focused on).	(AGENT–ACTION car, hit)	(AGENT–ACTION car, hit)	(GOAL–ACTION car, hit)	(GOAL–ACTION car, hit)
B Read sentence.	*The truck hit...*	*the car was hit...*	*the car hit...*	*the truck was hit...*
C Retrieve salient relation of sentence; if arguments are identical with those in A compare and proceed to E.	(AGENT–ACTION truck, hit)	(GOAL–ACTION car, hit)	(AGENT–ACTION car, hit)	(GOAL–ACTION truck, hit)
D (If arguments not identical) find less salient relation and compare with A.	(GOAL–ACTION car, hit)	—	—	(AGENT–ACTION car, hit)
E Respond according to match or mismatch in C or E.	"false"	"false"	"false"	"false"

In Table A.4 the eight sentences are ordered from top to bottom according to the order of latencies predicted by Principles 1–3, assuming that all subjects resorted to the less salient relation in Sentences (2) and (8). (The two pluses for the two sentences in the D column are parenthesized in order to indicate that an alternative strategy not involving this step is available; see footnote 2). The order in Table A.4 corresponds quite well with the empirically obtained one in Experiment 1, except for Sentences (2) and (8), which are actually easier than predicted by Principles 1–3. This discrepancy may have resulted from some subjects resorting to the strategy discussed in Footnote 2 in verifying these sentences, with the result that their mean latencies were shorter than predicted. Incidentally, the relative latencies of Sentences (4) and (8) are contrary to the predictions from Olson and Filby's model.

For Sentences (3) and (4), Principles 1–3 predict a difference in the same direction as Olson and Filby's model. It was the relative size of latencies of these two sentences on which they based their argument that in verification only surface structures are compared. By contrast, according to the alternative explanation presented above, I-marker relations are compared. The latter explanation hinges on the assumption, independently supported (see Section 1C), that relations in the I-marker differ in saliency and that the more salient aspects are utilized in the comparison. Since this can account for Olson and Filby's experimental results reasonably well, it may be concluded that their findings are not damaging to the theory of comprehension advanced in Chapter 6.

The assumption that, as far as possible, salient relations are activated first holds up well for the Olson–Filby experiment. The generality of this finding is another question. One may suspect that in this experiment, in which only two pictures were given as alternatives, it was practical to concentrate on the salient relation only and that in situations in which there are more alternatives, the

TABLE A.4
Factors Increasing Latency

Sentence	Step		
	B Passive sentence	D Comparing less salient relation	E Responding "false"
1			
7	+		
5			+
3	+		+
6		+	
4	+	+	
2		(+)	+
8	+	(+)	+

whole I-marker must necessarily become operative. On the other hand, the notion of differential availability of I-marker relations seems so well established (see also Sections 1C, 6E, and 9C) that it seems likely that even in the latter case salient relations are activated first and only subsequently — and perhaps more perfunctorily — less salient ones.

Relative saliency of different I-marker elements need not be constant over time. Specifically it should not be surprising to find that when the active or passive form of the comprehended sentence results in the agent or goal being salient, this effect wears off with time. This in fact occurred in a study by Garrod and Trabasso (1973) as well as in one by Anderson and Bower (1973, pp. 225–228). The latter also report that a delay of 2 min did not eliminate the "voice effect" for isolated sentences completely, whereas it did so for sentences in a narrative text. The explanation advanced by the above-mentioned writers is that while the surface structures are stored in short-term memory, the deep structures are normally stored in long-term memory, which are therefore available for comparison after delay. It seems to me, however, that an explanation is preferable which does not assume that verification proceeds without comprehension, which is what comparison of surface structures seems to imply.

APPENDIX B

Ambiguous Readings:
The Case of the Dative
Movement

Jackendoff and Culicover (1971) raise, among others, the problem of the doubtful acceptability of:

(B.1)   What was Mary bought by John?

In contrast to Example (B.1), the following sentence – to which the same transformations have been applied – seems perfectly acceptable:

(B.2)   What was Mary given by John?

Jackendoff and Culicover (1971, p. 410) find this case "to be a mystery," which they immediately set forth to explain. They suggest two factors for the questionable acceptability of Example (B.1):

a. The *for*-object of the verb *bought* in Example (B.1) is optional, whereas the *to*-object is obligatory with the verb *give* in Example (B.2).

This difference makes for the "slight unnaturalness," according to the authors, of the passive Example (B.3), which contrasts with Example (B.4):

(B.3)   Mary was bought a book.
(B.4)   Mary was given a book.

b. After perceiving *what was Mary,* one expects "a continuation along the lines of *what was Mary doing*";

and this expectation is disconfirmed in Examples (B.1) and (B.2).

Now, the authors argue, the combined effect of both factors (a and b) serves to "produce some confusion" in processing Example (B.1). On the other hand, there is no unnaturalness in Example (B.2), because only the second factor is operative there.

This explanation does not seem sufficient. Concerning the first factor, it can be shown that the optional–obligatory distinction is at best only a partial explanation of the unnaturalness of some passive sentences. Although they involve *to*-objects, Examples (B.5) and (B.6) are about as unacceptable as Example (B3) (as has been confirmed in a study reported on below):

(B.5)   Mary was thrown a book by John.
(B.6)   Mary was passed a book by John.

Likewise, the second factor fails to account for the relative unacceptability of Examples (B.5) and (B.6), because *Mary was* does not lead one to expect a continuation like *doing*. All this suggests that one should look for a common factor which underlies the unacceptability of passive sentences of Examples (B.5) and (B.6) as well as that of interrogative passives like:

(B.7)   What was Mary thrown by John?
(B.8)   What was Mary passed by John?

The explanation below is based on the treatment of the comprehension process in Section 10E. When hearing Examples (B.5)–(B.8), an interpretation suggests itself which has *Mary* as goal denoting the person to whom something is thrown or passed. Thus, in Example (B.5), *Mary was thrown* is tentatively interpreted as 'somebody threw Mary' (against the wall, perhaps), and in Example (B.6) *Mary was passed* as 'somebody passed Mary' (as on the road). Although the beginning of Examples (B.7) and (B.8), *what was,* might be supposed to rule out such a reading, this need not be so because an utterance does not invariably have to be processed from left to right (see Section 6A). Rather, the substring *was Mary thrown* or even only *Mary thrown* may be concentrated on and be assigned a reading, which subsequently clashes with a later, and final, reading of the utterance. Now, such an incorrect reading is obviated by semantic matching in the case of *Mary was given* in Examples (B.2) and (B.4); people are not something one is likely to give. Since no incorrect reading is constructed, no revision is required in Examples (B.2) and (B.4). These sentences are therefore easier to process, and hence more acceptable.

An apparent counterexample to this explanation is provided by the active sentences corresponding to Examples (B.7) and (B.8):

(B.9)   John throws Mary a book.
(B.10) John passes Mary a book.

These seem to be relatively acceptable in spite of there being no apparent reason why *Mary* as goal should not be attempted here as well. To explain this fact, an additional principle must be applied. Active sentences are easier to process than the corresponding sentences with passive or interrogative transformations (see Section 4D). Presumably, the difficulty of the passive and interrogative form is added to that resulting from the attempted incorrect interpretation of Examples

(B.5)–(B.8). Possibly, because of the lesser structural difficulty of active sentences, more structural steering occurs and no incorrect reading is arrived at.

SOME INFORMAL EXPERIMENTS

To obtain further confirmation for our explanation, acceptability judgements were obtained from native speakers of English who were ignorant of the hypotheses tested. Specifically, it was intended to investigate:

a. the acceptability of passive and interrogative–passive sentences with dative movement, like Examples (B.5)–(B.8), relative to that of the corresponding active ones, like Examples (B.9)–(B.10):

b. The effect of semantic constraints between action and goal (of the kind proposed for *give* in Examples B.2 and B.4 above) on the relative acceptability of different sentences with dative movement.

The explanation offered in the preceding section can be put to test by answers to (a) and (b). In addition, information was sought as to:

c. the relative acceptability of passive and interrogative–passive sentences with dative movement.

Note that the explanation given in the preceding section fails to make any prediction concerning the third question. Possibly, interrogative passives, being more complex than passives, will be more difficult to comprehend and this may affect their acceptability. On the other hand, the substring which is presumably incorrectly interpreted in the interrogative–passive sentence (*was Mary thrown*) is preceded by the disambiguating context (in *what was Mary thrown, Mary* cannot be the goal); this may be of greater help in avoiding the incorrect reading than the context following *Mary was thrown* in the passive sentence. Jackendoff and Culicover's explanation, however, can be tested by investigating the last problem, because their explanation should predict that interrogative–passive sentences will be decidedly less acceptable than the corresponding passives.

Three informal experiments were carried out. In the first, active, passive, and interrogative–passive sentences with dative movement were compared; these structures will be called A, P, and Q, respectively:

(B.11)   A: Ezra sold Martin the car.
         P: Arthur was sold the car by Ed.
         Q: What was Collin sold by Herbert?

Six different sentences were used, each in the three forms, A, P, and Q. The A-sentences included the one in Example (B.11) and the following:

(B.12)   Carl left Elsa the estate.
(B.13)   Jill passes Sue the salt.
(B.14)   David throws Peter the ball.

(B.15)   Paul hands Jack the ball.

(B.16)   Fred brings Danny the key.

Each of these A-sentences was turned into the corresponding P and Q forms. To alleviate somewhat the monotony of the judges' task, a different pair of names appeared in each of the resulting 18 sentences.

Six native English speakers served as subjects in the first experiment. Each subject was given a well-shuffled pack of 18 3 X 5-inch cards on each of which one of the sentences appeared. He was asked to sort the cards into 3 piles according to how good the sentence sounded.[1] After he had finished sorting, he was asked to go over the third pile – the one containing the sentences judged to be worst – and to sort these cards again into 2 piles according to how good they sounded. No restrictions were imposed either on the size of the piles or the time to sort the cards.[2]

The results can be analyzed in a number of ways. The findings below are pertinent to the questions raised above:

For each sentence the A form was judged more acceptable than either the P or the Q form. Only 1 subject judged an A sentence as less acceptable than the corresponding P sentence (this was for Sentence B.13). Ties between the A and Q forms appeared in the judgments of 2 additional subjects; all in all there were 5 such ties. Looking at the results from a different perspective, one may state that for 5 out of the 6 subjects, there were more sentences for which the A form was preferred than sentences in which it was not, or in which there was a tie between A and Q. The sixth subject preferred the A form in 3 out of the 6 sentences. Preference of the A form was statistically significant (at the .05 level by a one-tailed sign test).

Another way of looking at the data is to see which sentences were sorted into the first ("best") category. Four of the subjects included only A sentences in this category, and two of them also included some of the Q sentences (three Q sentences in all). None of the P sentences was put into this cateogry. All A sentences were sorted into the second category by two subjects, and the third by

---

[1] Relative rather than absolute judgments of acceptability were elicited in these experiments. People may be able to classify a few sentences as "acceptable" or "not acceptable" in an absolute sense; but as the number of sentences becomes larger and the distinctions to be made finer – as was the case in our experiments – they will in effect end up by classifying the sentences relative to each other (Bever, 1970, pp. 346–348).

[2] Subjects usually had no difficulty in following these instructions, with the following exceptions:

1. Two subjects ended up with only two groups in the first sorting. They were therefore asked to sort each of these into two piles according to the acceptability.

2. One of the subjects said he could not find any differences between the cards he had sorted into the third pile. For this subject, therefore, only three degrees of acceptability were available.

3. A fourth subject was dropped from the experiment because he insisted that only two categories of sentences could be distinguished. Another subject was substituted for him.

one of them. The answer to the first question posed above is therefore quite unequivocal: The A form is definitely preferred over both the P and Q forms.

The picture is less clear regarding the relative acceptability of P and Q sentences. Summing over all subjects, the Q form was preferred over the P form of the same sentence 12 times, while the reverse was the case 16 times (there were 8 ties between P and Q), but this difference was not statistically significant. On none of the 6 sentences was there unanimity between subjects in preferring either of the forms. While 2 of the subjects consistently preferred Q over P for all 6 sentences, there was one subject who consistently preferred P over Q; the 3 remaining subjects were not consistent in their preferences.

To obtain additional information concerning the relative acceptability of P and Q sentences, it was decided to run a second experiment. A slightly different procedure was adopted. Instead of handing the subject a pack of cards, the cards were spread out on the table in front of the subject. Doing so was thought to possibly make it easier for him to deliberate on the relative acceptability of these sentences.

In addition to the six sentences from the first experiment, two sentences were included in order to test the effect of semantic constraint (see b above). The P form of these sentences was

(B.17)   Ted was given a watch by Barbara.
(B.18)   Julia was lent a book by Evelyn.

Presumably, *Ted* and *Julia* are not construed as goals in Examples (B.17) and (B.18), because neither the giving nor the lending of people is customary.

The subjects were given 8 sentences, each appearing once in the P form and once in the Q form. The 16 cards containing these sentences were laid before the subject in 4 rows in a fixed, randomly determined order, with the P form of each sentence appearing directly above its Q form. Six native speakers of English sorted the cards into 3 piles and subsequently the third pile into 2, as in the first experiment.

In this experiment, the trend of preferring Q over P sentences was reversed. In 31 judgements the P form was preferred over the Q form for the same sentence, whereas the Q form was preferred only 8 times, and in 9 cases the P and Q forms of a sentence were sorted into the same pile. This difference was not statistically significant. Again, as in the first experiment, there was no single sentence for which all subjects preferred 1 of the forms. Only 1 subject was consistent in preferring the P form for all sentences, and none of the subjects consistently preferred the Q form.

The results of the two experiments, then, do not permit a firm conclusion regarding the relative acceptability of P and Q forms. Jackendoff and Culicover's explanation, which implies a clear preference of P over Q, is therefore not supported by the data. All that can be stated definitely is that both P and Q are, as predicted, significantly less acceptable than A.

After the first and second experiments, subjects were asked why they decided that some sentences did not sound right. Of the 12 subjects, 7 gave reasons to the effect that they first thought of the indirect object as the direct object; for instance, in the Q form of Example (B.11) it was Collin who was sold and not the car. The examples given by these subjects for this (incorrect) interpretation included both Q and P sentences. These introspective reports confirm the explanation given above. It is noteworthy that none of the subjects offered anything which might be construed as support for Jackendoff and Culicover's explanation.

Before discussing the effect of semantic constraints in the second experiment, a third informal experiment is described which also addressed itself to this problem. This was actually a continuation of the second experiment, conducted with the same 6 subjects. Each of them was handed 8 cards containing the A form of the sentences used in the second experiment. These he was asked to sort into two piles. (All 8 sentences were in the past tense, while in the first experiment some of the sentences were inadvertently constructed in the present tense.)

The results of this experiment can best be summarized by listing the sentences followed by the number (in parentheses) of subjects who sorted a given sentence into the "better sounding" category:

(B.19)   Dick gave Clement a plate. (6)
(B.20)   Phyllis lent Nancy a comb. (6)
(B.21)   Ezra sold Martin the car. (5)
(B.22)   Paul handed Jack the ball. (4)
(B.23)   Jill passed Sue the salt. (2)
(B.24)   David threw Peter the ball. (1)
(B.25)   Fred brought Danny the key. (1)
(B.26)   Carl left Elsa the estate. (1)

Intuitively it is understandable why Examples (B.23)–(B.26) were judged by most subjects to be less acceptable: The incorrect reading 'Jill passed Sue' (goal), 'David threw Peter' (goal – perhaps against the wall), and so on seems to be operative to some extent. This seems to affect their acceptability, even though these sentences are in the active form. (But remember that all A sentences were by far more acceptable than the P and Q sentences.) By contrast, the two sentences with *give* and *lent* were judged by all subjects, as expected, to be among the "better" ones. Here such an interpretation was presumably not considered; people are neither given nor lent. Nor is it likely that they are sold or handed – witness the judgements of Examples (B.21)–(B.22). The results thus accord with our intuitions as to what is plausible on pragmatic grounds.

The data on P sentences obtained in this experiment and on Q sentences can be ranked likewise. In general, these rankings accorded with the above intuitions of plausibility: the sentences with *give* and *lent* were the most acceptable; the sentences with *threw* were of least; and those with *handed* of intermediate acceptability – both in the P and Q forms. The remaining four sentences in the second experiment were of intermediate acceptability and their rankings differed from those of the corresponding A forms in the third experiment. Presumably, this discrepancy may be partly accounted for by the large variation between subjects. (Note also that in the case of *passed* and *left* the meaning of the verb in the hypothesized interpretation which has *Mary* as goal differs slightly from its meaning in the above P and Q sentences, where *Mary* is the indirect object. Conceivably, this may be a contributory factor to the lack of stability in judgements of these sentences.)

Some support is thus provided by the judgements of our subjects for our explanation of the acceptability of sentences with dative movement. Of the questions posed at the beginning of this section, the answers to the first two (a and b) were as predicted by this explanation, whereas the answer to the third (c) failed to support Jackendoff and Culicover's rival explanation. The introspective reports further confirmed the former. We next proceeded to carry out a more rigorously designed experiment to test the effect of pragmatic constraints. But before reporting on this, a methodological note seems in order.

?*WHY LINGUISTS SHOULD NOT BE LEFT SENTENCES TO JUDGE (AN ASIDE)

In many recent linguistic articles, one finds a generous sprinkling of question marks and asterisks, which serve to indicate several shades of acceptability of the sentences given as examples. Generally, no attempt is made to base the fine discriminations implied by this notation on anything but the writer's judgement. This practice of letting the linguist be the sole arbiter of acceptability I hold to be indefensible for reasons illustrated by the above data. Our results highlight the instability of acceptability judgements. The picture which emerges from the experiments is one of great variation between subjects. If a single person instead of all the six had judged the P and Q sentences, a different conclusion might conceivably have been arrived at. This is not the only study in which such a lack of reliability has been found. In an investigation by Quirk and Svartvik (1966) acceptability judgements were divided on many of the 50 sentences studied. Further, it appears that a given person's judgement is not very stable over time. In the case of our subjects, considerable changes in judgements had occurred after several weeks' interval.[3]

---

[3] Four subjects who were available at the time were retested with exactly the same procedure. One subject placed 9 of the 18 cards in a different category than he did in the first experiment. Another subject sorted the cards in the first experiment in a very systematic fashion: all A sentences in the "best" category, all Q sentences in the second, and all P sentences in the last two categories. He replicated this sorting almost perfectly. Two subjects from the second experiment sorted 10 and 14 cards (out of 16) respectively into a different category. The latter subject (14 cards) even reversed the relative position of the P and Q forms of the same sentence for 5 out of 8 sentences. For the other 3 subjects, such a reversal was observed only once.

It might be argued that, because of his training, a linguist will come up with more reliable judgements than a layman. However, the linguist cannot help being biased by the hypothesis he has in mind. Likewise, the reader of the linguist's paper may have become convinced by his arguments and consequently be biased in the same direction. Spencer (1973) found that while native speakers agreed among themselves on the acceptability or unacceptability of 80% of the sentences, their agreement with judgements found in articles of linguists was strikingly lower – about 50%. Statements concerning acceptability purport to be about views held by speakers of the language in general. Here, as for other psychological statements, a sample of one subject, even if he is unbiased, is not sufficient for arriving at any conclusion.

No psychologist would dream of submitting for publication results derived only from his own judgements, and linguists should be equally careful to eschew methodological sloppiness. Ideally, acceptability of sentences should be reported only when judgements have been elicited from a number of native speakers after necessary precautions have been taken to prevent the investigator's bias from affecting them. The number of judges and conditions under which judgements were obtained should be reported, because judgements may be sensitive to contextual effects, as pointed out by Bever (1970, p. 346–348), and demonstrated by Greenbaum (1973).

Lest these measures be considered too draconic, a different convention might be advocated. As a minimum precaution against unwarranted conclusions, the reader should be informed whether a given acceptability judgement is based on a reliable procedure. For instance, the asterisk or question mark preceding a sentence might be put in parentheses to indicate that this judgement is to be regarded as tentative, pending confirmation by several native speakers. To take my own medicine, I hasten to add that

(?) Nobody besides myself was given the sentence appearing as heading to this section to judge,

and to report on a more carefully controlled experiment.

A TEST OF THE SEMANTIC CONSTRAINT HYPOTHESIS

The semantic constraint hypothesis advanced above claims that the acceptability of sentences with dative movement is a function of the main verb: to the extent that the main verb and the object taken in isolation permit of a construal as action and goal, acceptability will be lowered. To test this hypothesis, two experimental forms containing lists of sentences were employed in both of which the same verbs appeared. In one form each verb appeared in a sentence without indirect object and in which the direct object was a person, and subjects were asked to rate the sentences as to their plausibility. In the second form the same verbs appeared in sentences with dative movement, and subjects were asked to rate the acceptability of the sentences. Since our informal experiments showed passive sentences to be less acceptable than active ones, all test sentences were in the passive. The following sentence frames were used:

(A) Paul was V + *en* by John.
(B) Paul was V + *en* a NP by John.

For example,

(B.27) Paul was sold by John.
(B.28) Paul was sold a book by John.

The semantic constraints hypothesis predicts that the median scores of implausibility on Form A should correlate positively with the median scores of acceptability for the corresponding sentences in Form B.

Special care was taken in constructing the test sentences so as not to bias the experimental results. We first searched books on English grammar (such as Quirk, Greenbaum, Leech, & Svartvik, 1972) for ditransitive verbs, like *give, sell,* and *throw,* which can take both a direct and an indirect object. All verbs resulting in sentences in which the direct object is deletable were discarded. Thus, *pay,* for instance, is not suitable for testing our hypothesis, because we have both Examples (B.29) and (B.30), with *Cyril* as indirect object:

(B.29) The man paid Cyril.
(B.30) The man paid Cyril the money.

As an additional check on possible construals of the verb and the noun phrase in Form B, we asked judges about each verb whether it had the same meaning in Sentence A and in the corresponding Sentence B. This was done as part of our procedure for obtaining plausible noun phrases for the Form B sentences: Each of 6 native speakers of English was presented with a list of sentences in Form B with a slot instead of NP for filling in "an appropriate word." Next he was asked to state whether the verb in the sentence "meant the same" with the filled in word as without it. If more than 1 of the 6 judges answered "yes" to this question, this was taken as an indication that the direct object might be looked on as deletable, as in Example (B.30); and the verb was discarded. This left us with the 21 verbs listed in Table B.1.

The NPs for the Form B sentences were selected from the words supplied by our judges. There was a striking degree of stereotyping in their suggestions. So that judgements of acceptability of Form B sentences should as far as possible not be affected by their inherent plausibility, we chose the most popular response. Also, we decided on the article which had to go with the noun[4] on the

---

[4] For *hand* there were as many judges who chose *a/the book* as *a/the pen,* and since the former noun was already chosen for *sell,* we opted for the latter. *The/a flat* had more responses than *a house* for *rent,* but the former is used differently by American speakers, and so was discarded. Finally, for the only verb on which every judge gave a different response, *save,* one response was selected arbitrarily.

TABLE B.1

Median Acceptability and Implausibility Ratings for 21 Verbs in Version 1

	Median implausibility on Form A	Median acceptability on Form B	Noun appearing in Form B as goal
mention	1.06	1.12	the incident
take	1.40	1.27	the check
make	6.19	1.31	a cake
return	5.53	1.50	the book
save	1.11	1.83	a candy
hire	1.11	2.00	a car
order	1.60	2.25	a sandwich
rent	6.56	2.31	a house
pass	3.80	2.32	the ball
buy	4.00	3.00	a present
sell	3.13	3.17	a book
throw	1.80	3.21	the ball
reserve	6.66	3.25	a seat
explain	4.63	3.40	the problem
read	6.38	3.50	a story
do	6.75	4.00	a favor
bequeath	6.57	4.50	money
hand	6.83	5.33	a pen
offer	4.25	5.67	a candy
give	6.54	6.00	a drink
call	1.21	6.50	a name

Note: Scores ranged from 1 ("completely unacceptable"/"completely plausible") to 7 ("completely acceptable"/"completely implausible").

basis of the completions supplied by the majority of judges. The list of nouns with their articles is given in Table B.1.

In the two experimental forms the same two nouns, *John* and *Paul*, figured in all sentences, since pretesting had suggested that acceptability judgements might be sensitive to such factors as the sound of the words. Instruction to the subjects typed on the list were as below

For Form A:

Kindly examine the following sentences. Some of them are plausible; some of them are not. You are asked to judge each sentence as to its plausibility by circling one of the numbers on the right from 1 (completely plausible) to 7 (completely implausible). Paul and John in these sentences are just two ordinary people; don't try to make up any special context for these sentences, but give your first reaction.

For Form B:

Kindly examine the following sentences. Some of them are acceptable English, some of them are not; i.e. some of them seem just right and some don't. You are asked to judge each sentence as to its acceptability by circling one of the numbers on the right from 1 (completely unacceptable) to 7 (completely acceptable).

The sequence of sentences in Form A was determined randomly. Two versions were prepared for Form A, which differed in the permutations employed. The constraint was observed that any two consecutive sentences in one permutation should not appear consecutively in the other version. The sentences for Form B also appeared in two versions, and in the same sequences as the corresponding sentences in the Form A version.

A third experimental form, C, was also used containing a list of sentences with the same verbs and nouns as List B and having the following form:

(C) NP was V + *en* for / to Paul by John.

(For *call* this form has different underlying relations and therefore no corresponding sentence was included.) The purpose of this form was to obtain acceptability judgements for sentences without dative movement corresponding to those in Form B and to assess the effect, if any, of the particular choice of words on the correlation between scores on Forms A and B. However, since the judgements on these two forms hardly correlated at all, the results for Form C will not be further reported here.

The rating sheets for the three forms, each in two versions, were shuffled and distributed to students enrolled at various departments of the Hebrew University, Jerusalem. On the rating sheet they stated in writing what their native language was. Below we report only on the results obtained for the 167 students who indicated that they were native speakers of English.

Spearman rank order correlations between the two versions, (which differ in sequence of sentences) were encouragingly high: .948 for Form A and .945 for Form B. It may be concluded therefore that: (1) our results are highly reliable; and (2) there was surprisingly little order effect for both the plausibility and acceptability judgments.

Table B.1 presents the median scores for one of the versions. Sentences are arranged according to ascending order of acceptability (Form B). Comparison with plausibility scores (Form A) shows that the greater the plausibility of a sentence in Form A, the lower the acceptability of the corresponding sentence of Form B, as predicted by the semantic constraint hypothesis. Spearman rank order correlations between the scores on Form A and on Form B were .487 for Version 1 and .447 for Version 2. Taken separately, the *p* values for these coefficients are .013 and .022, respectively (1-tailed test), but considering that the correlation has been replicated we are justified in regarding the hypothesis as corroborated.

The greatest divergence from what one might expect under the semantic constraints hypothesis is presented by the verb *call*: Example (B.32) in the B Form is completely acceptable, although Example (B.31) in the A Form is completely plausible. The reason for this may be that "call a name" is a frequently appearing collocation, and therefore Example (B.32) can resist intrusion by an interpretation appropriate to Example (B.31):

(B.31)   Paul was called by John.

(B.32)   Paul was called a name by John.

In retrospect it might have been wiser to exclude such collocations. The other discrepancy, *make,* also admits of a post hoc explanation. While the A Form is quite implausible, the B Form, Example (B.33), turned out to be quite unacceptable:

(B.33)   Paul was made a cake by John.

Presumably the first three words may have given rise to a different erroneous interpretation: 'Paul was made king (ambassador, etc.)'.

ACKNOWLEDGMENTS

I am indebted to Sidney Greenbaum for his detailed comments on a draft of part of this appendix and for helpful suggestions concerning the experiments. I thank Mordechai Rimor for his competent assistance in carrying out this experiment.

References

Anderson, J. R., & Bower, G. H. *Human associative memory.* Washington, D.C.: Winston, 1973.

Anisfeld, M., & Klenbort, I. On the functions of structural paraphrase: The view from the passive voice. *Psychological Bulletin,* 1973, *79,* 117–126.

Antinucci, F., & Parisi, D. Early language acquisition: a model and some data. In C. A. Ferguson & D. I. Slobin (Eds.), *Studies of child language development.* New York: Holt, Rinehart and Winston, 1973. Pp. 607–619.

Barclay, J. R. The role of comprehension in remembering sentences. *Cognitive Psychology,* 1973, *4,* 229–254.

Barclay, J. R. & Reid, M. Semantic integration in children's recall of discourse. *Developmental Psychology,* 1974, *10,* 277–281.

Bar-Hillel, Y. A demonstration of the nonfeasibility of fully automatic high quality translation. In Y. Bar-Hillel, *Language and information: Selected essays on their theory and application.* Reading, Mass.: Addison-Wesley, 1964. Pp. 174–179. (a)

Bar-Hillel, Y. A quasi-arithmetical notation for syntactic description. In Y. Bar-Hillel *Language and information: Selected essays on their theory and application.* Reading, Mass.: Addison-Wesley, 1964. Pp. 61–74. (b)

Bar-Hillel, Y. Do natural languages contain paradoxes? *Studium Generale,* 1966, *19,* 391–397.

Bar-Hillel, Y. Dictionaries and meaning rules. *Foundations of Language,* 1967, *3,* 409–419.

Bar-Hillel, Y. Universal semantics and the philosophy of language: Quandaries and prospects. In J. Puhvel (Ed.), *Substance and structure of language,* Berkeley: Univ. of California Press, 1969. Pp. 1–21.

Bennett, D. C. English prepositions: A stratificational approach. *Journal of Linguistics,* 1968, *4,* 153–172.

Bever, T. G. The cognitive basis for linguistic structures. In J. R. Hayes (Ed.), *Cognition and the development of language.* New York: Wiley, 1970. Pp. 279–362.

Bever, T. G., Garrett, M. F., & Hurtig, R. The interaction of perceptual processes and ambiguous sentences. *Memory and Cognition,* 1973, *1,* 277–286.

Bierwisch, M. Some semantic universals of German adjectives. *Foundations of Language,* 1967, *3,* 1–36.

Bierwisch, M. On certain problems of semantic representations. *Foundations of Language,* 1969, *5,* 153–184.

Bierwisch, M. Semantics. In J. Lyons (Ed.), *New horizons in linguistics*. Harmondsworth, Middlesex: Penguin, 1970). (a)

Bierwisch, M. Fehlerlinguistik. *Linguistic Inquiry*, 1970, *1*, 397–414. (b)

Bloom, L. *Language development: Form and function in emerging grammars*. Cambridge, Mass.: M.I.T. Press, 1970.

Bloom, L. *One word at a time*. The Hague: Mouton, 1973.

Bloom, L. Talking, understanding and thinking. In R. L. Schiefelbusch & L. L. Lloyd (Eds.), *Language perspectives: Acquisition, retardation and intervention*. Baltimore, Maryland: University Park Press, 1974.

Bloom, L., Miller, P., & Hood, L. Variation and reduction as aspects of competence in language development. In A. Pick (Ed.), *Minnesota symposium on child psychology* (Vol. 9). Minneapolis: University of Minnesota Press, 1975.

Blumenthal, A. L. Prompted recall of sentences. *Journal of Verbal Learning and Verbal Behavior*, 1967, *6*, 203–206.

Blumenthal, A. L., & Boakes, R. Prompted recall of sentences. *Journal of Verbal Learning and Verbal Behavior*, 1967, *6*, 674–676.

Bolinger, D. The atomization of meaning. *Language*, 1965, *41*, 555–573.

Bolinger, D. Adjectives in English: Attribution and predication. *Lingua*, 1967, *18*, 1–34.

Bolinger, D. Meaning and form. *Transactions of the New York Academy of Sciences*, 1974, *36*, 218–233. (a)

Bolinger, D. Transitivity and spatiality: The passive of prepositional verbs. In A. Makkai (Ed.), *Linguistics at the crossroads*. The Hague: Mouton, 1974. (b)

Bond, Z. S., & Gray, J. Subjective phrase structure: An empirical investigation. *Journal of Psycholinguistic Research*, 1973, *2*, 259–266.

Boomer, D. S., & Laver, J. D. M. Slips of the tongue. *British Journal of Disorders of Communication*, 1968, *3*, 1–12.

Bowerman, M. F. *Early syntactic development: A crosslinguistic study with special reference to Finnish*. Cambridge, England: Cambridge University Press, 1973. (a)

Bowerman, M. Structural relationships in children's utterances: Syntactic or semantic? In T. E. Moore (Ed.), *Cognitive development and the acquisition of language*. New York: Academic Press, 1973. Pp. 197–214. (b)

Bowerman, M. Development of concepts underlying language: Discussion summary. In R. L. Schiefelbusch & L. L. Lloyd (Eds.), *Language perspectives: Acquisition, retardation, and intervention*. Baltimore: University Park Press, 1974. Pp. 191–209.

Braine, M. D. S. Children's first word combinations. *Monographs of the Society for Research in Child Development*, 1976, Serial No. 164.

Bransford, J. D., Barclay, J. R., & Franks, J. J. Sentence memory: A constructive versus interpretive approach. *Cognitive Psychology*, 1972, *3*, 193–202.

Bransford, J. D., & Franks, J. J. The abstraction of linguistic ideas. *Cognitive Psychology*, 1971, *2*, 331–350.

Bransford, J. D., & Franks, J. J. The abstraction of linguistic ideas. A review. *Cognition*, 1972, *1*, 211–249.

Bransford, J. D., & Johnson, M. K. Contextual prerequisites for understanding: Some investigations of comprehension and recall. *Journal of Verbal Learning and Verbal Behavior*, 1972, *11*, 717–726.

Brown, R. *A first language: The early stages*. Cambridge, Mass.: Harvard University Press, 1973.

Brown, R., & McNeill, D. The "tip of the tongue" phenomenon. *Journal of Verbal Learning and Verbal Behavior*, 1966, *5*, 325–337.

Bühler, K. *Sprachtheorie*. Jena: Fischer, 1934.

Burgess, A. *Joysprick: An introduction to the language of James Joyce*. London: Deutsch, 1973.

Carey, P. W., Mehler, J., & Bever, T. G. When do we compute all the interpretations of an ambiguous sentence? In G. B. F. d'Arcais & W. J. M. Levelt (Eds.), *Advances in psycholinguistics*, Amsterdam, North-Holland Publ., 1970. Pp. 61–75.

Carroll, J. B. (Ed.) *Language, thought, and reality: Selected writings of Benjamin Lee Whorf.* Cambridge, Mass.: M.I.T. Press, 1956.

Carroll, J. B. Process and content in psycholinguistics. In *Current trends in the description and analysis of behavior.* Pittsburgh: Pittsburgh University Press, 1958. Pp. 175–200.

Carroll, J. B. Toward a performance grammar for core sentences in spoken and written English. In G. Nickel (Ed.), *Special issue of IRAL on the occasion of Bertil Malmberg's sixtieth birthday.* Heidelberg: J. Groos, 1973.

Carroll, L. *Alice in Wonderland.* London: Macmillan, 1948.

Cassirer, E. *The philosophy of symbolic forms. Vol. 1: Language.* New Haven: Yale University Press, 1953.

Chafe, W. L. Idiomaticity as an anomaly in the Chomskyan paradigm. *Foundations of Language,* 1968, *4,* 109–127.

Chafe, W. L. *Meaning and the structure of language.* Chicago: University of Chicago Press, 1970.

Chafe, W. L. Directionality and paraphrase. *Language,* 1971, *47,* 1–26.

Charniak, E. *Toward a model of children's story comprehension.* Cambridge, Mass.: M.I.T. Artificial Intelligence Laboratory, 1972.

Chase, W. G., & Clark, H. H. Mental operations in the comparison of sentences and pictures. In L. Gregg (Ed.), *Cognition in learning and memory.* New York: Wiley, 1972. Pp. 205–232.

Chomsky, C. *The acquisition of syntax in children from 5 to 10.* Cambridge, Mass.: M.I.T. Press, 1969.

Chomsky, N. *Syntactic Structures.* The Hague: Mouton, 1957.

Chomsky, N. On the notion 'rule of grammar.' In R. Jakobson (Ed.), *Structure of language in its mathematical aspects. Proceedings of symposia in applied mathematics.* American Mathematical Society, Vol. 12, 1961. Pp. 6–24.

Chomsky, N. *Aspects of the theory of syntax.* Cambridge, Mass.: M.I.T. Press, 1965.

Chomsky, N. Deep structure, surface structure, and semantic interpretation. In D. D. Steinberg & L. A. Jakobovits (Eds.), *Semantics: An interdisciplinary reader in philosophy, linguistics and psychology.* Cambridge, England: Cambridge University Press, 1971. Pp. 183–216.

Clark, H. H. Some structural properties of simple active and passive sentences. *Journal of Verbal Learning and Verbal Behavior,* 1965, *4,* 365–370.

Clark, H. H., & Clark, E. V. Semantic distinctions and memory for complex sentences. *Quarterly Journal of Experimental Psychology,* 1968, *20,* 129–138.

Clifton, C., Jr., Kurcz, I., & Jenkins, J. J. Grammatical relations as determinants of sentence similarity. *Journal of Verbal Learning and Verbal Behavior,* 1965, *4,* 112–117.

Clifton, C., Jr., & Odom, P. Similarity relations among certain English sentence constructions. *Psychological Monographs,* 1966, *80,* (5, Whole No. 613).

Cohen, E., Namir, L., & Schlesinger, I. M. *A new dictionary of sign language.* The Hague, Mouton, in press.

Collins, A. M., & Quillian, M. R. Experiments on semantic memory and language comprehension. In L. W. Gregg (Ed.), *Cognition in learning and memory.* New York: John Wiley, 1972. Pp. 117–137.

Cromer, R. The learning of surface structure clues to deep structure by a puppet show technique. *Quarterly Journal of Experimental Psychology,* 1972, *24,* 66–76.

Danks, J. H., & Sorce, P. A. Imagery and deep structure in the prompted recall of passive sentences. *Journal of Verbal Learning and Verbal Behavior,* 1973, *12,* 114–117.

Derwing, B. L. *Transformational grammar as a theory of language acquisition.* Cambridge, England: Cambridge University Press, 1973.

De Villiers, P. A., & de Villiers, J. G. Early judgment of semantic and syntactic acceptability by children. *Journal of Psycholinguistic Research*, 1972, *1*, 299–310.

Dingwall, W. O., & Shields, T. L. From utterance to gist: Four experimental studies of what's in between. Unpublished manuscript.

Dooling, D. J. Some context effects in the speeded comprehension of sentences. *Journal of Experimental Psychology*, 1972, *93*, 56–62.

Dougherty, R. C. Recent studies on language universals. *Foundations of Language*, 1970, *6*, 505–561.

Edwards, D. Constraints on actions: A source of early meanings in child language. Unpublished manuscript.

Empson, W. *Seven types of ambiguity*. New York: Meridian, 1955.

Engelkamp, J. Über den Einfluss der semantischen Struktur auf die Verarbeitung von Sätzen. Unpublished doctoral dissertation, Ruhr-Universität Bochum, 1972.

Engelkamp, J., Merdian, F., & Hörmann, H. Semantische Faktoren bein Behalten der Verneinung von Sätzen. *Psychologische Forschung*, 1972, *35*, 93–116.

Fillmore, C. J. The case for case. In E. Bach & R. T. Harms (Eds.), *Universals in linguistic theory*. New York: Holt, Rinehart & Winston, 1968. Pp. 1–90.

Fillmore, C. J. Types of lexical information. In D. D. Steinberg, & L. A. Jakobovits (Eds.), *Semantics: An interdisciplinary reader in philosophy, linguistics and psychology*. Cambridge, England: Cambridge University Press, 1971. Pp. 370–392.

Fodor, J. A. Current approaches to syntax recognition. In D. L. Horton & J. J. Jenkins (Eds.), *Perception of language*. Columbus, Ohio: Merrill, 1971. Pp. 120–139.

Fodor, J. A., Bever, T. G., & Garrett, M. F. *The psychology of language*. New York: McGraw-Hill, 1974.

Fodor, J. A., & Garrett, M. F. Some syntactic determinants of sentential complexity. *Perception and Psychophysics*, 1967, *2*, 289–296.

Fodor, J. A., Garrett, M. F., & Bever, T. G. Some syntactic determinants of sentential complexity. II: Verb structure. *Perception and Psychophysics*, 1968, *3*, 453–461.

Forster, K. I. The role of semantic hypotheses in sentence processing. In F. Bresson & J. Mehler (Eds.), *Current problems in psycholinguistics*. Paris: Centre National de Recherche Scientifique, 1974.

Forster, K. I., & Olbrei, I. Semantic heuristics and syntactic analysis. *Cognition* 1973, *2*(3), 319–374.

Forster, K. I., & Ryder, L. A. Perceiving the structure and meaning of sentences. *Journal of Verbal Learning and Verbal Behavior*, 1971, *10*, 285–296.

Francis, H. Sentence structure and learning to read. *British Journal of Psychology*, 1972, *42*, 113–119.

Fromkin, V. A. The non-anomalous nature of anomalous utterances. *Language*, 1971, *47*, 27–52.

Gardner, M. *The annotated Alice*. Harmondworth, Middlesex: Penguin Books, 1965.

Garrett, M. F. Does ambiguity complicate the perception of sentences? In G. B. F. d'Arcais, & W. J. M. Levelt (Eds.), *Advances in psycholinguistics*. Amsterdam: North-Holland Publ., 1970. Pp. 48–60.

Garrett, M. F. The analysis of sentence production. Mimeo, Massachusetts Institute of Technology, 1975.

Garrod, S., & Trabasso, T. Dual-memory information processing interpretation of sentence comprehension. *Journal of Verbal Learning and Verbal Behavior*, 1973, *12*, 155–167.

Gleitman, L. R., & Gleitman, H. *Phrase and paraphrase: Some innovative uses of language*. New York: Norton, 1970.

Goldman-Eisler, F. *Psycholinguistics: Experiments in spontaneous speech*. New York: Academic Press, 1968.

Goldman-Eisler, F., & Cohen, M. Is N, P, and PN a valid criterion of transformational operations? *Journal of Verbal Learning and Verbal Behavior,* 1970, *9,* 161–166.

Graf, R., & Torrey, J. W. Perception of phrase structure in written languages. *Proceedings of the 74th Annual Convention of the American Psychological Association,* 1966. Pp. 83–84.

Greenbaum, S. Informant elicitation of data on syntactic variation. *Lingua,* 1973, *31,* 201–212.

Greenberg, J. H. *Universals of Language.* (2nd ed.) Cambridge, Mass.: M.I.T. Press, 1963.

Greene, J. M. Syntactic form and semantic function. *Quarterly Journal of Experimental Psychology,* 1970, *22,* 14–27. (a)

Greene, J. M. The semantic function of negatives and passives. *British Journal of Psychology,* 1970, *61,* 17–22. (b)

Greene, J. *Psycholinguistics: Chomsky and Psychology.* Harmondsworth, Middlesex: Penguin Books, 1972.

Greenfield, P. M., & Smith, J. H. *The structure of communication in early language.* New York: Academic Press, 1976.

Greeno, J. G., & Noreen, D. L. Time to read semantically related sentences. *Memory and Cognition,* 1974, *2,* 117–120.

Haas, W. Meanings and rules. *Proceedings of the Aristotelian Society,* 1973. (a)

Haas, W. Rivalry among deep structures. *Language,* 1973, *49,* 282–293. (b)

Herriot, P. The comprehension of sentences as a function of grammatical depth and order. *Journal of Verbal Learning and Verbal Behavior,* 1968, *7,* 938–941.

Herriot, P. The comprehension of active and passive sentences as a function of pragmatic expectations. *Journal of Verbal Learning and Verbal Behavior,* 1969, *8,* 166–169.

Hockett, C. F. *A course in Modern Linguistics.* New York: Macmillan, 1958.

Honeck, R. P. Interpretive versus structural effects on semantic memory. *Journal of Verbal Learning and Verbal Behavior,* 1973, *12,* 448–455.

Howe, H. E., Jr., & Hillman, D. The acquisition of semantic restrictions in children. *Journal of Verbal Learning and Verbal Behavior,* 1973, *12,* 132–139.

Huttenlocher, J., Eisenberg, K., & Strauss, S. Comprehension: Relation between perceived actor and logical subject. *Journal of Verbal Learning and Verbal Behavior,* 1968, *7,* 527–530.

Ikegami, Y. The semiological structure of the English verbs of motion. Linguistic Automation Project, Yale University, 1969.

Ingram, E. A further note on the relationship between psychological and linguistic theories. *IRAL: International Review of Applied Linguistics,* 1971, *9,* 335–346.

Jackendoff, R., & Culicover, P. A reconsideration of dative movements. *Foundations of Language,* 1971, *7,* 397–421.

Jakobson, R. Closing statement: Linguistics and poetics. In T. A. Sebeok (Ed.), *Style in Language.* New York: M.I.T. Press and Wiley, 1960. Pp. 350–377.

James, C. T. Theme and imagery in the recall of active and passive sentences. *Journal of Verbal Learning and Verbal Behavior,* 1972, *11,* 205–211.

James, C. T., Thompson, J. G., & Baldwin, J. M. The reconstruction process in sentence memory. *Journal of Verbal Learning and Verbal Behavior,* 1973, *12,* 51–63.

Jarvella, R. J. Syntactic processing of connected speech. *Journal of Verbal Learning and Verbal Behavior,* 1970, *10,* 409–416.

Jarvella, R. J., & Collas, J. G. Memory for intentions of sentences. *Memory and Cognition,* 1974, *2,* 185–188.

Jarvella, R. J., & Herman, S. J. Clause structure of sentences and speech processing. *Perception and Psychophysics,* 1972, *11,* 381–382.

Jespersen, O. *Language: Its nature, development and origin.* New York: Norton, 1964.

Johnson, M. G. Syntactic position and rated meaning. *Journal of Verbal Learning and Verbal Behavior*, 1967, *6*, 240–246.

Johnson-Laird, P. N. The choice of the passive voice in a communicative task. *British Journal of Psychology*, 1968, *59*, 7–15. (a)

Johnson-Laird, P. N. The interpretation of the passive voice. *Quarterly Journal of Experimental Psychology*, 1968, *20*, 69–73. (b)

Johnson-Laird, P. N., & Stevenson, R. Memory for syntax. *Nature*, 1970, *227*, 412.

Kaplan, R. Augmented transition networks as psychological models of sentence comprehension. *Second International Conference on Artificial Intelligence*. London: British Computer Society, 1971. Pp. 429–443.

Katz, J. J. *Semantic theory*. New York: Harper and Row, 1972.

Katz, J. J., & Fodor, J. The structure of a semantic theory. *Language*, 1963, *39*, 170–210.

Katz, J. J., & Postal, P. *An integrated theory of linguistic descriptions*. Cambridge, Mass.: M.I.T. Press, 1964.

Kay, M. From semantics to syntax. In M. Bierwisch & K. Heidolf (Eds.), *Recent developments in linguistics: A collection of papers*. The Hague: Mouton, 1970.

Keyser, S. J., & Petrick, S. R. Syntactic analysis. Physical Sciences Research Papers, No. 324, Bedford, Mass.: Air Force Cambridge Research Laboratories, 1967.

Kintsch, W. *The representation of meaning in memory*. Hillsdale, New Jersey: Lawrence Erlbaum Associates, 1974.

Kintsch, W., & Monk, D. Storage of complex information in memory: Some implications of the speed with which inferences can be made. *Journal of Experimental Psychology*, 1972, *94*, 25–32.

Lakoff, G. Instrumental adverbs and the concept of deep structure. *Foundations of Language*, 1968, *4*, 4–29.

Leech, G. *Semantics*. Harmondsworth: Penguin Books, 1974.

Lindsley, J. R. Producing simple utterances: How far ahead do we plan? *Cognitive Psychology*, 1975, *7*, 1–19.

Lyons, J. *Introduction to theoretical linguistics*. Cambridge, England: Cambridge University Press, 1968.

MacKay, D. G. Mental diplopia: Towards a model of speech perception at the semantic level. In G. B. F. d'Arcais & W. J. M. Levelt (Eds.), *Advances in psycholinguistics*. Amsterdam: North-Holland, 1970. Pp. 76–98.

Macnamara, J., Green, J., & O'Cleirigh, A. Studies in the psychology of semantics: The projection rules. Unpublished manuscript.

Marks, L. E. Some structural and sequential factors in the processing of sentences. *Journal of Verbal Learning and Verbal Behavior*, 1967, *6*, 707–713.

Marks, L. E., & Miller, G. A. The role of semantic and syntactic constraints in the memorization of English sentences. *Journal of Verbal Learning and Verbal Behavior*, 1964, *3*, 1–5.

Martin, E. Towards an analysis of subjective phrase structure. *Psychological Bulletin*, 1970, *74*, 153–166.

Martin, E., Roberts, K. H., & Collins, A. M. Short term memory for sentences. *Journal of Verbal Learning and Verbal Behavior*, 1968, *7*, 560–566.

McNeill, D. *The acquisition of language: The study of developmental psycholinguistics*. New York: Harper & Row, 1970.

McNeill, D. Semiotic extension. In R. L. Solso (Ed.) *Information processing and cognition. The Loyola Symposium*. Hillsdale, N.J.: Lawrence Erlbaum Associates, 1975.

McNeill, D. The place of grammar in a theory of performance. Paper presented at the NYAS Symposium on Developmental Psycholinguistics, 1975.

Mehler, J. Some effects of grammatical transformation on the recall of English sentences. *Journal of Verbal Learning and Verbal Behavior*, 1963, *2*, 346–351.

Mehler, J., & Carey, P. Role of surface and base structure in the perception of sentences. *Journal of Verbal Learning and Verbal Behavior*, 1967, *6*, 335–338.

Mehler, J., & Carey, P. The interaction of veracity and syntax in the processing of sentences. *Perception and Psychophysics*, 1968, *3*, 109–111.

Miller, G. A., & Isard, S. Some perceptual consequences of linguistic rules. *Journal of Verbal Learning and Verbal Behavior*, 1963, *2*, 217–228.

Miller, G. A., & McKean, K. O. A chronometric study of some relations between sentences. *Quarterly Journal of Experimental Psychology*, 1964, *16*, 297–308.

Moore, T. E. Speeded recognition of ungrammaticality. *Journal of Verbal Learning and Verbal Behavior*, 1972, *11*, 550–560.

Noizet, G., Deyts, F., & Deyts, J. P. Producing complex sentences by applying relative transformations: A comparative study. *International Journal of Psycholinguistics*, 1972, *1*, 49–67.

Norman, D. A., & Rumelhart, D. E. *Explorations in cognition.* San Francisco: W. H. Freeman, 1975.

O'Connell, D. C., Kowal, S., & Hörmann, H. Semantic determinants of pauses. In G. B. F. d'Arcais & W. J. M. Levelt (Eds.), *Advances in Psycholinguistics.* Amsterdam: North-Holland Publ., 1970. Pp. 218–219.

Olson, D. R. Language and thought: Aspects of a cognitive theory of semantics. *Psychological Review*, 1970, *4*, 257–273.

Olson, D. R. Language use for communicating instructing and thinking. In J. B. Carroll & R. O. Freedle (Eds.), *Language comprehension and the acquisition of knowledge.* Washington, D.C.: Winston, 1972. Pp. 139–167.

Olson, D. R., & Filby, N. On the comprehension of active and passive sentences. *Cognitive Psychology*, 1972, *3*, 361–381.

Osgood, C. E. *Method and theory in experimental psychology.* New York: Oxford University Press, 1953.

Osgood, C. E. Where do sentences come from? In D. D. Steinberg & L. A. Jakobovits (Eds.), *Semantics: An interdisciplinary reader in philosophy, linguistics and psychology.* Cambridge, England: Cambridge University Press, 1971.

Osgood, C. E. Is behaviorism up a blind alley? Unpublished manuscript.

Paivio, A. *Imagery and verbal processes.* New York: Holt, Rinehart – Winston, 1971.

Paris, S. G. Integration and interference in children's comprehension and memory. In F. Restle, R. Shiffrin, J. Castellan, H. Lindman, & D. Pisoni (Eds.), *Cognitive theory* (Vol. 1). Hillsdale, N.J.: Lawrence Erlbaum Associates, 1975.

Paris, S. G., & Carter, A. Y. Semantic and constructive aspects of sentence memory in children. *Developmental Psychology*, 1973, *9*, 109–113.

Paris, S. G., & Mahoney, D. J. Cognitive integration in children's memory for sentences and pictures. *Child Development*, 1974, *45*, 633–642.

Piaget, J. *The language and thought of the child.* (3rd ed.) London: Routledge & Kegan Paul, 1959.

Potts, G. R. Information processing strategies used in the encoding of linear orderings. *Journal of Verbal Learning and Verbal Behavior*, 1972, *11*, 727–740.

Prentice, J. Response strength of single words as an influence in sentence behavior. *Journal of Verbal Learning and Verbal Behavior*, 1966, *5*, 429–433.

Quillian, M. R. Word concepts: A theory and simulation of some basic semantic capabilities. *Behavioral Science*, 1967, *12*, 410–430.

Quirk, R., Greenbaum, S., Leech, G., & Svartvik, J. *A Grammar of Contemporary English.* New York: Harcourt and Brace, 1972.

Quirk, R., & Svartvik, J. *Investigating linquistic acceptability.* The Hague: Mouton, 1966.

Rommetveit, R. *Words, meanings and messages.* New York: Academic Press, 1968.

Rosenbaum, P. S. *The grammar of English predicate constructions.* Cambridge, Mass.: M.I.T. Press, 1967.

Rosenberg, S., & Jarvella, R. J. Semantic integration as a variable in sentence perception, memory and production. In G. B. F. d'Arcais & W. J. M. Levelt (Eds.), *Advances in Psycholinguistics.* Amsterdam: North-Holland Publ., 1970.

Rubenstein, H. Psycholinguistics. In T. Sebeok (Ed.), *Current trends in linguistics* (Vol. 12). The Hague: Mouton, 1974.

Sachs, J. S. Recognition memory for syntactic and semantic aspects of connected discourse. *Perception and Psychophysics, 1967, 2,* 437–442.

Sapir, E. *Language: An introduction to the study of speech.* New York: Harcourt and Brace, 1921.

Savin, H. B. Meanings and concepts: A review of Jerrold J. Katz' *Semantic Theory. Cognition, 1973, 2,* 212–238.

Schank, R. C. Conceptual dependency: A theory of natural language understanding. *Cognitive Psychology, 1972, 3,* 552–631.

Schank, R. Identification of conceptualizations underlying natural languages. In R. Schank & K. M. Colby (Eds.), *Computer models of thought and language.* San Francisco: Freeman, 1973. Pp. 187–247.

Schank, R. C., & Rieger, C. J. Inference and the computer understanding of natural language. Computer Science Department, Stanford University, 1973.

Schleichert, M. Verstehen-Versuch eines Modells. In A. Diemer (Ed.), *Der Methoden-und Theorienpluralismus in den Wissenschaften.* Meisenheim am Glan: Hain, 1971.

Schlesinger, I. M. A note on the relationship between psychological and linguistic theories. *Foundations of Language, 1967, 3,* 397–402.

Schlesinger, I. M. *Sentence structure and the reading process.* The Hague: Mouton, 1968.

Schlesinger, I. M. On linguistic competence. In Y. Bar-Hillel (Ed.), *Pragmatics of natural languages.* Dordrecht: Reidel, 1971. Pp. 150–172. (a)

Schlesinger, I. M. Production of utterances and language acquisition. In D. I. Slobin (Ed.), *The ontogenesis of grammar.* New York: Academic Press, 1971. (b)

Schlesinger, I. M. The grammar of sign language and the problem of linguistic universals. In J. Morton (Ed.), *Biological and social factors in psycholinguistics.* London: Logos Press, 1971. Pp. 98–121. (c)

Schlesinger, I. M. Relational concepts underlying language. In R. L. Schiefelbusch & L. L. Lloyd (Eds.), *Language perspectives – Acquisition, retardation and intervention.* Baltimore, Md.: University Park Press, 1974. Pp. 129–151.

Schlesinger, I. M. Grammatical development: The first steps. In E. Lenneberg & E. Lenneberg (Eds.), *Foundations of Language Development.* New York: Academic Press, 1975. Pp. 203–233. (a)

Schlesinger, I. M. Why a sentence in which a sentence in which a sentence is embedded is embedded is difficult. *International Journal of Psycholinguistics, 1975, 4,* 53–66. (b)

Schlesinger, I. M. Is there a natural word order? Proceedings of the International Symposium of First Language Acquisition, Florence 1972, in press.

Schlesinger, I. M., & Namir, L. The grammar of sign language. In I. M. Schlesinger & L. Namir (Eds.), *Current trends in the sign language of the deaf.* The Hague: Mouton (in preparation).

Searle, R. J. *Speech acts: An essay in the philosophy of language.* Cambridge, England: Cambridge University Press, 1969.

Segal, E. M., & Martin, D. R. The influence of transformational history on the importance of words in sentences. Paper presented at the Psychonomic Society Meeting, October, 1966.

Segerstedt, T. T. *Die Macht des Wortes: Eine Sprachsoziologie.* Zürich: Pan, 1947.

Seligman, M. E. P. On the generality of the laws of learning. *Psychological Review,* 1970, *77,* 406–418.

Shafto, M. The space for case. *Journal of Verbal Learning and Verbal Behavior*, 1973, *12*, 551–562.

Shalom, C., & Schlesinger, I. M. Analogical thinking: A conceptual analysis of analogy tests. In R. Feuerstein (Ed.), *Studies in cognitive modificability*, Report No. 1, Jerusalem, 1972. (Mimeo)

Simmons, F. R. Semantic networks: Their computation and use for understanding English sentences. In R. C. Schank & K. M. Colby (Eds.), *Computer models of thought and language*. San Francisco: Freeman, 1973. Pp. 63–113.

Singer, M., & Rosenberg, S. T. The role of grammatical relations in the abstraction of linguistic ideas. *Journal of Verbal Learning and Verbal Behavior*, 1973, *12*, 273–284.

Slamecka, N. J. Recognition of word strings as a function of linguistic violations. *Journal of Experimental Psychology*, 1969, *79*, 377–378.

Slobin, D. I. Grammatical transformations and sentence comprehension in childhood and adulthood. *Journal of Verbal Learning and Verbal Behavior*, 1966, *5*, 219–227.

Slobin, D. I., & Welsh, C. A. Elicited imitation as a research tool in developmental psycholinguistics. In C. A. Ferguson & D. I. Slobin (Eds.), *Studies of child language development*. New York: Holt, Rinehart & Winston, 1973. Pp. 485–497.

Spencer, N. J. Differences between linguists and nonlinguists in intuitions of grammaticality–acceptability. *Journal of Psycholinguistic Research*, 1973, *2*, 83–98.

Stolz, W. S. A study of the ability to decode grammatically novel sentences. *Journal of Verbal Learning and Verbal Behavior*, 1967, *6*, 867–873.

Svartvik, J. *On voice in the English verb*. The Hague: Mouton, 1966.

Tannenbaum, P. H., & Williams, F. Generation of active and passive sentences as a function of subject or object focus. *Journal of Verbal Learning and Verbal Behavior*, 1968, *7*, 246–250.

Tejirian, E. Syntactic and semantic structure in the recall of orders of approximation to English. *Journal of Verbal Learning and Verbal Behavior*, 1968, *7*, 1010–1015.

Thorne, J. P. A computer model for the perception of syntactic structure. *Proceedings of the Royal Society of Britania*, 1968, *171*, 377–386.

Thorne, J. P., Bratley, P. & Dewar, H. The syntactic analysis of English by machine. In D. Michie (Ed.), *Machine intelligence* (Vol. 3). Edinburgh: Edinburgh University Press, 1968. Pp. 281–310.

Trabasso, T. Mental operations in language comprehension. In R. O. Freedle & J. B. Carroll (Eds.), *Language comprehension and the acquisition of knowledge*. New York: Winston, 1972. Pp. 113–137.

Turner, E. A., & Rommetveit, R. Focus of attention in recall of active and passive sentences. *Journal of Verbal Learning and Verbal Behavior*, 1968, *7*, 543–584.

Veneziano, E. Analysis of wish sentences in the one-word stage of language acquisition: A cognitive approach. Unpublished master's thesis. Tufts University, 1973.

Vygotsky, L. S. *Thought and language*. Cambridge, Mass.: M.I.T. Press, 1962.

Waismann, F. The resources of language. In M. Black (Ed.), *The Importance of Language*. Englewood Cliffs: Prentice-Hall, 1962.

Wang, M. D. Influence of linguistic structure on comprehensibility and recognition. *Journal of Experimental Psychology*, 1970, *85*, 83–89.

Wanner, E. *On remembering, forgetting and understanding sentences*. The Hague: Mouton, 1974.

Waryas, C. L., & Ruder, K. Children's sentence processing strategies: the double-object construction. Working paper, Parsons Research center, 1973.

Wason, P. C. The contexts of plausible denial. *Journal of Verbal Learning and Behavior*, 1965, *4*, 7–11.

Watt, W. C. On two hypotheses concerning psycholinguistics. In J. R. Hayes (Ed.), *Cognition and the development of language*. New York: Wiley, 1970. Pp. 137–220.

Watt, W. C. Competing Economy Criteria. Working paper, 5. School of Social Sciences, University of California, Irvine, 1972.

Wearing, A. J. The storage of complex sentences. *Journal of Verbal Learning and Verbal Behavior*, 1970, *9*, 21–29.

Webster's new dictionary of synonyms. Springfield, Mass.: Merriam, 1968.

Weisberg, R. W. Semantic factors in the storage of sentences by children. *Proceedings of the 79th Annual APA Convention*, 1971. Pp. 53–54.

Weisgerber, L. *Von den Kräften der deutschen Sprache.* Vol. 1: *Grundzüge der inhaltsbezogenen Grammatik.* Düsseldorf: Schwann, 1962. (a)

Weisgerber, L. *Von den Kräften den deutschen Sprache.* Vol. 2: *Die sprachliche Gestaltung der Welt.* Düsseldorf: Schwann, 1962. (b)

Wetstone, H. S., & Friedlander, B. Z. The effect of word order on young children's responses to simple questions and commands. *Child Development*, 1973, *44*, 734–740.

Wilson, N. L. Linguistical butter and philosophical parsnips. *Journal of Philosophy*, 1967, *64*, 55–67.

Winograd, T. Understanding natural languages. *Cognitive Psychology*, 1972, *3*, 1–191.

Woods, W. A. Transition network grammars for natural language analysis. *Communications of the ACM*, 1970, *13*, 591–606.

Wright, P. Transformations and the understanding of sentences. *Language and Speech*, 1969, *12*, 156–166.

Wright, P. Some observations on how people answer questions about sentences. *Journal of Verbal Learning and Verbal Behavior*, 1972, *11*, 188–195.

Author Index

Numbers in *italics* refer to the pages on which the complete references are listed.

Subject Index